English Historical Semantics

Edinburgh Textbooks on the English Language – Advanced

General Editor
Heinz Giegerich, Professor of English Linguistics, University of Edinburgh

Editorial Board
Laurie Bauer (University of Wellington)
Olga Fischer (University of Amsterdam)
Rochelle Lieber (University of New Hampshire)
Norman Macleod (University of Edinburgh)
Donka Minkova (UCLA)
Edgar W. Schneider (University of Regensburg)
Katie Wales (University of Leeds)
Anthony Warner (University of York)

TITLES IN THE SERIES INCLUDE:

English Historical Semantics
Christian Kay and Kathryn Allan

A Historical Syntax of English
Bettelou Los

Morphological Theory and the Morphology of English
Jan Don

Construction Grammar and its Application to English
Martin Hilpert

A Historical Phonology of English
Donka Minkova

English Historical Pragmatics
Andreas Jucker and Irma Taavitsainen

English Historical Sociolinguistics
Robert McColl Millar

Corpus Linguistics and the Description of English
Hans Lindquist

Visit the Edinburgh Textbooks in the English Language website at www.eup-publishing.com/series/ETOTELAdvanced

English Historical Semantics

Christian Kay and Kathryn Allan

EDINBURGH
University Press

To Jeremy Smith, colleague, teacher and friend

© Christian Kay and Kathryn Allan, 2015
© the chapters their several authors, 2015

Edinburgh University Press Ltd
The Tun, Holyrood Road,
12(2f) Jackson's Entry,
Edinburgh EH8 8PJ
www.euppublishing.com

Typeset in 10.5/12 Janson by
Servis Filmsetting Ltd, Stockport, Cheshire,
printed and bound in Great Britain by
CPI Group (UK) Ltd, Croydon CR0 4YY

A CIP record for this book is available from the British Library

ISBN 978 0 7486 4478 0 (hardback)
ISBN 978 0 7486 4479 7 (webready PDF)
ISBN 978 0 7486 4477 3 (paperback)
ISBN 978 1 4744 0912 4 (epub)

Contents

List of figures

Acknowledgements

Figure 4.1 *Oxford English Dictionary Online* entry for *manga²*, by permission of Oxford University Press.

Figure 5.1 Dating of semantic changes of the word *silly*, from M. L. Samuels, *Linguistic Evolution* (1972), Cambridge University Press, under their policy of allowing reproduction of a single figure without formal permission.

Figure 6.3 *HTOED* category 03.02.07.03.09.07.02 *Sofa / couch*; Figure 6.5 *HTOED* category 02.01.13.03 *Hold an opinion*; Figure 6.6 *HTOED* category *Bench* 03.02.07.03.09.07.03, all by permission of the University of Glasgow.

Unless otherwise indicated, quotations from Shakespeare's plays are taken from the First Folio of 1623 and retain the original spelling and punctuation. The First Folio is available at *Internet Shakespeare Editions*, University of Victoria, http://internetshakespeare.uvic.ca/, to whom we are grateful for providing this resource. Line numbers are taken from this site (accessed 16 February 2015).

Abbreviations and conventions

*	reconstructed form (hypothesised but not actually found) or unacceptable expression
\<a\>	enclose written forms
æ	Old English letter *ash*, pronounced like the \<a\> in *cat*
ȝ	Old English letter *yogh*, pronounced like the \<y\> in *yellow*
þ	Old English letter *thorn*, pronounced like the \<th\> in *think* or *this*
a.	*ante* 'before'
adj.	adjective
AND	*Anglo-Norman Dictionary*
BCC	Basic Colour Category
BCT	Basic Colour Term
c.	*circa* 'about'
cf.	compare
DOE	*Dictionary of Old English*
DOST	*A Dictionary of the Older Scottish Tongue*
DSL	*Dictionary of the Scots Language*
EModE	Early Modern English
HTE	*Historical Thesaurus of English*
HTOED	*Historical Thesaurus of the Oxford English Dictionary*
LModE	Late Modern English
ME	Middle English
MED	*Middle English Dictionary*
ModE	Modern English
ODE	*Oxford Dictionary of English*
OE	Old English
OED	*Oxford English Dictionary*
ON	Old Norse
PDE	present-day English
Roget	*Roget's Thesaurus of English Words and Phrases*
sic	'thus' (= 'as in the original')

SND   *The Scottish National Dictionary*
TOE   *A Thesaurus of Old English*

Dictionaries and thesauruses are listed by title in the first section of the References at the end of the book (pp. 191–2).

Bold type is used for technical terms which appear in the glossary and to indicate significant words in examples.

Italic type is used for example words and phrases.

SMALL CAPITALS are used for semantic components, basic colour categories and conceptual metaphors.

Dictionary citations are in the form (*OED purple*, noun 1a), showing the name of the dictionary, headword, part of speech and sense number.

HTOED headings are in italic with initial capital, e.g. *People.*

1 Introduction

The purpose of this book is to explore ways in which ideas from linguistics can be used to investigate and illuminate historical semantic data. It is aimed at people who have some knowledge of the history of the English language, or of theoretical Semantics, or both, and would like to study these topics in greater depth and examine how they impact on one another.

Semantics can be broadly defined as 'the study of meaning'. Linguistic meaning, in the sense of information conveyed by one speaker to another, can be studied within any of the generally recognised units of which discourse is composed: morphemes (the units of which complex words are constructed), words themselves, and longer units such as phrases, sentences and texts. Meaning also occurs in sounds and in non-linguistic contexts, such as gestures, signs and facial expressions, but these are outside the scope of this volume. Our main focus here is on the branch of Semantics known as **Lexical Semantics**, the study of word meaning, and within that on historical factors. We think that this aspect of Semantics has reached an exciting point in its development, and has the potential to develop much further in future. One reason for such optimism is that resources for the study of words, in the form of dictionaries and electronic text corpora, have both increased and improved immeasurably in recent years. Another is that two of the most interesting questions in Historical Linguistics, how and why languages change, can be approached through word meaning, taking account of changes both in the meanings of individual word forms and in larger areas of the lexicon. Lexical Semantics can also interact fruitfully with other areas of linguistics, such as **Etymology**, the study of the origins of words; **Sociolinguistics**, the study of language use among different groups in society; **Discourse Analysis** and **Text Linguistics**, the study of linguistic relationships within texts; and **Pragmatics**, the study of language in everyday interaction. As we shall see in the course of this book, Lexical Semantics also owes a large debt to two other subjects,

Anthropology, which has stimulated the comparative study of languages in ways that can be adapted to the study of different periods of a language, and Psychology, which inspired much of the initial linguistic work on how we categorise and understand our world.

This is a book on Historical Semantics, not a book on General Semantics, nor yet a History of Semantics. Over the years, there have been many theories of Semantics and many views on how languages develop. We have not limited ourselves to any one of these nor felt it necessary to mention all of them. Instead, we have looked for approaches and applications which are particularly relevant to historical work, and which are particularly interesting. At the same time we have placed emphasis throughout the book on finding and analysing data, whether in exemplification of particular points or in extended case studies. Two theoretical approaches predominate. We are both practising lexicographers as well as theoretical linguists, and have experience of dealing on a day-to-day basis with the vast and often unwieldy bulk of the English lexicon. The approaches that we have found most useful in our own work, and which we think students should be familiar with, are Structural Semantics and Cognitive Semantics. Although they are separated by time and by intervening models such as Truth-Conditional Semantics and Transformational-Generative Semantics, they can still be used in complementary ways. Structural Semantics provides the bedrock for any work in Lexical Semantics, and is implicit in many textbooks and histories of the English language. Whatever theory one may subscribe to, it is impossible to get very far in lexical studies without a grasp of such basic concepts as **synonymy**, **hyponymy** and **semantic field**; these concepts, and the issues associated with them, recur throughout the literature, sometimes, as in the case of *semantic field*, in a variety of guises. In other areas, such as the study of **polysemy**, **metonymy** and **metaphor**, Cognitive Semantics offers valuable new methods and insights.

At this point we would like to introduce two rather formidable but useful terms which have long been current in continental European linguistics but have only recently achieved much currency in English. These are **semasiology** and **onomasiology**. Semasiology is concerned with the meaning or meanings attached to individual word forms, as exemplified by the listings of form plus definition in an alphabetically-organised dictionary. Onomasiology, on the other hand, is concerned first with meaning, and then with the form or forms used to express that meaning, as in a conceptually organised **thesaurus** like *Roget's Thesaurus of English Words and Phrases (Roget)*. Dirk Geeraerts neatly sums up the difference: 'Between the two, there is a difference of perspective: semasiology starts from the expression and looks at its meanings, onomasiology starts from the meaning and looks at the different expressions' (2010: 23). Both of these approaches to meaning are important in this book, and both dictionaries and thesauruses are key tools. For semasiological work, our principal resource is the *Oxford English Dictionary* (*OED*). For onomasiological studies we draw mainly on the *Historical Thesaurus of the Oxford English Dictionary* (*HTOED*), which we were both involved in editing. The two approaches are not, of course, mutually exclusive, and many topics require a combination of both perspectives.

Two other contrasting terms you will encounter are **synchrony** and **diachrony**, which refer to one of the key oppositions made in Structural Linguistics. Synchronic research focuses on language at a particular point of time, or, more accurately, proceeds as if time is not a factor in the study. The term is often used as if it referred solely to the study of Modern English (ModE), but in fact it is perfectly possible to make a synchronic study of a historical period. A diachronic study, on the other hand, considers a longer period and takes full account of the passage and effects of time; this is the kind of study found in this book.

The structure of the book reflects the interests and points of view discussed above. Chapter 2 provides a framework for what follows in the rest of the book. Within a narrative history of the language from its beginnings in Anglo-Saxon England to the present day, we explore why the English lexicon is so large and rich in synonyms, and discuss how words are formed through processes such as **derivation** and **compounding**. Particular attention is paid to factors which influence lexical change, such as the effects of **borrowing** and of changing cultural contexts. In Chapter 3 we move into more theoretical territory. After an initial discussion of categorisation, we use a critical examination of structuralist concepts to establish a basic terminology, and then engage with some key concepts from Cognitive Semantics, such as **prototypes** and **domains**. Chapters 4 and 5 are largely semasiological in orientation. Chapter 4 is designed to help students take maximum advantage of the huge amounts of different kinds of information contained in the *OED*. Following an account of its origins and the changes which have occurred in subsequent editions, the structure and content of *OED* entries is explained through a detailed analysis of the nouns *manga* and *monster*. Other historical dictionaries and corpora are also discussed. The knowledge and skills accumulated so far are put to use in Chapter 5, which develops a typology of kinds of semantic change and discusses the key question of why words change meaning. From Chapter 6 onwards, an onomasiological perspective is developed. Chapter 6 parallels Chapter 4 in describing a key resource, *HTOED*, and the information it contains, using expressions for 'sofa' and 'hold an opinion' as examples. There is also further discussion of issues associated with categorisation. Chapter 7 is devoted to a case study of a single semantic field which has long been a focus of interest in Linguistics: the field of Colour. In the course of discussing the historical development of English colour terms, the chapter draws on comparative evidence from a range of languages. The importance of cultural context in understanding linguistic structure and change is discussed further in Chapter 8, with reference to work in anthropology, and an analysis of pronouns of address and material from the fields of Kinship and Time. Chapter 9 examines the role of metaphor and metonymy in semantic change, and further examines the link between language and culture in exploring what motivates the mappings between sources and targets in particular semantic fields. Finally, Chapter 10 summarises key points made in the book, suggests a follow-on activity which covers many of them, and considers some possible future research directions.

Students of Historical Linguistics are fortunate in that English has a long written history, stretching back over 1,300 years. These records are far from perfect, and in the early years they are sparse and restricted in the genres they represent, but they nevertheless form a basis for research. Students of Semantics are also fortunate in that lexical change is the most readily observable type of linguistic change, often being accomplished very quickly in modern conditions. It is therefore possible to apply the techniques of Historical Linguistics to observing innovation and change as they occur in modern media including the press and the internet. Some of the exercises in this book will encourage you to keep your eyes and ears open for current developments, such as words entering the language or changing meaning.

For convenience when studying its history, the English language is usually divided into three main periods. These dates are, of course, approximate and may vary in different textbooks. The dates used in this book are:

Old English (OE) 700 AD–1150 AD
Middle English (ME) 1150 AD–1500 AD
Modern English (ModE) 1500 AD to the present

Modern English is often further subdivided into:
Early Modern English (EModE) 1500 AD–1750 AD
Late Modern English (LModE) 1750 AD to the present

Present-day English (PDE), covering the English we speak
today, is sometimes distinguished as a sub-category of LModE

Technical terms, the **metalanguage** of the subject, are given in **bold type** throughout this book and are included in the glossary for easy reference. One confession we have to make is that we have retained the term **word** as part of that metalanguage. We are aware that this apparently straightforward term has been a source of unease and dispute throughout the history of modern Linguistics. For English, such unease has been partly based on the fact that not all lexical meanings are carried by single-word units: compare, for example, Latinate *capitulate* and native English *give in*, which express roughly the same idea in a different number of words. Multiword expressions such as idioms can also use several words to express a unitary idea. Alternative terms, most popularly 'lexeme', have been proposed but these are not used consistently throughout the literature, and we did not feel that there would be any great advantage in insisting on their use here.

Each chapter in the book is followed by suggestions for further reading and exercises. The latter generally take the form of hands-on experience of examining lexical data, but can also be used as a basis for classroom discussion.

We would like to thank the many students and colleagues who have, knowingly or unknowingly, contributed to the development of this book. In particular, we are grateful to Carole Biggam for her expert handling of Chapter 7; to Philip Durkin, Seth Mehl and Ai Zhong for comments and suggestions on draft chapters; to Justyna Robinson for trialling material in classes; to Marc Alexander for reading the draft and for technical assistance; to Kate Wild for her work on *Time*; to our anonymous reviewer for encouraging comments; and to Richard Strachan, Laura Williamson and all at Edinburgh University Press for their enormous patience and helpful input throughout the publication process.

2 A brief history of the English lexicon

2.1 Introduction

English today has an exceptionally large and varied vocabulary. Some of the words we use can be traced back to the Old English (OE) period; others have been imported from a variety of languages, notably French and Latin, over the succeeding years. The characteristics of the vocabulary of each period of the language, and the contexts in which the **lexicon** developed and changed, will be discussed below. We should remember, however, that our knowledge is only as good as the surviving records: many words may have occurred earlier or later than records show, or may have disappeared without being recorded. (The nature of the existing evidence is discussed further in Chapter 4.)

First we can gain a bird's eye view of a typical fragment of linguistic history by looking at a selection of words meaning 'merry' from the *Historical Thesaurus of the Oxford English Dictionary* (*HTOED*). The words are given in the order in which they are first recorded in English by the *Oxford English Dictionary* (*OED*), followed by any phrases. Before reading the paragraph following the example, you might find it interesting to think about how many of these words you know and how you would use them.

Words and expressions for 'merry'

Old English: blithe.
Middle English: lusty, playful, mirthful, jolly, gay, merry, jocund, galliard, jovy, jocant.
Early Modern English: pleasant, frolic, jolious, gleeful, buxom, jovial, gleesome, jovialist, jocundary, airy, festivous, hilarous, vogie (Scots), heartsome, high, as merry as the day is long, as merry as a cricket, as merry as a pismire (= ant), as merry/lively as a grig (= a dialect word for a cricket).

Late Modern English: festal, festive, laughful, hilarious, griggish, banzai, slap-you-on-the-back, as merry as a lark.

(Adapted from *HTOED* section 02.02.19.10 *Merry*)[1]

What strikes us about these words? Only one, *blithe*, has come to us intact from OE. It is still recognisable today, but is not in everyday use – the last *OED* example (sometimes referred to as a **citation**) is from an early nineteenth-century poem. However, several of the words first recorded in Middle English (ME) have OE **roots** (*lusty, playful, mirthful* and *merry* itself), and could have been in earlier use. Other ME acquisitions are of French origin (*gay, jocund, galliard, jovy, jocant*). The joker in this particular pack is *jolly*, which could come from French or from an Old Norse (ON) word related to English *yule* – sometimes we just don't have enough evidence to be sure. The meaning of *lusty* has clearly changed over the years, and *gay* is usually used nowadays with a primary meaning of 'homosexual' (see further section 5.2).

French words first recorded in ME may later develop new meanings, as *pleasant* does in Early Modern English (EModE). Other words appear in Modern English (ModE) in new forms (compare ME *jovy* with EMod *jovial* and *jovialist*, and *jocund* with *jocundary*). Latin is increasingly used as a source of new words, and several are first recorded here in EModE (*festivous, festal, festive, hilarous, hilarious*). Later in the history of English words are borrowed from a greater range of languages (*frolic* from Dutch, and, much later, *banzai* from Japanese). Words continue to be formed from OE elements (*gleeful, gleesome, heartsome, laughful*), and colloquial expressions (*slap-you-on-the-back*) and phrases are more likely to be recorded. These phrases remind us that the unit of meaning can be more than one word.

2.2 Old English (OE: 700–1150)

The language we refer to as OE can be traced back to the fifth century AD, when the people traditionally referred to as Angles, Saxons and Jutes began to arrive in England from parts of what are now Germany and Denmark, first as raiders, then as settlers. Their progress through England and southern Scotland can be traced through the study of place-names. Names containing elements such as *ing, ham* or *ton* (*Birmingham, Southampton*) indicate Anglo-Saxon settlement, while elements such as *aber* (*Aberdeen, Aberystwyth*) come from the Celtic languages spoken by the indigenous peoples. Our earliest written records are Kentish law codes from the late seventh century; by the tenth and eleventh centuries, the Anglo-Saxons had developed a rich literature in prose and poetry.

OE was a Germanic language, belonging to the **Indo-European** family of languages and closely related to modern languages such as Dutch and German. Its grammar was substantially different from that of ModE, since, like German, it used inflections on the ends of words rather than word order to express grammatical relationships. It is notoriously difficult to calculate how much OE vocabulary survives in later English. Baugh and Cable (2013: 52) estimate around 15 per cent based on a count of OE dictionary entries. Durkin (2014: 28–9) lists 9,600 words of OE origin among the 275,000 **headwords** in the *OED*, a total of only 3.5 per cent. However, this total does not include compounds or derived forms, such as *shoe-shop* and *shoed*. Either way, the total is small, but the effect of these survivors is often out of proportion to their number, since, with minor variations in pronunciation and spelling, they include many of the words for basic concepts that we still use in daily communication: *night* (OE *niht*), *day* (*dæg*), *father* (*fæder*), *fair* (*fæger*), *love* (*lufu*, noun, and *lufian* 'to love'), and so on.[2] Words such as these form the **core vocabulary** of a language, known by most speakers and used in most contexts, and are likely to remain stable over long periods of history. Words which enter a language in response to changing social, political or cultural conditions often have a shorter or less stable lifespan.

Many of our ways of deriving new words from root or **stem words** also date back to OE. Thus, through the use of **affixes**, in a process known as derivation, *freond* 'friend' produces forms like *freondlic* 'friendly', *freondscipe* 'friendship', *freondleas* 'friendless' and *unfreondlice* 'in an unfriendly way'. In these cases, and in others, the affixes have remained **productive**. We still form adjectives using the **suffixes** *-ly* (OE *-lic*) and *-less* (*-leas*), adverbs with *-ly* (*-lice*), nouns with *-ship* (*-scipe*), and negatives with the **prefix** *un-*. We also still make use of another type of word formation, compounding, where two (or occasionally more) independent words are joined to express a complex idea, as in *nihtlang* 'nightlong' and *dægtima* 'daytime'.

Compounding was commoner in Old English than in subsequent periods of the language, where the trend has been to import new words from other languages. Many OE compounds occur in poetry, for example *dægcandel* 'day + candle = the sun' or *swanrad* 'swan + road = the sea'. Metaphorical compounds such as these are called **kennings**.

The nature of OE poetic style helps to account for the large number of synonyms recorded for concepts commonly dealt with in the literature, such as various aspects of warfare and religion. *A Thesaurus of Old English* (*TOE*) records forty-seven words for 'battle' and forty for various kinds of sword. Elegant variation through the deployment of synonyms was a highly prized feature of literary style, and alliteration was a structural feature of both poetry and poetic prose.

In brief, the OE poetic line consisted of two half-lines linked by alliteration on stressed syllables, as in these examples from the epic poem *Beowulf*, with the alliterating syllables marked in bold type.

Hroþgar maþelode	**helm** Scyldinga
Hrothgar spoke	leader of the Danes (l. 371)
Wulfgar maþelode	to his **wine**drihtne
Wulfgar spoke	to his beloved leader (l. 360)
werodes **wis**a	**word**hord onleac
of the troop leader	store of words unlocked (l. 259)
the leader of the troop	unlocked his store of words (i.e., he spoke)

(Wrenn 1973)

Here we have three different ways of referring to the concept of a leader, enabling alliteration on **h** and **w**. Note too the compounds *winedrihten*, adding extra meaning to the concept, and *wordhord* in the sense of a person's vocabulary, occasionally occurring as an **archaism** in later English, but generally replaced by *vocabulary*, borrowed from Latin, or *lexicon* from Greek.

Three events had a profound effect on Anglo-Saxon life and the development of the OE lexicon. The first was the gradual conversion of the Anglo-Saxons to Christianity from the sixth century onwards. A good deal of Latin vocabulary was imported along with the Roman religion, for example words for church functionaries such as *abbod* 'abbot', *munuc* 'monk' and *nunne* 'nun'. Sometimes these words were combined with native elements, so that an archbishop could be referred to either by the Latin-derived *arcebiscop* or as *heahbiscop*, using OE *heah* 'high, principal, chief'.

Secondly, the relatively peaceful development of Anglo-Saxon society was shattered from the late eighth century by the attacks of Viking raiders from Scandinavia. Like the Anglo-Saxons themselves, many of these raiders turned into settlers. Their presence is indicated by place-names of Norse origin including those ending in *by* (Whitby) or *thorpe* (Scunthorpe). OE and the ON spoken by the Scandinavians were **cognate** Germanic languages, traceable back to a common source and sharing many features of grammar and vocabulary. For this reason, and because the two groups interacted in the course of daily life, some of our core words, such as *law* or *sky* or the verb *take*, are of Scandinavian origin. Sometimes we preserve both the OE and ON forms of a word with meanings which have differentiated over the years, as with *shirt* (OE) and *skirt* (ON) which originally referred to the same kind of garment.

The third event brings this part of our story to an end. In 1066, the English king, Harold, was defeated at the Battle of Hastings by William of Normandy, usually known as William the Conqueror. Anglo-Saxon social structures and institutions were largely replaced by Norman ones, and new vocabulary was imported from other languages, principally French. Linguistic change occasioned by a traumatic event such as this does not happen overnight, but gradually a very different form of English began to emerge.

2.3 Middle English (ME: 1150–1500)

The period when Middle English was spoken was one of great linguistic and **sociolinguistic** complexity. Although the Normans were themselves of partly Scandinavian origin (their name means 'people from the north'), by the time they arrived in England they spoke a variety of French. As the language of the new ruling class, this language was socially prestigious and was used in speech and writing alongside Latin in the administration of church and state. It is usually referred to as Anglo-French, or sometimes Anglo-Norman, to distinguish it from the French spoken in France. English continued to be the spoken language of the majority of the population, but suffered from diminished prestige and lost ground as a written language. Celtic and Scandinavian languages continued to be spoken in certain localities. The particular fascination of this period of linguistic history is observing how the competing languages interacted as English gradually reasserted itself.

The sociocultural situation affected language in various ways. The king and his court had little need to learn English, but the French knights who were assigned estates in England and parts of Scotland inevitably came into contact with the native population, the peasants and craftsmen who supplied them with food and services and with the labour and materials to build their castles, churches and cathedrals.

Many of these Normans must have learned at least a smattering of English or employed translators to act as intermediaries. (It is interesting that the surname Latimer, from a French word meaning 'clerk, interpreter', dates from this period.) Some married English women and employed English-speaking servants, including the nurses who brought up their children. People who wanted to advance in the world of business or the court needed to be competent speakers, readers and writers of English, Latin and French, and there was a good deal of translation of written materials. These sorts of multilingual situations, where increasing numbers of people primarily speak one of the languages but have some fluency in others, create ideal conditions for the transfer of vocabulary items: if you are speaking English but can't think of the right word, then you might try the French word and hope that the context makes clear what you want to say. Other factors also contributed to the increasing number of French words adopted into English, such as the translation of French literature and the use of French as the medium of instruction in English schools until the mid-thirteenth century.

Another consequence of this situation was the simplification of English grammar, a process begun during the OE period. Many grammatical inflections were lost, although we retain some of them, such as the possessive *'s* in *enemy's* or the plural -*s* in *friends*. French also had some direct effects on grammar, including the positioning of the adjective after the noun in phrases from areas of life where French was dominant, such as the law and the royal court, for example in the expressions *heir apparent* or *princess royal*. An interesting **pragmatic** development was in the use of personal pronouns, where the plural form *you* became used when addressing individuals of higher status than oneself, while the singular *thou* was used for intimates or people of lower status. Such usage persisted until the seventeenth century (see section 8.3). As a result of such changes, and of the retention of many French words in ModE, the language of a ME poet such as Geoffrey Chaucer (1342–1400) is much more accessible to us than the language of the *Beowulf* poet, writing in OE.

Many histories of English give long lists of French words borrowed into English; here we have space for only a few. These examples reflect the progress of the Conquest through the country, as can be seen by early borrowings in practical spheres of life, such as *war, baron, noble, messenger, servant*. Words recorded later in the period come from a large number of domains ranging from government (*parliament, realm, crown, treason*) to social life, the arts and health (*garment, cloak, dinner, music, beauty, medicine*). In the field of literature alone, a glance at *HTOED* shows such French-derived words as *poet, poetry, verse, refrain, metre, rime* (= *rhyme*), *allegory* and *simile*, reflecting cultural influence.

(The relationship between language and culture in such domains will be further examined in Chapters 6 to 8.) French also contributed new affixes, such as the suffixes -*ance*, -*(t)ion*, -*ity*, -*ment* used in the formation of abstract nouns (*allegiance, religion, authority, government*) and prefixes such as *con-, dis-, en-, pre-* (*conceal, distress, enclose, prefer*).

ME borrowings from French show the beginnings of one of the most characteristic features of ModE – its large and varied vocabulary, with the resultant potential for stylistic variation. In addition to having words for new concepts, speakers could choose among roughly synonymous words for familiar ideas. Such availability of synonyms may mean that one or more of the words drops out of use, but in other cases it is a trigger for **semantic change** (discussed further in Chapter 5). If two or more synonyms survive, their meanings are often differentiated, as in OE-derived *ask, hearty, might, wish* versus the originally synonymous French *demand, cordial, power, desire*, or they may be restricted to particular contexts or levels of style.

From the fourteenth century onwards, English increasingly resumed the functions of a national language spoken by most of the population, largely at the expense of French; Latin remained the language of religion and scholarship throughout Europe. As early as the thirteenth century, we find grammar books and wordlists for teaching French to English speakers, often aimed at people whose parents or grandparents were native French speakers but who had not themselves learned the language as children. As a result of Anglo-French wars, many Norman landowners lost their possessions in France, and the Anglo-French language became increasingly distinct from continental French, to the extent that Chaucer could poke fun at the provincial French of the Prioress in the *Canterbury Tales* (composed about 1387) by writing:

> And Frenssh she spak ful faire and fetisly,
> After the scole of Stratford atte Bowe,
> For Frenssh of Parys was to hire unknowe.
>
> (Robinson 1978: 188, 124–6)

> [And she spoke French very elegantly and properly
> After the school of Stratford at the Bowe
> For the French of Paris was unknown to her.]

Such exposure to different varieties of French also explains why English sometimes has two forms of French words, which may later have changed meaning or retained variant spellings, for example *warden* and *gaol* from Anglo-French, but *guardian* and *jail* borrowed later from central French (see further the discussion of *monster* in section 4.3.2.1).

In addition to its use in literature, English became the language of the law courts from 1362, and by the end of that century was generally used as the language of instruction in schools. Its position as the main written language of the country was consolidated in the fifteenth century, when it replaced French in many areas of local and central government. It was also increasingly used for private communication, such as letter-writing, by educated people who would previously have used French.

As in ModE, there was considerable diversity in the dialects of English spoken in the British Isles. Because French and Latin were the official written languages, there was no standard way of writing English, as there had been to some extent in the OE period, and scribes tended to spell words as they were pronounced. One extreme example is the approximately 500 ways of spelling the word *through* recorded in *A Linguistic Atlas of Late Mediaeval English* and 'ranging from fairly recognisable *thurgh*, *thorough* and *þorowe* to exotic-seeming *drowgh*, *yhurght*, *trghug* and *trowffe*' (Smith 1996: 68). Although this lack of consistent spelling can be frustrating for readers, it is helpful for modern scholars interested in reconstructing earlier forms of the spoken language.

By the end of the ME period, a more uniform written language was emerging, based on the dialect of London, which had become increasingly important as a centre of trade and commerce. There was greater physical and social mobility in the population and increased literacy in English. A key event was the introduction of the printing press to England by William Caxton in 1476, which eventually made books more easily available to more people than handwritten manuscripts had been. The printing of multiple copies of texts, in contrast to the production of hand-copied manuscripts, gradually led to the elimination of regional and idiosyncratic variation, and a standardised spelling system slowly began to emerge. Unfortunately for modern learners of English, this system predated various changes in the pronunciation of vowels, especially a series known as the Great Vowel Shift, leading to apparently illogical spelling variations such as *made/maid*, *flood/food* or *great/dream*. In the first pair, the vowels used to be different, whereas in the other two they were once the same. There is usually some historical reason for apparent illogicalities in modern spelling.

2.4 Early Modern English (EModE: 1500–1750)

EModE is a key time in the development of the English lexicon, with many new words added to the language. Two factors are of crucial importance in understanding this period. Firstly, the trends identified in section 2.3 above gained further momentum: the use of written English extended to most purposes, literacy in English increased, and the spread of printing made books more readily available. Secondly, the language was affected by a series of external events and by the increased mobility of its speakers both at home and abroad. Whereas French words entered ME as a result of conquest and subsequent political and cultural influence, speakers of EModE encountered a much greater range of languages through the growth of travel, trade and overseas settlement. By the end of this period, English was well on the way to becoming the world language we know today. It had also produced some of its greatest writers – Spenser, Shakespeare, Jonson, Milton and Dryden, to name but a few.

Probably the single most influential event was the Renaissance of learning in Europe. Following the sacking of Constantinople (now Istanbul) by the Turks in 1453, many Christian scholars fled westwards, taking their precious manuscripts with them. Whereas Latin works had circulated in medieval Europe, much of the new material was in Greek and had never been seen there before. Its gradual dissemination caused considerable intellectual excitement as scholars encountered new information and ideas in fields as diverse as art, architecture, history, mathematics, medicine, navigation, philosophy, science and warfare. The movement to promote these works and the ideas they contained is often referred to by later scholars as Renaissance Humanism. Highly-educated people became increasingly able to read in Greek as well as Latin and French; those who were literate only in English wanted access to this new knowledge, and a market developed for translation. Somewhat later, from the mid-sixteenth century, the Protestant Reformation led to translation of Latin and Greek versions of the Bible into vernacular European languages, and missionaries began to operate in more distant parts of the world.

Nothing reveals the deficiencies of a language more surely than translating into it. Since Latin was the language of scholarly writing, English had not developed the vocabulary or the prose style needed to express and discuss the new concepts. Translators faced a familiar choice: they could either coin new words from the resources of English or borrow from the source languages. On the whole, they chose the latter solution and many new words, such as *accommodation, alphabet, crisis, exaggerate* and *navigation,* entered the language from Greek or Latin. In discussing such words, we need to be aware that borrowing is not always a straightforward process of one language taking a word from another. Borrowings quite often occur in a chain, with several languages involved. For example, the word *alphabet* is undoubtedly formed from the names of the first two letters of the Greek alphabet, but it occurs in

Latin and French as well as Greek and may well have entered English via one of those languages rather than directly from its etymological source. It is often impossible to tell. A similar situation occurs in ME, where many Latin words entered English through the medium of French, and with the 'exotic' borrowings discussed below, which are often first recorded in Spanish or Portuguese.

The situation in EModE was somewhat unusual in that borrowing was primarily into the written language, although some words spread into spoken use. Often, however, these were restricted to more formal and technical **registers**, for example *efficacious* and *quadrilateral*. Sometimes there was a degree of experimentation over the form of a new word. In the sixteenth and seventeenth centuries, the *OED* records the following forms meaning 'splendid': *splendant, splendicant, splendidious, splendidous, splendiferous, splendious* and *splendorous*. *Splendid* itself is first recorded in 1624. Unsurprisingly, most of these forms were short-lived; no language needs quite so many similar words for the same concept.

At the same time as all this was happening, traders and travellers from Spain, Portugal and the Netherlands were reaching many parts of Africa, Asia and the Americas. Other nations were not far behind; the first British colonies in North America were established early in the seventeenth century. When confronted by strange landscapes, objects and customs, these explorers often adopted words from the equally strange-seeming languages of the indigenous people they encountered. Thus we find words such as *racoon, tomahawk* and *wigwam* from North America, *bungalow, chintz* and *typhoon* from India, *amok* and *teak* from Malaysia, and *ketchup* and *tea* from China. The English versions of these words are often first recorded in translations of travel writings. An alternative strategy was to apply names familiar from home: thus we find birds called *robins* in many places, including North America, the Caribbean, Australia and New Zealand, but none of these is zoologically equivalent to the British bird of that name. In terms of **prototypicality** (see Chapter 3), the key feature of a robin seems to be its red breast, followed by its song. Similar strategies applied in naming new places; for example, the New England towns of Plymouth and Boston were named after the towns in England from which settlers came, but the states of Connecticut and Massachusetts have names from American Indian languages.

A typical example of a word from this period is *hurricane*, borrowed into Spanish and Portuguese from the now extinct Carib language of the Caribbean islands. The variety of early spellings (for example, *furacane, haurachana, uracan, harrycain*) reminds us of the difficulty of transcribing words from unknown languages. Originally applied only to storms in the West Indies, the use of the word later broadened to such storms elsewhere. As it became established in English, it developed a short-lived verb form, compounds, and figurative uses, including a description of a large social gathering defined thus in 1746: 'A confused (= *disorderly*) meeting of Company of both Sexes on Sundays is called a Hurricane' (*OED hurricane*, noun 2b).

In the EModE period, as later, it was the custom of well-off people, mainly young men, to enhance their education with a Grand Tour of Europe. Judging by the words they brought back, for example from Italy, key interests included architecture (*balcony, cupola*), dancing (*carnival*), and music (*canto, madrigal, opera, trombone*). At the same time, French continued to be a major contributor to the English language, both in practical fields and, after the restoration of the monarchy in Britain in 1660, on the more pleasure-seeking side of life, with words such as *ballet, champagne* and *denim*.

One of the advantages of studying this period of English is that there was a good deal of debate about language at the time. Surviving texts show that not everyone was happy with the influx of new words. One commentator, Sir Thomas Wilson, wrote in *The arte of Rhetorique* in 1553:

> Emong al other lessons, this should first be learned, that we never affect any **straunge ynkehorne** termes, but so speake as is commonly received: neither sekying to be over fine, nor yet livyng over-carelesse, usyng our speache as most men do, and ordryng our wittes, as the fewest have doen. Some seke so far for **outlandishe Englishe**, that thei forget altogether their mothers language ... Some farre jorneid jentlemen at their returne home, like as thei love to goe in forrein apparell, so thei wil pouder their talke with **oversea language**. He that cometh lately out of Fraunce, wil talke Frenche English, and never blushe at the matter. Another choppes in with Englishe Italianated ... The unlearned or foolishe phantasticall, that smelles but of learnyng (such felowes as have seen learned men in their daies) wil so latine their tongues, that the simple cannot but wonder at their talke, and thynke surely thei speake by some Revelacion. (Burnley 2000: 217)

Outlandish here means 'foreign' (although it was also developing a negative sense) and refers to the smattering of a foreign language which a rich young traveller might pick up abroad or *oversea*. There was less opposition to the more obviously necessary words introduced by the explorers. The most serious complaint was against *ynkehorne* (inkhorn) terms, so-called because they were usually academic words from Latin and Greek whose meaning was obscure to those who didn't know these languages (an inkhorn being a container for ink that a scholarly writer might use). A few examples include *egregious* 'outstanding', *eximious* 'excellent', and *sternutation* 'the act of sneezing'. Less strange to us, but controversial at the time, are others such as *assassinate, clemency, exasperate* and *verbosity*, which are still in use today. It is often difficult to see why one word rather than another should have been accepted into general use, though we will look at some possible reasons in later chapters.

The new words and the old could be powerfully combined, as when Shakespeare writes in Macbeth's speech after the murder of Duncan:

> Will all great *Neptunes* ocean wash this blood
> Cleane from my Hand? no: this my Hand will rather
> The **multitudinous** seas **incarnadine**
> Making the green one, red.
>
> (*Macbeth* II, ii, 721–4)

The **polysyllabic** words in bold were probably both used first by Shakespeare in these meanings (and, helpfully, he gives the audience a clue as to the meaning of *incarnadine*: 'redden'). They contrast with the largely **monosyllabic** words in the rest of the passage and fit neatly into the iambic metre of the blank verse.

The two sides in the Inkhorn Controversy, as it is often known, were Neologisers, who believed that the English language could be improved by extending its vocabulary through borrowing, and Purists, who thought that any expansion should come from the language's own resources. The passage from Wilson quoted above is typical of purist attitudes. An extreme member of this group was Sir John Cheke, who attempted to translate the New Testament into English using only such 'English' words as *gain-rising* 'resurrection' and *byword* 'parable'.[3] Another was the poet Edmund Spenser, who quarried medieval litera- ture for words such as *wrizzled* 'wrinkled' and *yclad* 'clothed'. An early representative of the Neologisers was Sir Thomas Elyot, who explains in the preface to his book *The Governour* (1531) that he is writing in English rather than the Latin which might be thought more suitable for a well-educated classicist in order to encourage use of the language and reach a wide audience. His success is perhaps indicated by the fact that the *OED* credits him with 1,034 first uses of a word or sense, including *encyclopedia* and *participate*.

The Inkhorn Controversy was at its height from about 1525 to 1575, and then died down as it became obvious that the tide of new words was not to be resisted, especially by a language like English which had a long history of borrowing. Debates about language in the seventeenth century had a somewhat different focus. The Royal Society had been established in 1662 to promote the study of science. One of its concerns was the development of a suitable English prose style to replace the Latin in which many scholars still wrote; out of this arose a movement promoting the establishment of an English Academy to monitor and regulate the language in the manner of those in France and Italy. This movement was unsuccessful, and, as we shall see in section 2.5, attempts to regulate English took other forms.

Apart from the new words themselves, one lasting legacy of the EModE period was the impetus it gave to the development of the monolingual English dictionary, starting with Robert Cawdrey's *Table Alphabeticall* of 1604 (see also section 6.2). Bilingual dictionaries, aimed principally at the teaching of Latin, had appeared much earlier, but up until now people hadn't felt a need for dictionaries of their own language. Initially monolingual dictionaries of English included only 'hard words', responding to the needs of the less well-educated to understand and use their rapidly changing language. In the course of the seventeenth century, they became larger and more sophisticated, culminating in 1755 in Samuel Johnson's *Dictionary of the English Language*, which contained over 40,000 words compared to the 2,500 defined by Cawdrey.

2.5 Late Modern English (LModE: 1750 to present day)

Given the linguistic turmoil of the EModE period, it is perhaps not surprising that the later eighteenth century was a period of relative calm, characterised by a desire to tidy up the language or, in contemporary terminology, to 'ascertain' it. This process involved establishing rules, removing anomalies and 'fixing' the result so that the language would not deteriorate in future (something which worried some writers, who feared that their work might become as incomprehensible to later generations as Chaucer was to them). We thus see a move towards standardisation, and towards **prescriptivism**, the idea that there are right and wrong ways of using language. In the absence of an official body to make judgements and legislate for language (see section 2.4), the onus fell on individuals to develop dictionaries, grammars and manuals of pronunciation. The main focus was on grammar, usually with reference to the grammar of classical Latin, which was regarded as having reached a peak of perfection. It is to this period that we owe 'rules' made by analogy with Latin, such as 'It is I' is the correct form, whereas 'It is me' is wrong, and the condemnation of the 'split infinitive' as in 'to boldly go'. Such pronouncements are irrelevant to English, which is structurally different from Latin, but even in the twenty-first century we can still find them being discussed.

Probably because of the steady development of dictionaries during the seventeenth century, which increasingly provided authority on lexical issues, vocabulary was less subject to criticism than grammar. Many of the surviving comments simply reflect individual prejudices, for example against **clippings** (abbreviations) in popular use, like *incog(nito)* and *ult(imate)*, or apparently harmless words such as *banter*, *subject-matter* or *nowadays*, which were perceived to be vulgar or in some way illogical. Words continued to enter English from other European languages, especially French and Italian, and to be a focus of ridicule when spoken by affected young men, the 'fops' for whom an increasing number of words had entered the language, including *buck*, *dandy* and *macaroni* (originally applied to those who had toured Italy) in the eighteenth century.

The pinnacle of lexicographical authority was, of course, Samuel Johnson's *Dictionary of the English Language*, announced in 1747 and published in 1755. In the Preface to this work, Johnson says that his original intention had been to '. . . fix our language, and put a stop to those alterations which time and chance have hitherto been suffered to make in it without opposition'. However, as he somewhat reluctantly admits, the experience of compiling the dictionary made him realise that no lexicographer can 'embalm his language, and secure it from corruption and decay' (Burnley 2000: 305). Nevertheless, Johnson exercised censorship of a kind by basing his work on 114,000 quotations from the canon of English literature, either excluding words which he regarded as unsuitable or indicating his disapproval, as in *coax*: 'To wheedle, to flatter, to humour: a low word' (*OED coax*, verb 3a). Like many others both before and after, he wavered between prescriptivism and **descriptivism**, the view, which predominates among present-day scholars, that linguists should *describe* how language is used rather than *prescribe* a correct version.

While debates about the state and future of English were taking place, it continued to become established in overseas territories, often as the language of conquest, displacing native languages rather as French had displaced OE after 1066. Inevitably, these versions of English in different places diverged over time, so that we now regard American English, Australian English, British English, Indian English, and so on, as different varieties of the language traceable to a common ancestor. Following political independence from Britain, many Americans were keen to establish the independence of their English. Notable among them was Noah Webster, who published treatises on many aspects of language, culminating in *An American Dictionary of the English Language* of 1828, which promoted such distinctively American spellings as *color*, *center, traveler* and *check* (*cheque*). Lexical differences between American and British varieties grew over the years, though not to the extent of making the two languages mutually incomprehensible as has sometimes been predicted. Compare, for example, British *film, lift, lorry, luggage, petrol, post* with American *movie, elevator, truck, baggage, gas, mail*, many of which are at least known if not used on both sides of the Atlantic. Other Americanisms have filled gaps in British English, for example *escalator* (formerly called a *moving staircase*) and a university *campus* (formerly not really called anything at all in the UK). Similar patterns can be observed in other world Englishes, with distinctive vocabularies being developed and words being imported from one variety into another.

The next great influence on the growth of the English lexicon was the Industrial Revolution, which began in Britain in the late eighteenth century. As in the Renaissance, an explosion of knowledge, this time mainly in science and technology, stimulated lexical innovation. There are, for example, over thirty words for different branches of chemistry recorded in *HTOED*, starting with *zymology* 'the science of fermentation' in 1753. Other words relate to rapidly advancing medical science, such as *pathogenic* and *pathogenetic* 'causing disease', and *ophthalmoplegia* and *cyclitis*, both diseases of the eye (to pick a few examples at random from the thousands available). Sometimes we find formal and everyday terms for the same condition, as in *myopic* and *short-sighted*, used in different stylistic environments. Interestingly, both of these have developed similar metaphorical uses (on metaphor, see Chapter 9).

Many of the words we use routinely today, such as *telegraph, telephone* and *television*, date back to the nineteenth and twentieth centuries. Social factors, such as the arrival of railways, higher literacy rates through universal primary education, and better printing techniques, contributed to these developments in the nineteenth century just as air travel and electronic communications have in more recent times. In the nineteenth century, one outcome of such trends was a huge increase in the production of inexpensive popular reading matter, such as newspapers, magazines and novels. Another was the vocabulary developing around new phenomena such as railways. *Train*, a word with a long history and many meanings, is first recorded in the sense 'railway train' in 1814, and is soon followed by other words from this area of meaning, such as *railwayman* (usually *railroader* in the US) and *rolling stock*. Some scientific terms passed into general use, as with *traumatic* and *obsessive* from Psychology.

While borrowing continues to reflect contact with other cultures, many scientific words are not strictly speaking **loanwords**. Rather, they are constructed from roots adopted from the classical languages. This has the advantage of a degree of semantic transparency: if you know that *tele*, *graph* and *phone* come from Greek roots meaning respectively 'afar', 'writing' and 'sound', and *vision* from a Latin root meaning 'see, look', you can begin to understand *telegraph*, *telephone* and *television*. You can also coin other words using similar patterns, and possibly elements from other sources, as in *telebanking*. Sometimes such coinages can cause problems, as in an early confusion between *typist* and *typewriter*. *Typewriter* as the designation of a machine is first recorded in the *OED* in 1868, but for a short period from 1884 it also referred to the person operating the machine, as in this quotation from 1895, from a volume entitled *How to get Married*: 'The marriage of the type-writer and her employer is so frequent that it has passed into a joke' (*OED typewriter*, noun 2). Unsurprisingly in the light of such ambiguity, *typist*, first recorded in 1885, became the usual designation for a person.

Other, minor, types of word formation have become increasingly popular in modern English, for example **clipped** (shortened) forms (*fridge, lunch, phone*); **acronyms** composed of initials (*TV, VAT*); **blends** of parts of words (*brunch, guesstimate, motel*); **eponymous** forms from trade-names or the names of inventors or famous people (*cardigan, escalator, hoover, scrooge*); **conversions** from one part of speech to another (that's a big *ask*); and **back-formations** such as *administrate* from *administration* or *commentate* from *commentator*, where the verb is formed from the noun rather than vice versa. Some types, such as those with suffixes denoting a female **referent**, have fallen out of favour, as have words where a masculine form was deemed to include both sexes. One meets no *doctoresses* these days, and few *poetesses* or even *actresses*, while *chairmen* are generally referred to as *chairpersons* or *chairs*.

It is in the nineteenth century that we see the emergence of academic lexicology in Europe, the branch of linguistics concerned with the development of words. The main focus of this discipline in the nineteenth century was on the historical development of languages, especially the processes by which forms as superficially different as English *father*, French *père* and German *Vater* could be traced to a common ancestor. Interest grew in the history of the English language, leading to the editing of early manuscripts and to the compilation of the monumental *OED*, which traces the history of the general vocabulary of English from OE to the present day, except for words which died out before 1150. The first edition, compiled by a team of editors led mainly by Sir James Murray, was published in alphabetical parts between 1884 and 1928. Since then, Oxford University Press has continued to revise and update the dictionary and is now working on the fully revised online third edition. As the *OED* is a cornerstone of work in English

Historical Semantics, it will be referred to frequently throughout this book and discussed in detail in Chapter 4. At the time of writing, it contained 600,000 words from varieties of English around the world, and three million illustrative citations, which in themselves form a formidable historical text corpus. Following the example of the *OED*, historical dictionaries were later developed for different periods and varieties of English, for example the ongoing *Dictionary of Old English* (*DOE*), the *Middle English Dictionary* (*MED*) and the *Dictionary of the Scots Language* (*DSL*) (see section 4.4). There has also been progress in producing dictionaries and atlases of dialectal usage in Britain, the USA and elsewhere.

2.6 Conclusion: The present day

One advantage of studying vocabulary is that it changes more quickly and more obviously than other areas of language, such as grammar and speech sounds. New uses are all around us, though many are likely to be short-lived, such as the **vogue expressions** *over the moon* or 'we'll check that *going forward*' (= in future). Words continue to be needed for new concepts and activities such as space travel (*astronaut, cosmonaut, moonwalk, spaceman*) or computing (*bug, housekeeping, menu, mouse, virus*), the latter terminology coming from an extraordinary range of sources. Thanks to electronic media, new words spread very quickly, while the existence of resources such as text corpora and the internet makes it easier for lexicographers and others to track their progress. These resources have also enabled more attention to be paid to colloquial language and to the many geographical varieties of English.

   In a continually changing situation, certain constants can be observed. People encounter one another in many different contexts, from warfare to intellectual debate, and the transfer of vocabulary is often a result. Cultural change within a society also has an effect on its lexicon. However, within this situation, languages maintain an equilibrium, for example by discarding out-of-date or ambiguous words: the purpose of language, after all, is to enable us to communicate with one another.

Exercises

1. Section 2.1, *Words and expressions for* 'merry', gives only a fragment of the fascinating information about individual words to be found in the *OED*. Look up some of the words or meanings which are unfamiliar to you, and see if you can find reasons why this should be so. The words might be obsolete, or used only in dialect or limited contexts

such as poetry; or they might be very rare: for example, *griggish* is recorded only twice, both times in letters by the poet G. M. Hopkins. You might also like to find out whether Geoffrey Chaucer thought that *pismires* were merry.

2. Use *HTOED* to find some synonyms for people described as 'fops' or 'dandies', then use the definitions and citations in the *OED* to find out the sources of the words and work out what characteristics these people had (or were thought to have).

3. Use a dictionary to find out more about some of the italicised words in the paragraph below, for example their origins, structure and dates of use.

> Other, minor, types of word formation have become increasingly popular in modern English, for example **clipped** (shortened) forms (*fridge, lunch, phone*), **acronyms** composed of initials (*TV, VAT*), **blends** of parts of words (*brunch, guesstimate, motel*), and **eponymous** forms from trade-names or the names of inventors or famous people (*cardigan, escalator, hoover, scrooge*). Some types, such as those with suffixes denoting a female **referent**, have fallen out of favour, as have words where a male form was deemed to include both sexes. One meets no *doctoresses* these days, and few *poetesses* or even *actresses*, while *chairmen* are generally referred to as *chairpersons* or *chairs*.

Some online exercises on the history of English using *HTOED* are available at *Word Webs: Exploring English vocabulary*.

Further reading

There are many histories of the English language, which deal with the lexicon to varying extents. The most comprehensive is Baugh and Cable (2013 and previous editions). A good short introduction is Barber et al. (2009); Mugglestone (2006) contains chapters on the history of English by a variety of authors. Topics in this chapter are covered in Kay and Allan (forthcoming 2015). For an overview of vocabulary, see Jackson and Amvela (2000) and Hughes (1988 and 2000); on borrowing, see Durkin (2014) and on word-formation, Minkova and Stockwell (2009) and Plag (2003). For a fuller discussion of the OE lexicon, see Kay (2012). Burnley (2000) offers extracts with commentaries from linguistically important texts. For a discussion of the historical relationship between names and general vocabulary, see Hough (2012). On historical pragmatics, see Jucker and Taavitsainen (2013), especially chapter 5 on terms of address, and on syntax see Los (2015).

Notes

1. Numerical references are to the print edition of *HTOED* (2009, ed. Christian Kay et al.). Spellings follow the *OED* headwords.
2. The OE script contained some forms we no longer use including æ, called ash and pronounced like the <a> in *cat*, and þ, thorn, pronounced like the <th> in *breath* or *breathe*. Edited OE texts often place a length mark over certain vowels, but that is not done in this book.
3. Cheke wrote this in about 1557, but his work was not published in his lifetime. An extract is given in Baugh and Cable (2013: 422–3).

3 Categories of meaning

3.1 Introduction

One of the ways in which we make sense of the world is by sorting things into categories. Basically, a category is a set of things which have enough in common to differentiate them from other sets of things. Thus, if confronted by a room full of tables and chairs, most people would have no difficulty in recognising two distinct groups of objects and sorting them out accordingly. The criteria they used, whether consciously or unconsciously, might include appearance (does the object have a back or not?) and function (is it for sitting on or laying things on?). These criteria would probably not include number of legs, since both tables and chairs often have four legs and this would be a poor way of discriminating between them. Furthermore, such criteria might not be wholly successful: lurking in a corner might be an object which could be a large stool (backless, but used for sitting on) or a small table (also backless, but used for laying things on). The absence of clear lines of demarcation among potential members of a set can be a problem for anyone who tries to classify things, whether they are objects in the external world or words in a language.

Categorisation is an important cognitive ability. We can see it developing in children, who may initially operate with different categories from those of adults, for example calling all their drinks *juice.* Later, as they learn the categories normally operated by adults, they will exclude milk and other non-fruit drinks from this category. Categories can also vary more broadly across time and space; many Glaswegians, both children and adults, use the term *ginger* to refer to all sorts of soft drinks, not just those with a ginger flavouring. Such usage can be confusing for outsiders, who may misinterpret utterances because they are familiar with different categories. Knowledge of this kind is equally important in interpreting historical texts. In earlier periods of English, for example, the colour term *purple* referred to shades of red closer to what we would now call *crimson* or *scarlet*, often with reference to the robes worn by cardinals or Roman emperors (see further section 7.5). The *OED* identifies another meaning in this area: 'Of the colour of blood; bloody, blood-stained' (*purple*, adj. 2c), and this is probably the meaning Shakespeare intended when he wrote:

> See how my sword weepes for the poore Kings death.
> O may such **purple** teares be alway shed
> From those that wish the downfall of our house.
>
> (*Henry VI, Part 3*, V, vi, 3138–40)

Categorisation is of key importance in **Cognitive Semantics**, a branch of **Cognitive Linguistics** which has become increasingly influential since the 1980s. Cognitive Linguistics combines insights from the disciplines of Linguistics and Psychology, on the basis that our mental processes and our production and understanding of language are closely linked. Two of its key insights which are particularly relevant to Historical Semantics are the recognition of the importance of context and encyclopaedic knowledge, emphasised throughout this book, and the development of prototype theory (see section 3.3). Cognitive Linguistics has also been extremely influential in the development of metaphor theory (see Chapter 9). This book is written mainly from a Cognitive Semantics perspective, but it also incorporates some earlier ideas and theories about word meaning which you are likely to come across when reading about the subject. We will therefore begin this chapter by looking at some traditional views and introducing you to some terminology which is in general use. While a good deal of work has been done recently on synchronic Lexical Semantics (e.g. Murphy 2003), we'll restrict ourselves here to some basic notions.

3.2 Traditional approaches to Semantics

3.2.1 Reference

One of the most basic concepts in Semantics is **reference**, the relationship between the words we use (**referring expressions**) and the things we are talking about (the **referents** of the words). Some expressions have **constant reference**, i.e. refer to a unique entity, as *the moon* and *the sun* do when we are talking about our world, but the majority have **variable reference** and refer to sets of individuals. A word like *house* or *student* can identify thousands of possible referents; in this respect they operate in much the same way as the category labels described in section 3.1. If we want to be more precise, we have to identify the individual more specifically, as in *that house* or *the students in my class*.

The further we take the notion of reference, the more problematic it becomes. A key problem is that reference is essentially a theory that makes sense for nouns, which comprise the majority of the words we use to identify things in our universe. The clearest cases are nouns that refer to concrete objects. These words can be learned by **ostensive definition**: we can physically point to something and say to a child or a learner 'That's an apple' or 'This is a dog'. Ostensive definition is less effective, or indeed impossible, when it comes to nouns which refer to abstractions such as *happiness* or *ineptitude*, or to other parts of speech. For adjectives referring to qualities like colour or shape, such as *blue* or *round*, it might be possible to assemble a collection of blue or round objects and invite our listeners to apply their classificatory skills to deciding what they have in common, but this would be a hit-or-miss procedure and would often lead to disagreements over less clear examples. It would not help us much if we were trying to explain the italicised words in sentences like 'John *is thinking*' where there are no guaranteed physical signs of the activity.

Help is at hand from an important cognitive skill, our ability to think beyond the world of our immediate experience. We can imagine things we have never seen, share the feelings of other people, and discuss events in the past or future of which we have no actual experience. As children, we happily accept imaginary worlds inhabited by supernatural creatures such as elves, wizards or talking animals. As adults, we probably don't actually believe in such worlds, but we can still envisage how they operate: we could all write a fairy story or a story about life on another planet or set in another period of history. Such knowledge is part of the cultural context in which language is used, and an appreciation of it is crucial in Historical Linguistics, where we have to take account of changing world-views over time. Of equal importance is our capacity for metaphorical thinking, which enables us to perceive connections between the material world and abstract concepts, and thus to discuss such non-material things as ideas and feelings (see Chapter 9).

A more general problem for theories of reference is the fact that the boundaries of sets are rarely clear-cut, and can vary from speaker to speaker or era to era, as in the example of the *purple-red* boundary above. Another issue that historical semanticists have to bear in mind is that the referents themselves may have changed over the ages. Someone using the word *car* in the fifteenth century could have been referring to any of a range of wheeled vehicles from a cart to a chariot, but obviously not to a motor car, while his *pen* would have been a feather with a sharpened end. Likewise, if you encounter the word *potato* in a mid-sixteenth century text, it might be worth knowing that it probably referred to the sweet potato, which was prized at the time as an aphrodisiac. Luckily for us, many such pieces of information can be gleaned from the *OED*.

3.2.2 Sense

Linguistics has a particular problem with its metalanguage, the terminology used to discuss the subject. In a nutshell, the problem is that the object of discussion (in our case the English language) is the same as the medium of discussion (the English language). The words used as technical terms are part of everyday language but are used in a more specialised way. For example, in everyday use *meaning* is a more general term than *sense*, but in some contexts they are interchangeable: we can talk about a word having several *meanings* or several *senses*. In this section, however, following the structuralist approach described in section 3.2.2.1, we use **sense** as a technical linguistic term to refer to the relationships which words have with other words in the language system, their **sense relationships**. Sense is thus a much wider concept than reference: all words have some relationship to other items in the language. The fact that many words denote abstractions ceases to be such a problem if we analyse them in these terms; *love* and *hate* may have no referents, but they are opposites of each other and both denote kinds of *emotion*.

When considering sense relationships, two things have to be borne in mind:

1. When a word form has only one sense, it is described as **monosemous**; the condition is called **monosemy**. Many words, however, exhibit polysemy, the condition that occurs when a single form has more than one sense. The word *run*, for example, is multiply **polysemous**. As a verb, it can apply to swift movement, as in 'to run a race'; or to a badly applied dye, as in 'the colours have run'; or to organising or managing something, as in 'to run a business'. As a noun, it can mean a place where animals are kept, e.g. a *chicken run*, or a fault in a piece of cloth, e.g. a *run* in a pair of tights. In Semantics, each of these meanings of *run* is treated as a separate sense, entering into sense relationships with other meanings. Forms may have been polysemous throughout their history in English, or may start from a single meaning then develop others. The noun *saucer*, for example, was borrowed from French in the mid-fourteenth century with the single meaning 'a dish at table containing sauces and spices', whereas the

verb *stun*, also from French, is recorded some fifty years later with both literal and figurative meanings already in place.

2. Traditionally, the meaning of a single sense is thought of as having two overlapping aspects. Its **denotative meaning** is its basic core meaning or **denotation**, free from any meanings associated with particular styles, groups of speakers, or individuals; these meanings are generally agreed by speakers of a language and appear in dictionaries. They enter into relationships with other meanings, forming a network of sense relationships in the language. **Connotative meanings**, on the other hand, vary more from speaker to speaker, and occur in particular contexts. They're related to pragmatic questions like 'Who used the word?', 'What was the occasion?', 'What was the relationship between the participants in the conversation?' For example, take these three words for 'dog': *dog, doggie, pooch*. The referent is the same in all three cases: they refer to the same kind of animal in the real world. However, the **connotations** are quite different. You could use the word *dog* in any context, but *doggie* has connotations of childishness while *pooch* is a slang term with somewhat derogatory connotations. Dictionaries often deal with such information by labelling words *slang, colloquial*, etc.; such labels indicate how a word is used but don't affect its core meaning. Some scholars use the term connotation slightly differently: for example, Lynne Murphy makes a three-way distinction between denotative meaning, connotative meaning and 'social meaning', defining connotations as 'loose associations' which can be included in dictionary definitions and social meaning as 'what an expression can tell you about the person who is saying it and the social situation they are in' (Murphy 2010: 33).

For historical linguists dealing with written texts, connotative meanings can be particularly hard to tease out. In upper-class British English in the twentieth century, for example, certain words such as *toilet* (rather than *lavatory*) or *glasses* (for *spectacles*) had connotations of lower-class vulgarity. Academic papers written by linguists don't often arouse public controversy, but Alan Ross's article characterising certain words as Upper Class or U (*looking-glass, table napkin, writing-paper*) and others as Lower Class or Non-U (*mirror, serviette, note-paper*) led to considerable debate about their acceptability (1956: 28). In the mouth of a character in a novel or play from the period, such words may invite a negative assessment of that character's social standing which is relevant to an understanding of the text as a whole.

3.2.2.1 Sense relationships

Sense relationships are based on perceptions of degrees and kinds of sameness or difference among meanings. Their study was pioneered by one of the most important figures of modern Linguistics, Ferdinand de Saussure (1857–1913), whose *Course in General Linguistics* was published posthumously in 1916, and whose work forms the basis of **Structuralism** in linguistics and other disciplines. The type of Semantics he developed is usually described as **structuralist**. Saussure made a distinction between two different kinds of relationships, **syntagmatic** and **paradigmatic**, which is fundamental in many branches of linguistics.

Syntagmatic relationships are formed by items which can occur together in a grammatical structure and are often referred to as **collocations**. Thus the adjective *sensible* forms collocations with the nouns *man* and *decision* in sentences like (1): 'He was a *sensible man* who made *sensible decisions*' or 'That *remark* wasn't *sensible*', where the **collocates** (sometimes also called **collocators**) are *man, decision* and *remark*. In the course of its complex history *sensible* also collocates with a wide range of other terms, as shown in these entries from *OED2*: *sensible earthquake* (sense 3, 'Easy to perceive, evident'), *sensible distance* (sense 4, 'Large enough to be perceived'), *sensible talk* (sense 5, 'Easily understood, making a strong impression'), and *sensible grief* (sense 6, 'Such as is acutely felt'). Such collocations can sound strange to modern ears, or even be misinterpreted as instances of the modern meaning. The availability of electronic text corpora makes the study of collocations much easier, since key word in context (KWIC) searches can identify all the collocates of a given word (see, for example, Anderson and Corbett 2009). The resulting wealth of information may offer a better understanding of how a word is or was used, but it also makes the researcher appreciate the extent to which word meaning varies according to context, and the uphill task lexicographers face when trying to organise meanings into a manageable set of senses.

Paradigmatic relationships, by contrast, are formed by items which can occur in the same position in a grammatical structure, sometimes changing the meaning, sometimes not. In a sentence such as (2) 'She was feeling really *miserable*', we could replace *miserable* with a range of other words, for example *sad, unhappy, blue*, without greatly changing the meaning of the whole. Such words would commonly be regarded as **synonyms** of one another in this particular sense. On the other hand, we could change the meaning of the sentence completely by substituting **antonyms** such as *happy, joyful, ecstatic* (which we are therefore claiming are synonyms of one another). Some people might question the inclusion of *ecstatic* in this list, arguing that it refers to a much stronger feeling, and that takes us to the heart of the problem of synonymy: when, if ever, do two words 'mean the same'? This is a particularly pertinent question for the English language, which has accumulated large quantities of approximately synonymous words in the course of its history, offering speakers subtle choices in how they communicate (see further Chapter 2). Two or more words may temporarily share an exact meaning, but speakers often have no real need for a choice between such words, with the result that meanings may change or disappear over time, as discussed more fully in Chapters 5 and 6.

There has been considerable discussion of synonymy and other sense relationships in the Linguistics literature, with writers such as Cruse (1986) and Murphy (2003) investigating different ways of distinguishing types of synonymy. Some writers abandon the term altogether. The linguistic anthropologist Eugene Nida, who worked on meanings in New Testament Greek, calls such words overlapping terms, which may be a better description of their relationship (Nida 1975). We will not engage in this discussion here, however, but will use the term synonymy to refer to words which can substitute for one another in at least some contexts without causing significant meaning change.

Some words are close in meaning but are clearly not synonyms. In sentence (3) 'She wore an old *red* coat', we could alter the meaning of the whole by substituting other colour terms such as *green, blue* or *yellow*. These are related to each other in that they are colour terms and so form a set with *red*. This set is connected to the set which contains the more general word *colour* itself. What we have here is a relationship between the general and the specific, known as hyponymy or **inclusion**, which identifies hierarchies of meaning. If we move further down the *red* line of the hierarchy, as in Figure 3.1, we find *scarlet, vermilion* and *crimson*, which have a **hyponymous** relationship with *red* as being particular kinds of red; in other words, the meaning of *red* is *included* within the meanings of *scarlet, vermilion* and *crimson*. These relationships can be represented diagrammatically in Figure 3.1.

Colour, the most general term in the group, is called the **superordinate** or **hyperonym** of the whole group, while *red* is the superordinate of *scarlet, vermilion* and *crimson* at the next level in the hierarchy. Terms such as these, which occur at the same level in the hierarchy, are **co-hyponyms** of one another, just as *green, blue* and *yellow* are co-hyponyms of *red*. The relationship between co-hyponyms is variously referred to as **contiguity, partial synonymy** or **incompatibility**. A somewhat similar sense relation is **meronymy**, the relationship between wholes

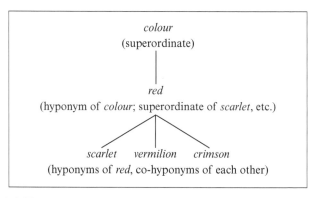

Figure 3.1 Hyponymy

and parts, as in *leg* and *arm* being **meronyms** of *body*. Hyponymy and meronymy are key relationships in the structure of thesauruses (see Chapter 6) and in explications of semantic change. As we will see in Chapter 5, narrowing of meaning is one of the commonest forms of semantic change among words which start off as synonyms. Thus OE *hund* referred to any dog and *fugol* to any bird, but their meanings narrowed in competition with other words such as *dog* and *bird*, and their later **reflexes** *hound* and *fowl* are now hyponyms of the more general terms.

Antonymy can be seen as a special type of contiguity in that the meanings of antonyms overlap to some extent with one another. For example, *loud* and *quiet* are both used to describe noise, but the degree of noise differs. *Boy* and *girl* are both hyponyms of *child* but differ in the feature of sex. Two different kinds of antonyms are usually identified. **True antonyms**, also called **binary antonyms** or **complementary terms**, describe an either/or situation: someone is either *alive* or *dead*, *male* or *female*, *married* or *single*. A sub-group of this type is **converse terms** or **conversives**, which denote a reciprocal relationship, as in *above/below*, *husband/wife*, *parent/child*; as in these examples, many words of this kind refer to spatial positions or human relationships. The majority of antonyms, however, are what are called **graded antonyms** or **polar terms** and refer to positions on some kind of scale. *Hot* and *cold*, for example, can refer to a range of temperatures depending on what one is talking about; in absolute terms, a hot stove has a higher temperature than a hot bath, but both can be described as *hot*. Grading is often reinforced by intermediate terms on the scale such as *warm* and *cool*.

Interpreting adjectives of this kind can be challenging for historical linguists. If life expectancy for most people is 40 or 50 years in a particular period, then *old* and *young* are likely to refer to lower ages than would nowadays be the case. In Jane Austen's novel *Persuasion*, published in 1818, both the heroine, Anne Elliot, and her sister Elizabeth are considered *old* in that they are increasingly unlikely to attract husbands at the ages of 27 and 29 respectively. Taylor (2003a: 276) points out that for young children *old* is often synonymous with *big*, since for children 'bigness' is a primary characteristic of adults. On another scale of judgement, 'early in the morning' may mean something entirely different to a medieval monk or peasant and a modern-day student!

You may have been unconvinced by the examples given above of true antonyms: nowadays we recognise different types of sexuality, and being married is not the only alternative to being single; such examples show how changing social conditions can affect vocabulary. Even the classic pair *dead* or *alive* is not immune from challenge. The adjective *half-dead* first occurred in OE and demonstrates our capacity to exaggerate and to play with language, as does the equally impossible phrase 'more dead than alive'. The condition may seem physically impossible, but the expression nevertheless exists.

3.2.3 Components, sets and fields

Attempts have been made over the years to formalise the differences in meaning outlined above, usually by 'breaking down' the meaning of individual words into **components** – units of meaning smaller than a word. Such attempts are generally known as Feature or **Componential Analysis (CA)**. Quite a lot of work of this kind was done in the 1960s and 1970s, often by anthropologists investigating areas such as kinship systems in different societies. CA provides a kind of shorthand which allows researchers to formulate the essential characteristics of concepts like 'mother' or 'family' (see further Chapter 8). As an illustration, take the four words *man, woman, boy, girl*, which are all hyponyms of *human being*. One of their essential semantic features is a component [+HUMAN], which differentiates them from *ape, gerbil, blackbird*, etc. which are [-HUMAN]. In order to distinguish them further, we need to make choices from two other sets of components: MALE/NOT MALE and ADULT/NOT ADULT. With these two pairs of components, we can formulate definitions which will sort out the four words to show their shared features and differences of meaning, as in Figure 3.2.

Our componential definitions would then be:

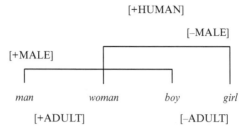

Figure 3.2 Componential analysis of *man, woman, boy, girl*

Man [+HUM +MALE +ADULT]	*Woman* [+HUM -MALE +ADULT]
Boy [+HUM +MALE -ADULT]	*Girl* [+HUM -MALE -ADULT]

A methodology like CA is superficially attractive, and seems at first glance to work well for the set of words above, but it runs into problems as soon as we try to extend it into larger or less clearly structured areas of meaning. Our four sample words are all polysemous, and the definitions cover only the most general uses. Some of the components are themselves unclear; for example, the age at which a child becomes an adult may not be a fixed point and varies from culture to culture and context to context. Further complications arise if we add words to the set with even fuzzier meanings, such as *baby, child* and *teenager*. As with true antonyms, the CA system requires us to make binary choices – a person is either an adult or not – but cases in the real world may be less clear-cut than this suggests. Nevertheless, thinking componentially can be a useful linguistic shorthand.

As we shall see in Chapter 6, what a thesaurus-maker is doing, consciously or unconsciously, when establishing a category such as 'roundness' is using a component [ROUND] as a basis for gathering up all the expressions which include this concept. Similarly, when analysing word meanings either diachronically or synchronically, it may be possible to express the difference between senses componentially, though without necessarily setting up binary oppositions like the ones expressed above. For example, the word *proud* goes back to OE *prud* in the meaning 'Having a high or exalted opinion of one's own importance. Usually in negative sense . . .' (*OED* adj. 1a). It could be distinguished from later meanings indicating 'proper' or justified pride, as in *proud parents*, by the use of a component such as [BAD], thus linking it with words such as *conceited* and *arrogant*.

Within the network of sense relationships, words can be organised into larger groups called **lexical sets**. Thus we can identify a lexical set of colour terms (*red, green, blue, crimson, light, dark*, etc.), culinary terms (*cook, bake, flambé, appetiser, ingredients*, etc.), and so on. These sets build up into bigger units known as **lexical** or **semantic fields**, covering much larger areas of meaning. Underlying the lexical field is a **conceptual field**, the domain of activity in the external world. Since we are dealing mainly with the lexicon here, we will use the term lexical field. The set of colour terms might form part of a lexical field of vision terms (colour is something that we see) or of light terms (as part of the field of physics terms). Such units have no fixed boundaries; the core of a set or field may be obvious enough, but there are usually controversial items on the periphery which might arguably belong to other fields. Does ten-pin bowling, for example, fit into a category of games or one of sports? Membership of sets and fields can also vary over time, sometimes in response to changing knowledge. An Anglo-Saxon classifying the word *whale*, for example, would put it with other terms for *fish*, since, not unreasonably, that is what people at the time thought it was.

One way of seeing how sets and fields work in practice is to look at the scheme of classification which appears in the front matter of thematic thesauruses such as *HTOED* or *Roget*. In structuralist terms, the entire vocabulary of a language occupies something which can be conceptualised metaphorically as **semantic space**. The thesaurus makes a 'map' of this space by organising the lexicon according to the relationships described above. All the meanings fit into it, but how they fit in will vary from thesaurus to thesaurus. Adrienne Lehrer, whose article on cookery terms uses structuralist principles to sort out that particular set of words (Lehrer 1969), summarises the situation thus in her subsequent book:

> Theories of semantic fields assume . . . that the vocabulary of a language is structured, just as the grammar and phonology of a language are structured – the words of a language can be classified into sets which are related to conceptual fields and divide up the *semantic space* or the semantic domain in certain ways. (1974: 15)

The concept of fields and domains, though not this view of the structuring of their content, remains important in Cognitive Semantics.

3.2.4 A note on homonymy

Traditionally a distinction is made between polysemy (see section 3.2.2), where meanings can be traced back to a single source, and **homonymy**, where two words share the same form, but go back to quite different roots. For example, all meanings of the form *right* can be traced back to OE *riht* 'law', and the form is therefore deemed to be polysemous. These include senses related to entitlement (human *rights*, television *rights*), direction (on your *right*), and politics (the far *right*), as well as 'a stag's full complement of antlers' (*OED* noun 10d). The form *bat*, on the other hand, has two etymologically unrelated meanings, the animal and the sports bat, and is therefore homonymous. According to the *OED*, *bat*[1] (the animal) first appeared in ME as *bakke* and derives from a Scandinavian word. *Bat*[2] (originally a stick or short piece of wood) may have come into ME from French *batte* or derive from an unrecorded OE word **bat*, possibly derived from Celtic. As a result of spelling changes the words have ended up with identical forms but have no semantic connection. Such accidents of history are of intrinsic interest to historical linguists and can be a factor in semantic change if the meanings are close enough to be confused (see Chapter 5).

3.2.5 A memory aid

A lot of terminology has been presented in this chapter. Although the words themselves are not usually Greek in origin, many are coined from Greek elements which have been widely used in English, especially in the development of scientific terminologies (on coinage, see section 2.5). Prefixes used in Semantics include:

- *poly* 'many', as in *polysyllable*. When combined with the root *seme* 'a unit of meaning', we get polysemy, **polyseme**, an individual word form which exhibits polysemy, and the adjective **polysemous**.
- *mono* 'one, single', as in *monosyllable*, gives us the parallel set monosemy, **monoseme** and **monosemous**.
- *hypo* 'lower, below', as in *hypodermic* 'below the skin', combines with *nym* 'name' to give hyponymy, **hyponym** and hyponymous or **hyponymic**, which have a lower position in taxonomies of meaning.
- *hyper* 'above', as in *hypersensitive* and *hyperbole*, gives us the parallel set hyperonymy, hyperonym (sometimes hypernym) and hyperonymous. In this book, superordinate is generally used for hyperonym.
- *homo* 'same', as in *homosexual*, plus *nym* 'name', yields homonymy, **homonym** and homonymous. This prefix can also be combined with a root meaning 'to write' to produce **homography**, and with one meaning 'sound' to produce homophony, and their associated forms. Homography applies to words which are spelled the same but pronounced differently, **homographs**, as in the substance *lead*

and the verb *to lead*, which can be ambiguous in written language. Homophony refers to the opposite situation, potentially ambiguous in spoken language, where words are pronounced the same but spelled differently, as in *right, rite, write, wright* – these are **homophones**.

- *mero* 'part' yields meronymy, **meronym** and meronymous, contrasted by some writers with coinages featuring *holo* 'whole', as in holonymy, **holonym** and holonymous.

3.3 Categories and prototypes

Two themes have emerged from our discussion so far. The first is the importance of sets and categories in semantic thinking. The second is the difficulty we often encounter in both life and language in deciding what belongs to a particular category. Our understanding of both these themes can be enhanced through ideas from Cognitive Semantics.

Interest in categorisation can be traced back to the early Greek philosophers, especially Aristotle, who developed a system of classification which persisted almost to our own day (see Taylor 2003a: 19–40). Aristotle was interested in the essential properties of objects, that is the features which define an object and allow it to be assigned uncontroversially to a particular class. These include **necessary conditions**, the set of criteria used to define members of a category, and **sufficient conditions**, the set of criteria deduced from these which defines the category itself. Aristotle's famous example is the definition 'Man is a two-footed animal', where the necessary conditions 'two-footed' and 'animal' are sufficient to define the 'essence' of man (in the sense of 'people') and thus the category. Other properties, such as the fact that an individual member of the set (i.e. a person) may be red-haired or well-educated or knock-kneed, are accidents or accidental properties and are irrelevant to the definition. Aristotle's theory is known as **classical categorisation theory**. Like componential analysis, it's a binary theory, offering either/or choices: either something belongs to a category or it does not. As a result, categories have firm boundaries and membership is clear-cut; if any entity meets all the criteria, it belongs to the category, but it cannot belong if it does not meet the criteria. Furthermore, all members of a category belong to it equally: something can't be more or less a member or a better or worse member. Thus Winston Churchill is clearly a member of this category and a horse equally clearly is not. Problems arise, however, when we come to cases which we might intuitively want to include: what do we do with a one-footed man (or woman), for example? At this point,

we may begin to question the validity of Aristotelian categories; in
the real world, categories may have clear cores but they tend to have
fuzzy edges.

Dissatisfaction with Aristotelian categories led people to look around
for new ideas. A useful concept proved to be that of the **fuzzy set**, introduced by the mathematician Lotfi Zadeh in 1965. According to fuzzy
set theory, items can have degrees of membership in a set, ranging from
best examples to least good examples (Zadeh 1965). Such ideas were
developed in Psychology, especially in the work of Eleanor Rosch,
who observed that people seem to have fairly clear ideas of the 'best'
(most typical) examples of a category, and that these best examples
are more important than a checklist of criteria in shaping our ideas
about set membership (Rosch 1973). Many categories of objects in the
real world are relatively clear-cut, for example the category of cats.
We've all seen hundreds, if not thousands, of cats in our time, yet we
rarely have any difficulty in assigning an individual to the category
regardless of differences in appearance, size, lifestyle, etc. We can say
therefore, using Rosch's terminology, that cats form a 'natural category',
one that we know from experience because it exists in the real world.
In linguistic terms, our word *cat* accesses a mental concept of a typical
cat which we have developed from our encounters with actual cats.
This typical example, the most cat-like cat, is called the prototype, and
is the standard against which potential members of the category are
measured. A list of defining features can be abstracted from the prototype and is sometimes called a **stereotype**; for British cats, this might
include the facts that they normally have four legs, a tail, fur of certain
colours, say miaow, and so on. Less typical examples, such as the breeds
Sphinx (which has no fur) or Manx (which has no tail) meet some but
not all of these criteria. This way of looking at categorisation, which
was adopted in linguistics in the 1980s, is sometimes called **prototype
theory**.[1] Unlike classical theory, prototype theory does not require us
to make binary choices, but rather to decide on degrees of likeness, so
that a category has clear members at its core but can also include less
clear examples.

3.3.1 Prototypes in action

The term prototype has several applications in Cognitive Semantics,
none of which is exactly the same as its use in everyday language to
denote 'The first or primary type of a person or thing; an original on
which something is modelled or from which it is derived; an exemplar, an archetype' (*OED* noun 1a), as in the prototype of a new kind of

aeroplane. As discussed above, the term is applied to typical members of categories of objects and other things in the experiential world, and by extension to the words denoting them. Prototypes may vary to some extent from speaker to speaker and culture to culture, but are similar enough to allow us to operate within the same language system, so that when someone uses the word *tree* or *happiness*, we know what they are referring to, even if, for a speaker of Canadian rather than British English, the prototypical tree might be a pine tree rather than an oak or an elm. They may also vary diachronically: the prototypical ship of an Anglo-Saxon or a Viking would be very different from ours, but would nevertheless retain its core meaning of 'a conveyance for taking people across water'.

There has been considerable interest, especially in Psychology, in identifying the factors which define prototypes. As in other Psychology experiments, the assumption is that it will be easier, which usually means faster, to identify core members of a set than peripheral members. Some of the early experiments involved inviting people to write down the first examples which came into their heads of a particular category, such as vegetables, fruits or birds. The results showed considerable agreement over the first few words given, at least among the American college students who took the tests. The following lists come from experiments reported in Battig and Montague (1969):

Vegetables, order of preference
1. carrot, 2. pea, 3. corn, 4. bean, 5. potato, 6. tomato, 7. lettuce, 8. spinach.
least cited: garlic, leek, black-eyed pea.

Fruits, order of preference
1. orange, 2. apple, 3. banana, 4. peach, 5. pear, 6. apricot, 7. tangerine, 8. plum.
least cited: nut, gourd, olive, pickle.

Birds, order of preference
1. robin, 2. sparrow, 3. bluejay, 4. bluebird, 5. canary, 6. blackbird, 7. dove, 8. lark.
least cited: ostrich, titmouse, emu, penguin, bat.

Various things can be deduced from these lists and subsequent experiments, none of them uncontroversial. Prototypical features of birds seem to be small size, feathers and the ability to fly; the preferred birds also seem to have a particular shape which ostriches, emus and penguins do not share. Prototypical fruits are soft and sweet. The prototypical vegetable is more mysterious: what common properties can we extract from things as different as carrots and spinach? It may be that this is not a natural category but a functional one containing things which are eaten as vegetables. That would explain the inclusion of *tomato* in the list, even though most college students probably know that technically it's a fruit, not a vegetable, just as they probably know that a bat is a mammal, not a bird. (On different types of categories, see section 6.3.) Cultural differences are also obvious from the list; if you try this experiment on speakers of other languages or varieties of English, you'll find that they produce different lists, but there will probably be a relatively high level of agreement between speakers from a single culture about most of the items on the list. However, even if speakers across cultures produce the same words, the referents may be different. As we saw in section 2.4, the American robin is a different creature from the British one, although the stereotype of both contains features such as having a red breast and a distinctive song.

Prototypes can also form the basis of categories of synonymous words. In *HTOED*, for example, the category *Cat* contains eighteen words, some of which are obsolete or more restricted in meaning than *cat* itself, such as *pussycat* or *moggie*, the latter defined in the *OED* as '*colloq.* (chiefly *Brit.*) A (domestic) cat, *esp.* a non-pedigree or otherwise unremarkable one' (*OED* noun 3). As the most neutral term in the set, *cat* can be described as its core member, and would probably be picked as the heading in a thesaurus. There are also hyponymous sub-categories for concepts such male cat, female cat and kitten. As the editors wrote in the Introduction to *HTOED*:

> Within each heading in *HTOED*, meanings are grouped according to a loose principle of synonymy. There is no claim that these words are exactly synonymous, i.e. could replace one another in all contexts (if such a condition exists), but rather that they share enough of their meaning to be classified together. Although the project was started before the current cognitive semantics paradigm became dominant, that paradigm has retrospectively proved sympathetic to the problems involved in categorizing large quantities of lexical data. The development of prototype theory, which allows for fuzzy sets containing both good and less good examples of the central concept, challenges the either/or basis of Aristotelian category assignment and liberates semanticists from a narrow notion of synonymy as an organizing principle. (*HTOED* 2009: xix)

3.3.2 Lexical prototypes

With reference to the development of individual words, the word itself is seen as a category and each distinct meaning of that word is said to have a prototype. The simplest kind of word is a monoseme, which constitutes a monocentric category with a single prototype. So many words develop additional meanings over time that it's quite difficult to think of examples, but three possibilities are *telephone*, *word-processor*, *giraffe* – all fairly recent additions to the English vocabulary. The majority of words, however, are polysemous and constitute polycentric categories with more than one prototype. Such words start out with a single prototype, in either English or their source language. When a new meaning develops, the original prototype might disappear, or gradually shift towards the new meaning, or it might continue to exist alongside the new meaning. If both old and new meanings survive, **prototype split** has taken place, and the form now has two prototypes. In words with a long history, prototype split can take place many times over, with variable numbers of prototypes surviving. For example, the word *sad* developed various meanings over the years, and has recently developed a new one. These meanings are given in chronological order of their development, summarising the information in the *OED*:

1. satisfied, sated
2. steadfast, settled
3. strong, capable
4. orderly, serious
5. miserable
6. pathetic (as in people described as 'sad anoraks', or comments such as 'In the evenings, I wash my socks – how sad is that!')

In this case, we can probably see how the meanings have developed. Some speakers focus on part of meaning (1), which develops into meaning (2) (if you're satisfied you tend to be settled); that usage spreads to other speakers and eventually a new prototype emerges. In this case, though not always, the process is repeated: a settled person is seen as strong, a strong person as serious, and a serious one as sad. The earlier prototypes, (1) to (4), gradually drop out of use, leaving only (5) and (6) in ModE. This type of process is referred to as **chaining** (or sometimes **radiation**); if we have enough information, we can see how one meaning develops out of another like a series of links in a chain (though this progression isn't always clear-cut; see Chapter 5). Taking a term from the philosopher Wittgenstein, the chain is sometimes referred to as a 'family resemblance' structure: like members of a family, the meanings bear some resemblance to one another although they are clearly not identical and do not share all the same features (see Taylor 2003a: 42–3, 110–11).

3.3.3 Homonymy revisited

In section 3.2.4 we discussed the difference between polysemy and homonymy. A frequently raised question in Cognitive Semantics is whether this distinction is worth making at all. As historical semanticists, we may be interested in the fact that all the meanings of *staff* noun,[1] including 'a stick carried in the hand to assist walking' and 'a body of persons employed by an organisation', ultimately derive from a Common Germanic word represented by OE *stæf* 'stick'. Many people, however, do not know this and would not find the information particularly interesting or useful. Semanticists sometimes argue that a distinction should be made between cognitive polysemy, where the connection between senses is apparent to most speakers of the language, and etymological polysemy, where a word's complete history is considered. A more drastic view is that the concept of polysemy should be abandoned altogether, and all cases of multiple meanings treated as homonymy. This would certainly make life easier for lexicographers, who generally group polysemous meanings under a single headword with multiple senses but give homonyms separate entries. However, even this approach is not as straightforward as it sounds. Meanings may go back to different roots in OE but the same root in earlier Common Germanic, or to different roots in one of the Romance languages but the same root in Latin, because the meanings had already diverged by the time English or French or Italian became separate languages. Sometimes the root of a meaning is not known, and there is not enough evidence to reconstruct its history. There is no single solution to these difficulties, but, as we shall see in succeeding chapters, the distinction between polysemy and homonymy is useful in explaining intrinsically diachronic processes such as semantic change and the development of metaphor.

3.4 Domains and frames

One of the main advantages of Cognitive Semantics is that it emphasises the role of knowledge and experience of the world in producing and understanding language. Structuralists and others working in the twentieth century were often keen to exclude extralinguistic knowledge, sometimes referred to as encyclopaedic knowledge, from Semantics, on the grounds that it could never be subjected to the kind of quasi-scientific analysis we looked at in section 3.2.3. Cognitive Semantics, on the other hand, recognises that we arrive at meanings by drawing on whatever relevant information we have. As Taylor says, 'Word meanings are cognitive structures, embedded in patterns of knowledge and belief; the context against which meanings are characterized extends beyond the language system as such' (Taylor 2003a: 87). Such an approach is especially advantageous for historical semanticists; with limited textual evidence and no native speakers to interrogate, we need to take help wherever we can find it when trying to elucidate meanings.

Knowledge and meaning are understood in terms of **semantic domains**, which are rather like semantic fields in that they identify areas of human experience, such as Time or Space or Emotions. As with the lexical fields discussed in section 3.2.3, underlying the semantic domain is a **conceptual domain**, the domain of activity in the external world. Unlike fields, however, which tend to be structured by the basic sense relationships of synonymy, hyponymy, etc., domains are structured by the different ways in which knowledge can be presented. Expressions like *hour, week, day, month* and *year* are part of the large semantic domain of Time, here structured or **profiled** in units of increasing size which are themselves treated as domains with their own structures or **profiles**. Many domains have more than one possible profile; our selection from these depends on how we want to present our information. The domain of the year, for example, can be profiled as twelve months or four seasons. The domain of the week can be profiled as seven days or as a vaguer system of weekdays and weekend. As we will see in section 8.5, profiles of these and other domains have changed in the course of the history of English; in order to understand such changes we need to draw on our knowledge of how people lived at the time. Where a word is polysemous, i.e. has more than one meaning, these meanings are described as being profiled against multiple domains, and are understood through a background of conceptual knowledge that relates to different areas of experience. Thus *day* could be profiled as a part of the domain of the week, or, in contrast with *night*, as part of the domain of light, or as part of the domain of the lifecycle, as in 'he's had his day'; these constitute its **domain matrix** (see Taylor 2003a: 87–94).

Any particular profile of a domain is referred to as a **schema**. A schema is essentially an abstract model of the configuration of a domain, what we might call a blueprint of its structure. Depending on how we want to profile our information, we can apply a bounding schema which imposes boundaries or divisions on the year, a sequencing schema, which presents things in a particular order, as in the names of the months and seasons, or a part-whole schema relating parts and wholes, as in *week, month, year, century*. Other important schemas are the containment schema, referring to things being inside or outside other things, and the journey schema identifying such things as source, path, goal. The last two of these are especially important in the understanding of metaphor (see Chapter 9).

Many writers use the term **frame** for the body of knowledge needed to process a particular situation. In interactions with others, we draw on conventional frames which are part of our shared culture when talking about activities or events such as shopping or travelling; with people we know well we may draw on individual experiences. Accompanying these frames in attempts to describe them is what's called a script, which draws on the knowledge in the frame to indicate everything associated with a particular occasion. Two of the best-known examples are for restaurant meals and plane journeys, which read rather like instructions for theatrical performances and are described in detail in Ungerer and Schmid (2006: 212–17).

Below we have a rather idealised version of a frame and script for a lecture:

Frame: Lecture
Props: Room, desks, seats, whiteboard, data projector, pens, paper
Roles: Lecturer, students
Entry conditions: Lecturer has knowledge; students want to acquire knowledge
Results: Students have acquired knowledge; lecturer has earned salary

Script: A lecture at University X

Scene 1: Preliminaries	Scene 2: The Lecture
Students enter lecture room	Lecturer enters room
Students decide where to sit	Lecturer distributes handouts
Students go to seats	Lecturer distributes attendance list
Students sit down	Lecturer takes out notes
Students take out pen and paper	Lecturer lectures

And so on, and on, and on. You can probably see that this is rather an inadequate representation of what actually happens at a lecture. There's quite a lot of possible detail missing: nobody takes their coat off, nobody arrives late. There's also a rather simple-minded analysis of motive – students may have quite a variety of reasons for attending lectures as well as acquiring knowledge, such as seeing their friends or getting out of the rain. However, it's a start and can help to explain how we interpret some utterances. For example, if Student A says to Student B 'My pen has run out', we draw on our knowledge of the need to take notes at lectures and probably interpret this to mean that Student A would like to borrow a pen.

Frames and scripts can date quite quickly: you might want to point out that students increasingly use laptops rather than pens and paper to take notes at lectures. It can therefore be difficult to construct them for activities in past periods. Sometimes writers can be helpful, as in this extract from *Pride and Prejudice* (1813) where Elizabeth, the heroine, dances with the haughty Mr Darcy, who has previously shown no interest in her. We can deduce quite a lot from this 'script' about polite behaviour at dances. We also learn that it is usual to have a partner for two dances at a time, and that these last about half an hour.

> They stood for some time without speaking a word; and she [Elizabeth] began to imagine that their silence was to last through the two dances, and at first was resolved not to break it; till suddenly fancying that it would be the greater punishment to her partner to oblige him to talk, she made some slight observation on the dance. He replied, and was again silent. After a pause of some minutes she addressed him a second time with:
>
> 'It is *your* turn to say something now, Mr Darcy. – *I* talked about the dance, and *you* ought to make some kind of remark on the size of the room, or the number of couples.'
>
> He smiled, and assured her that whatever she wished him to say should be said.
>
> 'Very well. – That reply will do for the present. – Perhaps by and bye I may observe that private balls are much pleasanter than public ones. – But *now* we may be silent.'
>
> 'Do you talk by rule then, while you are dancing?'
>
> 'Sometimes. One must speak a little, you know. It would look odd to be entirely silent for half an hour together, and yet for the advantage of *some*, conversation ought to be so arranged as that they may have the trouble of saying as little as possible.'
>
> Jane Austen, *Pride and Prejudice* (1813: chapter 18)

3.5 Conclusion

This chapter has been concerned with relationships among word forms and their meanings. We have looked at individual word forms, and discussed how meanings relate to one another in situations such as polysemy and homonymy. We have also discussed how these meanings relate to those of other forms with which they share some meaning. In so doing, we have drawn selectively on developments in Semantics in the last fifty or so years, concentrating on theoretical insights which are particularly relevant to Historical Linguistics. We have concluded that Cognitive Semantics is a particularly helpful approach which increases our understanding of both word meaning and larger areas of meaning such as semantic domains. It even helps us to solve one of the key problems of early Semantics, the meaning of *synonym* itself, since we can now say that within a prototype category of synonyms, some are prototypical and others less so!

Exercises

1. Look at the entries for the senses of the adjective *sensible* listed as 14 a–c in the *OED*, and make lists of their collocations. Examine how these support (or not) the division of the word into these senses. If you have access to an online corpus, check the range of collocations found there. These corpora are readily available from Brigham Young University:
British National Corpus http://corpus.byu.edu/bnc/
Corpus of Historical American English http://corpus.byu.edu/coha/
Corpus of Contemporary American English http://corpus.byu.edu/coca/.

2. Sometimes, and confusingly, words which look like antonyms are in fact synonyms. This is the case with *inflammable*, first recorded in 1605, and *flammable*, first recorded in 1813. Oxford Dictionaries Online explain:

> The words **inflammable** and **flammable** both have the same meaning, 'easily set on fire'. This might seem surprising, given that the prefix **in-**normally has a negative meaning (as in **indirect** and **insufficient**), and so it might be expected that **inflammable** would mean the opposite of **flammable**, i.e. 'not easily set on fire'. In fact, **inflammable** is formed using a different Latin

prefix **in-**, which has the meaning 'into' and here has the effect of intensifying the meaning of the word in English. **Flammable** is a far commoner word than **inflammable** and carries less risk of confusion.

Use the *OED* definitions and citations to examine some other words with the core meaning 'not easily set on fire', such as *incombustible, non-inflammable, uninflammable, non-flammable, non-flam*. Consider whether they are denotatively synonymous, and whether their connotations differ. When are they first recorded in English and why are there so many of them? You might also like to look at other words listed in the *HTOED* for *flammable* and *incombustible* to see whether any more are still in use. You could also compare the pair *ebriate/inebriate(d)*.

3. Go through the entry for the adjective *right* in the *OED* and work out the semantic connections among the senses. Note which ones have been present since Old English, and when newer senses have developed. The easiest way to get an overview of what has happened to this word might be to make a chart.

4. Consider the group of words below and decide (a) whether each one is monosemous or has multiple meanings, and (b) if the latter, whether it is polysemous or homonymous. Do this without consulting a dictionary and then check the *OED* to see whether your judgement is etymologically correct or reflects some link that you have perceived between the meanings. You might also find it interesting to check whether a modern dictionary agrees with you.

Bikini   cross   giraffe   ear   wake   die   band   mean

Further reading

Murphy (2010) is a useful general synchronic overview of Lexical Semantics. Also useful for discussions of key terms are the glossaries by Murphy and Koskela (2010) and A. Cruse (2006). For prototype theory and other aspects of Cognitive Semantics, see Geeraerts (2010) and Taylor (2003a). Lehrer (1969) uses CA for a detailed synchronic analysis of cookery terms, stressing the importance of real-world knowledge. Kay (2000) discusses the use of semantic theory generally and CA in particular in historical lexicography.

Note

1. There is some debate in the early linguistics literature over whether the prototype has actual existence in the real world. The answer to this is basically no. If we went out and rounded up a lot of cats, we could probably agree on which were prototypical, but there isn't a single prototype sitting smugly out there waiting to be discovered.

4 Tracing the development of individual words

4.1 Introduction

In this chapter we look at some of the resources available to research-ers interested in studying the history of individual English words, and especially at historical dictionaries. Since historical dictionaries differ considerably in both content and presentation from modern synchronic dictionaries, we'll also spend some time discussing the purpose of such dictionaries and how they are compiled. Our main focus will be the *OED*, which is generally recognised as the most important of all English historical dictionaries, and has been the inspiration and model for sub-sequent dictionaries such as the *A Dictionary of the Older Scottish Tongue* (*DOST*) (see section 4.5). The *OED* is the largest historical dictionary of English and contains detailed information on all the words in general use in ME and later varieties, including words and senses which have become obsolete. It is thus an enormously valuable tool for anyone interested in language change.

Historical dictionaries try to present the most complete picture pos-sible of the formal and semantic development of the words they record. In the *OED*, entries for individual words include information about etymology (the origin of the word), forms (spelling and grammatical variation), pronunciation, and meanings recorded in different periods. In common with other historical dictionaries, the *OED* supports its defi-nitions of senses with quotations from contemporary texts showing how particular meanings were or are used in context. In section 4.3, we'll look at how all this information can be used in lexical research. Before that, however, we'll look at the long and fascinating history of the *OED*, which is a major research project in its own right. We'll also see how it has developed over the course of three major editions.

4.2 Introducing the *OED*

The idea of the *OED* dates back to the 1850s, when interest in the history of languages was firmly established around Europe. Scholars of English became concerned that there was no available dictionary that presented a complete picture of the historical development of individual English words. This kind of dictionary was already being written for other languages: for example, the first part of the *Deutsches Wörterbuch*, a large-scale historical dictionary of German, was published in 1852. In 1859, the Philological Society, a group devoted to Philology (the study of the histories and structures of languages) started a project to compile a dictionary, to be called *A New English Dictionary on Historical Principles*. Oxford University Press subsequently took over responsibility for the project (long before any of the dictionary appeared in print), and later it was officially renamed *The Oxford English Dictionary*.

4.2.1 OED1

Originally it was expected that it would take ten years to finish the *New English Dictionary*, but in fact it was a very much longer and more difficult process than anyone had anticipated. The early editors of the dictionary quickly realised that collecting the material they would need to describe and illustrate word histories would be a huge task. They faced a number of problems. An important aspect of the dictionary was that it should be evidence-based, with the entries written on the basis of actual uses of each word; it should also give a sense of when particular words and word meanings were in use. The editors therefore needed to find written examples of all of the forms and senses of each word, including the earliest and latest instances of each, so that the dictionary would give a full picture of the historical development of the word. It would be difficult and time-consuming enough to find these examples in available published texts, but they faced an additional complication: if they were to trace the earliest uses of words they would need to collect examples from OE and ME texts, and many of these existed only in obscure manuscripts which were not catalogued or edited, and were therefore difficult to identify and use. Of course, all of the work for the first edition, including data collection, had to be done without the aid of computers, so even finding an example of a word in a printed text involved careful and painstaking effort.

The first editor of the *OED*, Herbert Coleridge, began by making public appeals to recruit large numbers of volunteers, who would read published texts and copy out quotations which showed the uses of each word. Initially, readers were asked to read texts of their own choice, and to note interesting and unusual word uses. In later years, more targeted reading was commissioned, for example asking people to read particular kinds of source texts or to look for particular words or senses (such as more common words or very established senses, which were neglected by early volunteer readers). Coleridge enlisted large numbers of readers, but died after only two years, and a second editor, Frederick Furnivall, was appointed in 1861. Furnivall was editor of the dictionary for eighteen years, and continued to recruit volunteer readers in both the UK and the USA. His major contribution to the project, however, was to found the Early English Text Society, a scholarly society of medievalists who produced editions of OE and ME texts from manuscript sources and thus made these texts accessible to dictionary editors. Furnivall was a great publicist for the dictionary, but he was less enthusiastic about lexicography itself, and soon tried to find someone else to take over the project. In 1879, he persuaded James Murray to become the third editor of the dictionary, and it was under Murray's editorship that the major editorial work of the project was completed, and the bulk of the dictionary was produced.

The dictionary was published in fascicles, or sections, which each contained entries from a portion of the alphabet: the first fascicle, published in 1884, included entries in the range *A – Ant*. In 1888 a further editor, Henry Bradley, was appointed to lead the editing of parts of the dictionary. It was not until 1928, thirteen years after Murray's death and sixty-nine years after the first editor was appointed, that the final part of the first edition was published, under the editorship of William Craigie and C. T. Onions, who had both worked with Murray and Bradley. Each of the editors had a large team of assistants; although people often think of the first edition as Murray's creation it is the work of hundreds of scholars and enthusiasts, whose number grew as the dictionary evolved.

Inevitably, such a long period of production meant that entries in the later part of the alphabet were based on much better and more complete data than entries in the first part. Much more reading had been done by the time the final fascicles were published, including the reading of many more OE and ME texts, which had been edited during the late nineteenth and early twentieth centuries. As well as this, the dictionary editors were more experienced by the final stages. As a result, some of the content of the first edition was effectively out of date as soon as the whole work was finished. To remedy this, the final fascicle was followed in 1933 by a supplement to the dictionary, which mainly included entries for words and senses from across the alphabet which had been omitted from the first edition. A second supplement was published in four volumes between 1972 and 1986.

4.2.2 OED2

By the time the second supplement to the *OED* was completed in 1986, the dictionary had become somewhat unwieldy; the original 128 fascicles, which were published in ten volumes in 1928, had been joined by the five volumes of supplements (one from 1933 and four from 1972 to 1986), which weren't integrated into the alphabetical sequence of the first edition. Anyone looking up a word in these volumes might have to look in three books to find the information they needed. As well as this, many new electronic tools were available to lexicographers and dictionary users by the 1980s, and large-scale reference works could be published and accessed electronically rather than in cumbersome print copies. A new edition of the dictionary, which integrated all of the published material into a single sequence, was published in hard copy in 1989 and on CD-ROM in 1992 (the editors were John Simpson and Edmund Weiner). *OED2* included some very limited revision of the first edition and some new supplementary material, including new entries and a few revised definitions, but generally very little was changed. Most second edition entries are the same as their first edition or supplement counterparts, and where they are different the differences tend to be very minor. This means that the bulk of the material in the second edition dates from the late nineteenth century. Three volumes of additions to the second edition were published between 1993 and 1997.

4.2.3 OED3

A major new project to revise the whole dictionary thoroughly was begun in the 1990s, and is likely to go on for some time. The Chief Editor of *OED3* was John Simpson until his retirement in 2013, when Michael Proffitt took over. The project occupies more than seventy full-time members of staff, including editors for new words and etymology (each with their own team of editors), a bibliography team and an archivist. A glance at the full list of dictionary staff and the much longer list of consultants, advisers and contributors gives a sense of the scale of the project (see Further reading).

OED3 is currently being published in small sections which are released online rather than in hard copy; the first revised entries, for the range *M – Mahurat*, appeared in 2000. It may seem odd to start at the letter M rather than the letter A, but there were two particular reasons for this. By the time they reached the letter M in the middle of the alphabet, the editors of the first edition were relatively experienced, and had established good working practices to deal with the problems different types of entries presented; these entries therefore provide a reliable starting point for the revised entries. Furthermore, words beginning with M in English are a mixture of native words (such as *mother* and *mouse*) and words borrowed from a variety of different languages (such as *magnanimous*, borrowed from Latin, *macron*, borrowed from Greek, and *meerkat*, borrowed from Dutch). Not all letters show this kind of variety in English: for example, the letters J and X were not used in early English, so most words beginning with these letters are borrowed from other languages.

Although the *OED*3 editors started by working through the alphabet from M, they changed their practice when they had completed the letter R. The batches released every three months now consist of entries from across the alphabet; for example, the batch released in March 2012 included *ant, education, feminism, locomotive, time, veggie* and *you*. In revising the second edition material for *OED*3, the editors have been able to integrate new research into the project, and have carried out very extensive research of their own. They have, for example, added new entries and new senses for existing entries, they have completely revised etymologies and they have given more detailed information on pronunciation in different accents of English. They have found earlier and later quotations to illustrate usage of most words and senses, thus changing our knowledge of the period of currency of a word. All definitions have been reconsidered and in most cases revised. Even with the new electronic tools available to them, and all the new research on English they can draw from, the scale of the revision explains the large number of staff and long timescale of the project.

4.3 What the *OED* tells us

Nowadays, many scholars find the electronic edition, *OED Online*, the most convenient version of the *OED* to use. Because *OED*3 is an ongoing project updated every three months, the online edition is a mixture of second and third edition entries. These are signalled in a column on the right of the screen, in blue for updated entries and in red for non-updated ones. The 'entry profile' gives a summary of information about the word and where appropriate there is a link from *OED*3 to *OED*2 entries. As a user of *OED Online*, it is important to be aware that there are some differences between the two editions in the information given and in the way it is presented. In general, it is helpful to spend some time familiarising yourself with the way information is presented in whichever edition of the *OED*, or indeed any other dictionary, you use.

The amount of information presented in each *OED* entry can be daunting for anyone who is not familiar with the conventions used. A very short and simple entry, for the noun *manga*, is reproduced in Figure 4.1 – we will use this to demonstrate exactly what information is presented in the entry. In section 4.3.2 we will look at a longer and more complicated entry, for the noun *monster*. Symbols and abbreviations used in the entry for *manga* are explained below; full lists of all the *OED* symbols and abbreviations are given on the *OED* website (see Further reading). We will refer to *OED Online* throughout, so if you have access to it, you might like to look at the entries there.

4.3.1 manga²

4.3.1.1 Headword
The word at the top of each entry is generally referred to as the headword. Following this is a part of speech label, *n* (for *noun*), and a superscript ² which indicates that there is a separate entry for *manga n¹*, a homonym of *manga n²*. In other words, there is another noun which happens to have the same form as this one, but is not etymologically related to it so is treated separately (on homonyms, see section 3.2.4). Deciding whether or not two forms are homonymous is usually straightforward, as here, but can be a problem for lexicographers dealing with older words with uncertain etymologies.

4.3.1.2 Information about editions
The label on the right tells us that *manga n²* is a third edition entry, published online in 2000. Under 'publication history' we learn that some further minor change has been made to the entry more recently, so that a later date is given for the current version. Since it was a new word in the third edition, there is no 'previous version' link to *OED2* (compare the entry for *monster*).

4.3.1.3 Pronunciation
In this case, three alternative pronunciations are indicated, transcribed in the alphabet of the International Phonetic Association (IPA), one for British English, and two for US English. The mark ' at the beginning of *manga* indicates a stressed syllable. *OED2* entries tend not to list US pronunciation, but *OED3* entries give more information about differences in these two major varieties. *OED3* occasionally also gives pronunciations for other major varieties of English, such as Australian

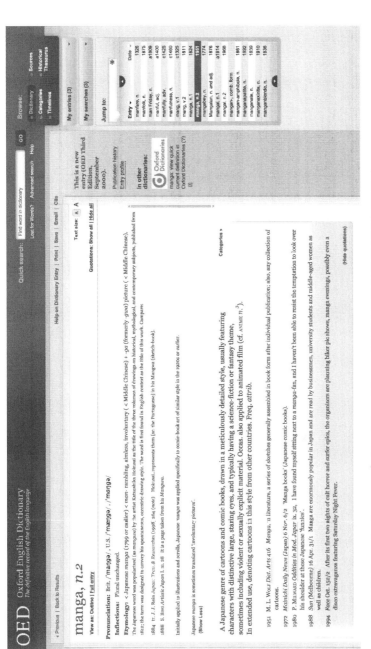

Figure 4.1 *OED Online* entry for *manga*[2]. (Reproduced by permission of Oxford University Press.)

and South African English, but only where a word is principally used in that variety (e.g. *galah* or *Ndebele*). Received Pronunciation and General American are usually given for British and US English respectively, since these are the most generally-known accents in these varieties, and are often treated as 'reference accents' in terms of which other accents are described. Widely-used variants in the pronunciation of a word, such as the vowel in *bath* in British English, are often given as well, but not all possible pronunciations for regional varieties of British and US English are given; for example, Scottish pronunciations, which often have different vowels from other varieties of English and often include final -*r* (e.g. in the word *car*), tend not to be given.

4.3.1.4 Inflections
Information about the inflected forms of words, such as the plural form for nouns or the past tense of verbs, tends only to be given where the inflected form is irregular. The plural of *manga* is *manga* rather than *mangas*, so this is noted explicitly; by contrast, the plural of *meerkat* is not given in its entry, since it follows the usual pattern in English, *meerkats*.

4.3.1.5 Forms
manga is found with only one spelling in English, so there is nothing to say about its form, but many words are attested with a variety of different spellings, particularly in earlier English. If you scroll down to the entry for *mangal n*[1], using the word list on the right in the online edition, you'll see that several different forms are listed, along with information about when these are recorded. For example, '18 **mangale**' means that the spelling *mangale* is attested in the 1800s; '18 – **mangal**' means that *mangal* is attested from the 1800s onwards. If you click on 'previous version', you'll see that *OED2* followed a slightly different convention: here, 9 **manggall** means that this form is attested in the nineteenth century, that is the 1800s.

4.3.1.6 Etymology
The first part of this section, in larger type, gives the basic facts of the history of the word. *OED3* works backwards from the present-day form, giving the most recent history of the word first. The sign < means 'from', so in this case the etymology tells us that English *manga* is a borrowed form of Japanese *manga*, which is recorded (in a Japanese text) in 1799, but may have occurred earlier. The etymology then traces the origins of the Japanese form, which is a compound of a Middle Chinese adjective *man-* 'rambling, aimless, involuntary', and a Middle Chinese noun -*ga* 'picture'; the earlier form of -*ga* in Middle Chinese is -*gwa*. The rest

of this section, in smaller type, gives more information about the word's history in both English and Japanese.

4.3.1.7 Definition

This is perhaps the most straightforward part of the entry, in that it is the most familiar; not all dictionaries contain the kinds of information we've already seen in the *OED*, but all of them define the words they include. In this entry, only one definition is listed for *manga*, and it covers a number of slightly different but closely related and overlapping senses. Firstly, the entry notes that *manga* is 'Occas[ionally] also applied to animated film', and directs the reader to compare the word *anime*, which is the more common term for this sense ('cf.' means 'compare'). Secondly, the definition notes that the word is also in 'extended' use: it is sometimes used with a more general meaning for non-Japanese cartoons of a similar kind. If this extended sense was more established and in more widespread use it would be defined separately, but here it is simply noted within the same definition. Thirdly, the definition notes that the word is 'Freq[uently] *attrib[utive]*', meaning that the noun *manga* can be used to modify another noun as if it were an adjective, in a phrase like *manga book* or *manga fan*.

4.3.1.8 Quotations

This section gives some examples of the use of the word. These examples are sometimes referred to as citations. The date of publication and full reference of each one is given (with a link to the full title where abbreviations have been used), so that anyone reading the entry can find the published source and see the larger context of the quotation. The first quotation under each meaning is always the earliest that the dictionary team has found (in English, of course; the etymology section has already noted that *manga* is found earlier in Japanese). The quotation with the latest date in this entry is very recent, from 1994, showing that the sense is still in use. For senses that are no longer current, the latest available attestation will be given. The quotations often make interesting reading in themselves, as you'll see when we come to *monster* in 4.3.2.

4.3.1.9 Other links

The entry for *manga* includes a link to a modern dictionary. For older words, links may be offered to other historical dictionaries (see section 4.5). The link called 'categories' beside the definition leads to a broad subject classification, in this case 'Arts, Literature, Science Fiction'. *Manga* was added to the *OED* after *HTOED* data collection was

finished, but other words, such as *monster*, have 'thesaurus' links attached
to senses which appear in *HTOED*.

4.3.2 monster

In section 4.3.1 above we looked at a straightforward entry for a word
with only one defined sense. Entries get much more complicated,
but also much more interesting, when we look at words which have
changed meaning through time, and which may be polysemous in different periods. In this section, we will look at a much longer entry, for
monster, and explore the relationship between its current and past senses.
Unfortunately, the *OED* entry is too large to reproduce here, so we'll
concentrate on general points. You may find it helpful to look at the
'outline' version of *monster* in *OED Online* to get an idea of the structure
of the entry.

There are two *OED* entries for *monster*, which is first recorded in ME:
one is for the relatively rare verb *to monster*, and the other covers the
noun, adverb and adjective uses. These are all included in the same
entry because the adverb and adjective uses are very closely related to
the noun. The adverb, listed at branch B of the entry, is only attested
twice, in both cases as the first element in adjectival compounds
(*monster-eating* and *monster-neighing*). The definition for the adjective
at branch C notes that the adjectival use developed from the noun use
(branch A) and is recorded much later. We will therefore concentrate on
the noun form in our discussion, first considering its formal history and
etymology, and then looking in more detail at its semantics.

4.3.2.1 Formal history and etymology of monster
The list of spelling variants in the first part of the entry shows that
monster is found in English from the ME period onwards. As we would
expect from our discussion of ME in section 2.3, there are several spelling variants in the ME period, but most of these are not generally found
after the 1500s. After the 1600s, the only form that is commonly attested
in most varieties is the current spelling *monster*. Scots shows some later
variation; this is unsurprising, since Scots underwent only very limited
standardisation before it was replaced by Standard English in most of its
written functions during the 1700s.

The etymology of *monster* is also consistent with larger trends in the
history of English. As we saw in Chapter 2, the ME period is marked
by a high level of borrowing from French, and *monster* is one of these
borrowed words: the immediate donor languages are Anglo-Norman
(referred to as Anglo-French elsewhere in this book), the variety of

French used in England after the Norman Conquest, and Middle French, the variety used in France in the same period. The *OED* often lists both varieties since both are likely to have influenced the borrowing process: Anglo-Norman was the variety that many English speakers would have heard through contact with Norman French speakers, but many would also have read texts written in Middle French, and thus come across forms of the same word in the two varieties.

The rest of the etymology section lists the meanings found in French in different periods, which therefore have the potential to be borrowed into English, and gives the earlier history of the form, which was taken into French from Classical Latin. Finally, it lists cognates in other Romance languages for comparison.

4.3.2.2 Semantic history

A look at a current synchronic dictionary shows that in PDE *monster* has several established senses, which gives us a helpful starting point for considering the semantic history of the word. The *Oxford Dictionary of English* (*ODE*) lists the following senses and sub-senses for the noun.[1]

1. A large, ugly, and frightening imaginary creature
1.1 An inhumanly cruel or wicked person
1.2 A rude or badly behaved person, typically a child
2. A thing of extraordinary or daunting size
3. A congenitally malformed or mutant animal or plant

This entry separates the meanings of *monster* into three branches: (1) senses relating to scary creatures, or to people compared to scary creatures; (2) a sense relating to noteworthy or unusually large size; and (3) a technical sense relating to animals or plants. From a historical point of view, we want to discover whether all three senses have always been present in English, whether there were other early meanings that have died out, and how the senses are related.

In the *OED*, the noun is split into seven senses, some of which are divided further into sub-senses, giving a total of eleven definitions. The definition for sense 1a reads:

> Originally: a mythical creature which is part animal and part human, or combines elements of two or more animal forms, and is frequently of great size and ferocious appearance. Later, more generally: any imaginary creature that is large, ugly, and frightening.

This definition incorporates two slightly different but closely related meanings which are covered by the first part of sense 1 of the *ODE* definition. The first attestation for the sense is a manuscript of Chaucer's

Canterbury Tales from *c.*1375. *OED* sense 1b is defined as 'In extended and figurative use', and in most of the quotations abstract qualities or concepts, such as ingratitude, gluttony, war, life and death, are figuratively described as *monsters*. In 1667, for example, the poet John Dryden described the Great Fire of London as a living being, a *monster* who 'walk'd boldly upright'. These uses seem to develop directly from the 'mythical or imaginary' creatures in 1a, although it is important to remember that the figurative sense might not be an innovation in English but might have been borrowed from the donor language. The dates of the quotations show that both 1a and 1b are attested from the ME period until the present, with no significant gaps (of a century or more) in the record of their use in writing, and that both are common in PDE.

There is an interesting note attached to the definition of 1b: 'Formerly also in collocations like *faultless monster, monster of perfection*, indicating an astonishing or unnatural degree of excellence'. This usage, exemplified in a quotation from 1682, contrasts strongly with the collocations in 1a, where the monster is *wicked, terrible* and *hideous, a thing of dread*, and something which *eats children* or has to be *tamed* or *beaten.* The *OED* compares sense 1b to sense 2 'Something extraordinary or unnatural; an amazing event or occurrence; a prodigy, a marvel', recorded from *c.*1384–1710. The use of *monster* in either of these senses would be highly unusual nowadays. They are not mentioned in *ODE*, and Google searches for *faultless monster* and *monster of perfection* uncover mainly quotations from earlier periods or uses in poetic language. Nevertheless, the desire to find some good in monsters seems to persist, as shown in the originally American sense 7, 'An extraordinarily good or remarkably successful person or thing', recorded from 1968 mainly in show-business contexts, and from 1931 in adjectival use. This is perhaps a metaphorical development from sense 4, 'A creature of huge size', since such a person is *big* or *huge* in a metaphorical sense.

ODE sense 3 and *OED* 3a 'A malformed animal or plant; (Med[ical]) a fetus, neonate, or individual with a gross congenital malformation, usually of a degree incompatible with life' cover roughly similar ground. *OED* 3a overlaps with *OED*2 in that it refers to an unnatural thing of a particular kind. The sense appears to be borrowed from the donor language since the etymology section notes that the meanings 'disfigured person' and 'misshapen being' are attested earlier in French, in the first half of the thirteenth century. For many early texts, including the first citation here, two dates are given: the first, *a.*1400, is the manuscript date, and the second, (*a.*1325), is the date of composition of the text (*a* = *ante* 'before'), as the pop-up bubble from the symbol ▶ indicates. As we will see in section 4.3.3, such dates are usually approximate and the fact that two are given shows that identifying any single sense as the earliest in English is not straightforward. We might also conclude that, in cases like this, identification of the earliest use is neither particularly important nor particularly interesting. The first three senses of *OED monster* exist in the donor language, and all three are found around the same time in surviving written English, so the order in which they happen to be evidenced is perhaps not much more than an accident of history.

The latest date of attestation for *OED* sense 3a (1996), and the inclusion of this meaning as *ODE* sense 3, suggests that it is still current, but a closer look at the *OED* quotations and a comment in the definition appears to offer counter-evidence. The definition notes that the medical sense is 'Now *rare* . . . because of its pejorative associations'; the final three attestations (from 1897, 1968 and 1996) are all from specialist medical texts, suggesting that non-technical use of this sense is either rare or obsolete, possibly as a result of changing social attitudes. The extended and figurative uses in sense 3b are attested from around 200 years later than the first quotation in 3a, and the most recent examples could be interpreted as extensions of other meanings of *monster* such as sense 1a or perhaps 4, since these include the idea of an unnatural or abnormal being. Tracing extended meanings when several senses are involved is no easier than tracing earliest attestations!

The remaining *OED* senses are found in PDE, attested by twentieth- and twenty-first-century quotations, although not all are in widespread use. What is interesting is the way in which each of these meanings relates to a particular aspect of earlier meanings of *monster*, by processes of semantic change such as widening from a specific to a more general meaning or extension through metaphor (on such processes, see Chapter 5). *OED* sense 4 focuses on the component of large size, initially in reference to creatures. Much later, the application widens to include a range of objects and abstractions such as a desk, a bell and fuel bills, and then becomes a technical term in Mathematics (which then brings forth a 'baby monster'). Because this last use is restricted to a specific type of discourse, it is not recorded in all dictionaries (*ODE* 2 doesn't mention it, for example). It is also a very recent sense, and can be traced back to a definite source, so that we can be confident about the date of its first use.

OED sense 5 defines a monster as 'A person of repulsively unnatural character, or exhibiting such extreme cruelty or wickedness as to appear inhuman; a monstrous example of evil, a vice, etc.' (equivalent to *ODE* 1.1). This sense seems to develop by metaphor from sense 1a, perhaps influenced by 2 and 3a; rather than describing a mythical or imaginary creature, it refers to a human who behaves like this kind of creature in some way, and who therefore seems non-human. Interestingly, there is no equivalent in the *OED* of the weakened sense *ODE* 1.2 'A rude or badly behaved person, typically a child'; the *OED* may not yet have found enough examples to justify including it. Sense 6 'An ugly or deformed person, animal, or thing', labelled as *gen[eral]* (as opposed to technical), shows widening from 3a, extending the meaning to anything (but usually a living thing) that is physically ugly or deformed. This sense is very clearly negative; its definition uses the pejorative words *ugly* and *deformed* rather than the more neutral *malformed* of sense 3a.

Finally, if we look at the adverbial and adjectival senses of *monster* in branches B and C of the entry, we see that they connect to only a small number of the noun senses. The rare and obsolete adverbial use in B, 'In the manner of a monster', derives from sense 1a, while the adjectival uses in C relate to noun senses 4 and 7. The entry also lists a number of compounds (C1) in which the *monster* element mainly denotes an imaginary creature, something large, or something very successful (though there are a couple of notable exceptions, such as the one-off phrase *monster-little-man*, 'an abnormally small person'). The more you use the *OED*, the more you'll notice that words develop in very different ways.

4.3.3 Overview

Reading an *OED* entry to get a sense of the history of a word can be tricky, and takes practice. However, we hope that our analysis of *monster* has shown how we can use the *OED* to trace a path through the complexities of lexical relationships. The different aspects of each entry – etymology, definitions and quotations – can be fitted together like jigsaw pieces (though not always as neatly!). It's important to remember that they offer clues rather than definitive information, and we cannot always take these clues at face value. The reason that the *OED* presents so much information is to enable readers to examine it for themselves, so we must be critical and cautious in evaluating the evidence.

We have already noted in our discussion of *monster* that we cannot take dating evidence at face value, for three reasons:

- Firstly, quotation dates are often marked with *c.* for *circa* or *a.* for *ante*, indicating that they are approximate. It is usually impossible to date early manuscripts with the same accuracy as modern printed texts, and such dates should be taken as 'best guesses' based on available evidence. If we look at the *OED2* entry for *monster* by clicking on 'previous version', we can see that several of the texts that provide attestations have been re-dated (because the scholarly view of these manuscripts has changed), and that the first three senses are presented in a different order in the unrevised entry, reflecting different interpretations of the data.

- Secondly, we can never be sure that the *OED* editors have found the very first attestation for each sense, particularly for earlier periods. Many texts exist in only a single manuscript, which might not be edited or generally known to scholars, and many manuscripts have been lost, so that evidence of earlier usage may simply have disappeared. We should never assume that a first *OED* attestation is the first use of a word in a particular sense. An attestation is proof that a meaning is in use by a particular date, but lack of an earlier attestation is not proof of lack of use.

- Thirdly, when a word is borrowed, more than one sense in the donor language may well be borrowed along with the form, but not all of these may be recorded. Later evidence is less problematic than early evidence, but we also need to be careful with more recent dates of attestation. In particular, we need to remember that all of the attestations in the *OED* are from written English, but evidence from other areas of linguistics indicates that change, including semantic change, can often be found in spoken language first. Exceptions in English, where first occurrences can be found in written language, include the inkhorn terms discussed in section 2.4 and many technical terminologies.

For all of the reasons given above, the dates in the *OED* need to be treated carefully, although they are still extremely useful for obtaining a general sense of how the lexicon has developed. It is also important for us to remember that analysing word meaning, whether synchronically or diachronically, is a matter of interpreting data rather than uncovering the 'true' meanings of words in different periods. When we looked at the different senses of *monster* and the relationships between them, it was noticeable that some senses shaded into others and that different connections could be made for extended uses; the precise sense intended in a particular instance of use can often be a matter for debate. Similar issues affect lexicographers, such as those working on *OED2* and *OED3*, when they are trying to sort a batch of quotations into senses in the first place; the divisions they end up with will be the ones which they consider best represent the data they have, but they are well aware that other divisions are possible.

4.4 Some other historical dictionaries

The different possibilities in the ways in which word meaning can be handled, and the lack of any definitively 'correct' way of dividing senses, becomes even clearer if we compare entries in the *OED* with entries in other historical dictionaries. In this section we'll focus on specialised dictionaries that deal with shorter periods or particular varieties of English. These can often supplement the information in the *OED* or give a slightly different view of a word.

4.4.1 Middle English Dictionary *(MED)*

The *MED* covers the period 1100–1500. In print form, it is around 15,000 pages long, but it also exists in a searchable electronic format which is freely available online (http://quod.lib.umich.edu/m/med/) and can be accessed via links in *OED Online* entries. The main content of the *MED* was completed in 2001, so it is an up-to-date resource which is enormously valuable to scholars researching words in this period. *OED3* entries take account of the evidence in *MED*, but it was not available when *OED2* was being produced, so it often provides a more informative and more accurate account of words in the unrevised portion of *OED Online*.

One thing to note about the *MED* is that it uses ME forms of words as its headwords: *monster* is therefore found under *monstre*. Each entry gives variant spellings for the period, provides brief information on etymology, and splits the senses into lettered branches. Like the *OED*, the *MED* is evidence-based, and the entries include quotations as examples of each sense. Because it focuses on a shorter period than the *OED*, it is able to include a larger number of quotations for that period, and it tends to present most of the existing ME examples for all but the commonest words.

Definitions are listed for three different senses of *monstre*, and these are quite different from the senses identified in the *OED*. Sense (a) 'A deformed human being or animal, a monstrosity; a mythological or allegorical monster' seems to cover *OED* senses 3a 'a malformed animal or plant' and 1 'a mythical creature'; several of the same quotations are used, though some are dated slightly differently. Sense (b) '*fig.* the goddess Fortuna' does not have any parallel sense in the *OED*, providing us with a good example of the difference between the *OED* and a specialised dictionary which deals with a narrower slice of time. The quotation from Chaucer which occurs in *MED* (b) appears in the *OED* under sense 2 'Something extraordinary or unnatural; an amazing event or occurrence; a prodigy, a marvel'. In the context of the whole history of the word, the three examples of this narrowed meaning do not provide enough evidence for the *OED* to treat it as an independent sense; it does not aim to give an exhaustive picture of infrequent uses of this kind. By contrast, in the context of the ME period, the three examples (out of twenty-six attestations for the entry as a whole) give enough evidence for it to be regarded as a relatively important sub-sense which is worth defining explicitly. Likewise, some of the quotations that attest *MED* sense (c) 'a wonder, prodigy, monstrous thing or event; omen, portent' can be found under *OED* sense 2. The different scope of the *MED* therefore results in a slightly different treatment of the meanings of *monster*, but there are clear correspondences between it and the *OED*.

4.4.2 Anglo-Norman Dictionary (AND)

A parallel resource for the ME period is the *AND*, which covers the French used in England to varying extents from the time of the Norman Conquest until about the middle of the fifteenth century. It can be interesting to check meanings recorded here against those which are treated as borrowings in ME. *AND* is freely available at the Anglo-Norman Online Hub (http://www.anglo-norman.net/) along with information about this language. It is complete but currently under revision as material is added from a greater variety of sources, especially non-literary works. Its text-base is, unsurprisingly, smaller than that of the *MED* or *OED*, and it has only one entry for *monstre* (*monster*), with six quotations in the sense 'monster, aberration of nature'.

4.4.3 Dictionary of the Scots Language (DSL)

Historical dictionaries which focus on particular varieties rather than particular periods can also be enormously valuable to scholars, whether they are researching dialect words or comparing the way word meaning has changed in different places. One dictionary that is particularly worth mentioning in this context is the *Dictionary of the Scots Language* (*DSL*; http://www.dsl.ac.uk). This is a freely available electronic resource which pulls together two major Scots dictionaries into one package: *A Dictionary of the Older Scottish Tongue* (*DOST*), which covers Older Scots, from 1200 to 1700, and the *Scottish National Dictionary* (*SND*), which covers Modern Scots, from 1700 to the present. It is comparable to the *OED* in that it covers the entire recorded history of a variety. Its entry for the noun *monster* has ten senses and sub-senses based on a different set of attestations from those in the *OED*, divided and ordered somewhat differently. For example, it has a separate sense (4a) 'Applied to persons as a strong term of opprobrium in various . . . senses'.

4.4.4 Dictionary of Old English (DOE)

If we want to step further back into the history of English, another very useful historical dictionary is the online *DOE*, which covers the period 600–1150. It is based on evidence from the *Dictionary of Old English Corpus*, which contains at least one copy of every surviving OE text, and presents a selection of examples from this corpus in each entry. The *DOE* is designed to complement the *MED* and *OED*, and has many similar features, but because it deals with English when it was a different type of language (see section 2.2) it also gives other kinds of information, especially about grammar. Like the *OED*, the *DOE* is an ongoing project, but is in the middle of the first stage, so not all of the alphabet has been completed. At the moment, entries in the letters A–G are complete (these were published electronically in 2009), and work continues on the rest of the alphabet. Completed entries can be accessed via *OED Online* or on CD or by subscription from http://www.doe.utoronto.ca/

Because *monster* is found in English only from the ME period, we cannot take our comparison of entries for this particular word any further. As an example of the loss of OE lexis after 1066, we can note that the OE section of the *HTOED* category *Hybrid creature/monster* contains seven entries, of which only one survives into ME. This is *feond-sceaþa* (recorded in *HTOED* and the *OED* in its ME form *fiend-scathe*). *DOE* records three occurrences of this word in extant OE poetic manuscripts, and defines it as 'enemy, hostile ravager'. The *OED* uses one of these quotations and one from early ME, and defines it simply as 'a monster'.

4.4.5 Other dictionaries

Attempts have been made to compile a dictionary of EModE (1475–1700), but these did not come to fruition. Data from the proposed project have been incorporated into *OED* revisions. A recent addition to online historical dictionaries is *A Dictionary of Canadianisms on Historical Principles*, based on a print dictionary from 1967 and containing nearly 10,000 headwords illustrated by quotations from 1505–1965.

4.5 Historical corpora

Dictionaries nowadays, both synchronic and diachronic, depend heavily on electronic text corpora for their source material. Like dictionaries themselves, corpora have to be approached with care. The *DOE* Corpus and the *MED* Corpus are both available to scholars but are difficult to use for those without fairly advanced knowledge of these stages of the language. This is because words in these corpora are not lemmatised, i.e. the variant spellings and grammatical forms aren't collected up under a headword as they are in a dictionary, and there is no attempt at sense division. Edited corpora of historical texts are relatively rare. The best-known is the multi-genre Helsinki Corpus of English Texts, the pioneer in the field. It was published in 1991 and contains around 1.5 million words extracted from OE, ME and EModE texts. Its team has also produced a range of more specialised corpora, such as the Corpus of Early English Correspondence and the Corpus of Early English Medical Writing. A useful item on its website is the Corpus Resource Database (CoRD), which lists details of Helsinki projects and of historical corpus projects carried out elsewhere.

Scots is relatively well served for corpora, with the Helsinki Corpus of Older Scots (1450–1700; 800,000 words), the Corpus of Modern Scottish Writing (1700–1945; 5.5 million words), and the Scottish Corpus of Text and Speech (1945 to present; 4 million words, written and spoken). On a grander scale is the Corpus of Historical American English which contains 400 million words covering the period 1810–2009 and offers a range of sophisticated searches and connections to other corpora. On the same website at Brigham Young University are a number of corpora for more recent English which still have interest for historical linguists, such as the TIME Magazine Corpus of American English, 100 million words from the 1920s to 2000s. Vast databanks of texts are also becoming available, such as the Google Books Corpus (155 billion words of texts from the USA and 34 billion from the UK), and the Early English Books Online project which has digitised 125,000 printed books from the period 1475–1700. Corpora have certainly got larger, but size brings its own problems. While a corpus of a few million words is often not large enough to reveal significant results for any but the commonest words (as opposed to much more frequently recurring grammatical patterns), billion-word corpora may produce more results than the analyst can cope with other than by a process of sampling. Alexander notes that a search in a 1-million word corpus for *inside* produced 178 example results, whereas the Google Books Corpus produced 10,057,203 (2015: 50). It will be interesting to see how corpora develop in future, but one thing is certain: historical semanticists will soon begin to wonder how they ever managed without them.

Exercises

1. Look at the *OED* entry for *meerschaum* and prepare a summary of its history, taking account of the kinds of information discussed in the entry for *manga* in section 4.3.1. If you want to look at something more challenging, you could try one of the following entries: *knight, magazine, novel.*
2. Study the compound words in *OED monster* branch C (1) and try to sort them into groups based on semantic aspects of the nouns, such as large size, success, or evil character. Take account of the dates of the source sense, and discuss any instances where you found it difficult to make a decision.
3. Make a detailed comparison of the treatment of *monster* in the *OED* and the *DSL*.
4. Use a corpus such as the Time Magazine Corpus of American English or the Corpus of Historical American English to see whether you can find any evidence for *ODE* sense 1.2 'A rude or badly behaved person, typically a child'.

Further reading

A good deal of information about the history and current practices of the *OED* is available at http://www.oed.com/ – spend some time browsing the site and finding out more about this remarkable dictionary.
The URLs mentioned in Chapter 4 are:
list of dictionary staff:
http://www.oed.com/public/oedstaff/staff-of-the-oxford-english-dictionary/
list of consultants, advisers and contributors: http://www.oed.com/public/advisers/consultants-advisers-and-contributors/
symbols:
http://public.oed.com/how-to-use-the-oed/key-to-symbols-and-other-conventions/
abbreviations:
http://public.oed.com/how-to-use-the-oed/abbreviations/

Brewer (2007) is an account of the history and development of the *OED*; Mugglestone (2005) is a collection of chapters on various aspects of the project. Murray (1995) is an interesting, informal account of the early days of the project by James Murray's granddaughter, and Winchester's biography of one of the contributors (1999) and history of the *OED* (2003) are both highly-readable, popular introductions. Kay and Mackay (2005) celebrates the publication of *DOST* with chapters by a variety of scholars.

Note

1. We have used the *ODE* here because, like many recent dictionaries, it is corpus-based; this means that it lists senses on the basis of contemporary evidence, and so can provide reliable information about which senses are in widespread current use. Like the *OED*, it includes attestations drawn from its corpus, although not for all senses, as this entry shows. It is available via links in *OED Online* entries.

5 How and why words change meaning

5.1 Introduction

In the last chapter, we examined the semantic history of a single word, *monster*, by tracing the account of its development in the *OED*. In this chapter, we'll think about patterns of change across groups of words, and then consider the most interesting question of all: *why* do words change meaning? Throughout the chapter, we'll explore examples of words which have changed semantically, looking at data from the *OED* alongside evidence from books, newspapers and the internet. Close attention to individual word histories is crucial for the study of semantic change: any generalisations we can make about tendencies in change and motivations for change can only result from specific examples collected together to give a broader picture.

5.2 The significance of meaning change

There has always been widespread interest in how and why words change meaning, and evidence of this can be seen all around us. Discussions about word meaning can frequently be seen and heard in the media and on the internet. For example, in March 2012 there were a number of reports in British newspapers and on the BBC Radio 4 news programme *Today* about the meaning of the word *literally*, prompted by British Deputy Prime Minister Nick Clegg's use of the word in an interview about taxation. Clegg said: 'It makes people so incredibly angry ... you are paying your taxes and then you see people *literally* in a different galaxy who are paying extraordinarily low rates of tax' (*Daily Telegraph*, 10 March 2012). Here Clegg used *literally* with an intensifying sense, meaning something like 'virtually', rather than in its earlier meaning of 'in a literal or actual sense'. This 'new' meaning is not an innovation: the *OED* notes that it is 'Now one of the most common uses', and records examples from the mid-eighteenth century onwards (*literally*, adverb 1c). Despite this, it is perceived by many speakers to be an incorrect use of the word, particularly because it appears to directly conflict with the earlier meaning.

The response that followed Clegg's comment shows that speakers have strong feelings about this kind of language change, and often have a sense of unease. In the *Today* programme feature, one contributor, Paul Parry, said that 'this is probably the worst thing Nick Clegg has ever done' (perhaps not entirely seriously), and talked about 'epidemic levels' of 'misuse' of *literally*. An editorial in the *Daily Telegraph* noted that Clegg's use of the word was not new, but maintained that it was still unacceptable, saying that 'The word has been deployed to intensify meaning for many years, but we must still try to defend its literal meaning' (13 March 2012). Reports that specifically asked whether it mattered how *literally* was used generally agreed that it did, although they did not all agree on why. In the *Today* programme, Parry suggested that the intensifying sense could cause communicative problems, since 'There is no other word that means *literally* and if the word *literally*'s meaning is eroded by all this misuse then there is nothing to replace it . . .' (reported in the *Telegraph* online, 12 May 2012). A reaction piece in *The Times* echoed this view, but gave a different kind of reason, concluding that 'Language constantly evolves and some people misuse it deliberately for emphasis, but we can't have the country sounding like airhead Rosie Webster from *Coronation Street*' (a British television soap drama; 15 March 2012).

Changes in the way words are used are particularly noticeable to a language community when they involve meanings that are sensitive and highly charged. For example, a fairly recent but well-established semantic change, and one which many speakers are still conscious of, has affected the word *gay*. *Gay* was borrowed into English from French in the ME period; its most common meaning in earlier times was 'bright, happy, carefree', reflecting its early meaning in French. It has had many other meanings in the course of its history, but the most frequent sense of the word in PDE is 'homosexual', attested in the *OED* from the early 1940s onwards, though mainly used within the homosexual community until significantly later (*OED* adj. 4d, noun 5). Many speakers are still aware of the earlier meaning, although it is relatively rare in actual use; it is still found in contexts such as traditional songs, including the Christmas carol *Deck the Halls*, which includes the line 'Don we now our *gay* apparel'.

As the new meaning became more generally known, particularly after homosexuality was decriminalised in the UK, a great deal of concern was expressed in public debate, often in highly inflammatory language.

In a House of Lords debate from 1979 (entitled 'The English language deterioration in usage'), one member talked of the development of the new meaning of *gay* as 'very distressing' and said that the word had been 'used for propaganda purposes in a way which has destroyed its useful meaning in English';[1] in a House of Commons debate the following year, an MP commented that 'the very use of the word "gay" is an affront to the meaning of the word, and to ordinary, normal people'.[2] Although it is difficult to imagine such statements being made publicly nowadays, it is still possible to find discussions on the internet and in the media about the 'hijacking' of the word *gay* by the homosexual community. In this case, anxiety about meaning change cannot be separated from anxiety about social change and attitudes to sexuality; for example, an article on the conservative Christian website *Dakota Voice* complains about this 'hijacking' in an article that also talks about 'the mainstreaming of deviant sexual behaviour' (*Dakota Voice*, 13 December 2011).

A subsequent semantic development which is also problematic is an additional, newer meaning for *gay*, 'pathetic, stupid'. This meaning does not appear to be widespread across the community of English speakers (at least not in 2015), but is associated with the slang of younger speakers, particularly teenagers. It appears to have its origins in children's use of homophobic insults, so has developed out of negative views of homosexuality, but it is no longer restricted to people or things which are seen as 'camp'; for example, in the 2011 film *The Dilemma*, electric cars are described as *gay*. Many speakers who use the meaning claim that it does not have any connection to the sense 'homosexual', and that *gay* 'pathetic, stupid' is established to the point that it is independent of its source. In linguistic terms, the argument here is that the two meanings can synchronically be viewed as homonyms, even if *gay* is historically polysemous (see sections 3.2.4, 3.3.3). However, this view is controversial, and other speakers maintain that the newer meaning is offensive. Whichever side of the argument speakers support, their views show that meaning and meaning change can be a highly emotive issue when it relates to social and cultural change.

5.3 Studying semantic change

Despite the high levels of interest in meaning change shown by the public, it has been a relatively neglected area of study within linguistics. In the 1950s and 1960s, when modern linguistics was becoming established, there was very little research on semantic change, or indeed on Semantics, compared to other areas of the discipline such as Phonetics or Syntax. More recently, there has been a resurgence of interest in the subject. One reason for this may be the availability of better resources, such as dictionaries and large online corpora (see Chapter 4). Another is the increasing dominance of Cognitive Semantics, with its interest in the relationship between mental processes and linguistic expression. Concepts such as fuzziness in meaning, prototypicality and the tracking of chains of meaning in polysemous word forms (see section 3.3, especially 3.3.2) offer convincing ways of approaching the 'messiness' and unpredictability of lexical semantic change – characteristics which perhaps deterred earlier scholars. Further impetus has come from the discipline of Pragmatics, especially in theories developed from the notion of '**invited inferencing**', where speakers produce, and possibly intend, meanings beyond the straightforward meaning of an utterance. Because there is a degree of ambiguity in such utterances, listeners have a choice of interpretations. As with the tendencies in change discussed in section 5.5, inferred meanings may gradually be incorporated into the core meaning of an expression and a new sense develops. One example is the phrase *as long as*, which originally referred to temporal and spatial dimensions (e.g. 'I'll stay *as long as* you need me), then assumed a meaning of 'provided that' in metaphorical expressions like '*as long as* you don't mind' (Traugott and Dasher 2005: 36–8). *Since* shows a similar path of development, with an early temporal meaning 'from that time', in expressions like 'I have been waiting *since* this morning', giving rise to a causal meaning 'because' in expressions like '*Since* it was raining, I got wet.' As with *as long as*, both meanings survive in PDE, and in some current and earlier uses both appear to be involved simultaneously. Geeraerts gives the following example:

> Since you lost your favourite fountain pen, you seem to have been suffering from writer's block. (Geeraerts 2010: 147)

Here, *since* clearly refers to a period of time, but a causal sense is also implied by the context: if you have had writer's block from the time you lost your pen, the loss of the pen appears to be responsible for the condition. This kind of example acts historically as a 'bridging context' between the earlier sense and a new sense. As Traugott puts it, 'The hypothesis is that invited inferences that arise on the fly may become conventionalized ... [i.e.] semanticization of a formerly pragmatic meaning ...' (Traugott 2012: 168).

Some types of change in language follow clear patterns, so that a change which affects a single word can be observed to take place across a large group of words, with predictable results. For example, some sound change works in this way, so that in a certain phonological context a sound will change in all words which show that context.

In OE, a number of words began with the cluster *hl-*, including *hlaf* 'loaf', *hlæder* 'ladder', *hlædel* 'ladle', *hlid* 'lid' and *hlud* 'loud'; in PDE, this cluster has been lost, so that any words which survive from OE and had this initial cluster now begin with *l-*, as these examples show. This is a predictable pattern which affects the whole set of OE *hl-* words without exceptions. It is not possible to find examples of this kind of phenomenon in semantic change. If we consider words that have a similar meaning to *gay* before it shifted semantically to meaning 'homosexual', we can see that they have not changed in the same way. In the example from *HTOED* discussed in section 2.1, *gay* is listed alongside partial synonyms including *blithe, jolly, merry* and *gleeful*. Though some of these have changed in meaning or show new senses, none of them has followed the same pattern as *gay*.

This point has been discussed by many scholars; for example, in his book on etymology, Durkin says:

> Semantic changes are notoriously difficult to classify or systematize ... although some semantic changes occur in clusters, with a change in one word triggering a change in another, we do not find anything comparable to a regular sound change, affecting all comparable environments within a single historical period. In this respect semantic changes are more similar to sporadic sound changes, but with the major difference that they are much more varied, and show the influence of a much wider set of motivating factors. Additionally, semantic change is much more closely connected with change in the external, non-linguistic world, especially with developments in the spheres of culture and technology. (Durkin 2009: 222–3)

We will explore such comments further in the rest of this chapter. The difficulties that the study of semantic change presents to scholars should not be underestimated, but the 'wider set of motivating factors' that Durkin mentions, along with the connection between semantic change and change in the 'external, non-linguistic world', are part of what makes semantic change so intriguing.

5.4 The process of semantic change

The example of *gay* discussed above provides an interesting illustration of semantic change in progress. We have seen that the most recent meaning, 'pathetic, stupid', is not used by the whole community of English speakers. It is not certain exactly when or where the new sense was first used: the *OED* marks the meaning as '*slang* (chiefly *U.S.*)', and gives a first quotation from 1978, but it may well have been used in speech before then (see section 4.3.3). Its adoption by a relatively large number of speakers is likely to have been gradual. Early adopters would have used it alongside the dominant sense, 'homosexual', and those in contact with these early adopters would have become aware of the new use and perhaps started to use it themselves. Others may have resisted its use; these may have been older speakers who viewed it as belonging to a different speech community, and therefore avoided it, or people who thought it was inappropriate or offensive. Their resistance may have weakened as more speakers adopted the new meaning. However, undoubtedly there are still some speakers who are currently unaware of the new meaning, and who may remain unaware of it.

This example (and the spread of dates in polysemous entries in the *OED*) points to the fact that changes in language tend to occur relatively slowly and unevenly. Like other kinds of change, semantic change tends not to be observable in all speakers or writers at the same time or may not take place in all varieties of a language. In some cases, a new meaning may co-exist with an established meaning or meanings. In others, one or more meanings may be lost over time, and may or may not be replaced by new meanings. The process is rarely straightforward.

5.5 Categories of meaning change

Although semantic change is not predictable or regular in the way that some sound change is regular, it is certainly not random, and there is convincing evidence that there are some common tendencies. An understanding of these tendencies can help us to make sense of the changes that affect a single word over time. Many attempts have been made to identify and classify common tendencies, with the inevitable result that you may find different definitions and names for them depending on what you read. An early and influential attempt was that of Ullman (1962), whose work is still followed to varying degrees in many histories of the English language. In this section, we'll look at the kinds of change that are widely identified in the literature and supported by extensive lexical evidence.

5.5.1 Widening (or broadening or generalisation) and narrowing (or specialisation)

The tendency in semantic change referred to as **widening**, **broadening** or **generalisation** occurs when the meaning of a word (or of one of its senses) becomes more general, so that it can be used to refer to a broader, less specific concept. One often-cited example is the word *bird*, the reflex of OE *brid*. The earliest attestations are for the sense 'young bird, young of a bird' (*OED* noun 1a), which seems to have been the only meaning in OE. In later English, *bird* is not restricted to the young of the species, but applies to all feathered vertebrates (*OED* noun 2). This meaning is first attested in the *OED* in the early thirteenth century, and co-exists for some time with both 'young bird' and a related sense which shows widening in a slightly different direction, 'the young of other animals' (*OED* noun 1b). Nowadays most speakers would not recognise either of these early uses, although the *OED* and some other sources (including the *Oxford Book of British Bird Names*, published in 1984) record the expression *a hen and her birds*, found in some Northern varieties of British English.

A second example of a word which has widened in meaning is *caddy*, borrowed into English from Malay and attested from the late eighteenth century onwards. *Caddy* has shifted from its early meaning, 'a small container for tea', to that of a more general kind of storage container. Present-day searches for *caddy* on retail websites recover products as diverse as disk-drive caddies, diaper (or nappy) caddies, utility caddies (to store tools, nails, etc.) and remote control caddies (which attach to armchairs).

The opposite tendency to broadening is **narrowing**, also called **specialisation** by some scholars. Narrowing occurs when the meaning of a word (or one of its senses) becomes more restricted and specific over time, so that it refers to only a subset of the concept described in its earlier meaning. A well-known example of narrowing is *meat*, the PDE reflex of OE *mete*, which was a rough semantic equivalent of PDE *food*, as this quotation from around 1450 shows: 'þi mete schal be mylk, hony, & wiyn' (*OED meat*, noun 1a). Here, *mylk, hony, & wiyn* 'milk, honey and wine' are described as types of *meat*. Uses like this are found as late as 1996, although latterly the sense seems largely to be restricted to varieties of English such as Scottish English or Caribbean English. The much more specific PDE meaning of *meat*, 'flesh from animals' (*OED* 4a), has almost completely replaced the earlier meaning, although traces of it can still be found, particularly in fixed phrases like the proverb 'one man's meat is another man's poison' (*OED* 1c), and compounds such as *sweetmeats* 'preserved or candied fruits, sugared nuts, etc.', marked 'chiefly archaic' by the *OED*.

A word which has narrowed in meaning more recently is the mass noun *sport*. Etymologically, *sport* is a shortened form of *disport*, a word borrowed in the fifteenth century which is more or less obsolete in PDE, though may still be part of the **passive vocabulary** of some speakers. Initially, *sport* was used to describe a range of leisure activities, as well as 'fun' or 'enjoyment'; for example, a definition in a Latin–English glossary collection from the early fifteenth century uses the expression 'sporte of redying [reading]' (*OED* noun 1). In present-day use, *sport* usually refers to a specific kind of activity which involves physical exertion and skill, such as football or tennis (*OED* noun 4a).

Overall, narrowing is a commoner form of change than widening. There are various reasons for this. One is the changing nature of our society and its ever-increasing complexity, which generates a need for new forms of expression for novel or more precisely specified concepts. Another is the availability of synonyms in English, which allows a meaning to be narrowed while synonyms continue to cover the general concept. *Sport* may have become specialised, but we can still talk about *fun, enjoyment, pleasure,* and so on.

5.5.2 *Amelioration (or elevation) and pejoration (or deterioration or degeneration)*

Two further tendencies in semantic change are **amelioration** (occasionally called **melioration** or **elevation**) and its opposite process, **pejoration** (sometimes called **deterioration** or **degeneration**). These occur when a sense of a word becomes more or less positive over time as changes in its connotations become conventionalised and part of its denotative meaning. Amelioration is the tendency shown when words acquire more positive connotations, either from a negative or neutral meaning to a positive one, or from a negative meaning to something neutral. A classic example is the adjective *mischievous*, borrowed into English from Anglo-French in the fourteenth century with the meaning 'Of an event or occurrence: unfortunate, calamitous, disastrous. Of a person: miserable, needy, poverty-stricken' (*OED mischievous*, adj. 1). Citations in the *OED* show that words collocated with *mischievous* in early use include *misery* and *death* (or *end*). By the fifteenth century, its meaning had broadened to a general meaning of 'harmful', which is used in a wide range of contexts and still has some currency (*OED* senses 2 and 3). In the seventeenth century the original meaning became obsolete and the process of amelioration began, resulting in the meaning 'Of a person, behaviour, etc.: characterized by acts of childish naughtiness or petty annoyance; inclined to mischief' (4a), the main present-day meaning. In the eighteenth century we find (4b), 'In more positive sense: charmingly roguish; playful, teasing'. These two senses refer mainly to the activities of children, which are relatively harmless on a scale of wickedness, and this may have driven the process of amelioration. Overall, the senses of the entry can be understood as a chain of meaning showing gradual prototype shift, with each sense bearing a fairly obvious relationship to its chronological neighbours.

A more dramatic example from the same semantic domain can be found in the history of *wicked*, attested from the thirteenth century in a variety of highly negative meanings, particularly 'evil, cruel'. This sense is still common in PDE, most often in fairy tales and children's stories (e.g. the characters of the Wicked Stepmother in *Cinderella* and the Wicked Witch of the West in *The Wizard of Oz*) and in religious language. A related sense, 'malicious, mischievous', often intended humorously, which the *OED* describes as 'weakened or lighter' (3a), is found from the seventeenth century in expressions including *wicked tongue*, and shows a degree of amelioration. In the twentieth century, a further sense, 'great, excellent', emerged, initially in US slang; this is generally the sense intended when speakers use *wicked* to describe aspects of contemporary culture, such as music or cars. In this case the negative meaning 'evil, cruel' has not been replaced, but another sense has emerged alongside it and has become just as established for some speakers at least. The words *bad* and *sick* have followed a similar negative to positive trajectory, evidenced in slang and the usage of younger speakers. Such usage may reflect one of the functions of slang, which is to establish in-groups and protect them from outsiders through linguistic mystification, such as saying the opposite of what you mean.

The word *nice*, another borrowing from French, has had several negative meanings during its long history, and is a good example of how difficult it can be to plot the development of a highly polysemous word where the links between senses are less clear. It first appears in early ME with the meaning 'foolish, silly, simple' (*OED* sense 1). From the end of the fourteenth century until the mid-seventeenth century, it is attested with the meaning 'wanton, lascivious' (*OED* 2). Around the same time, a further branch of meaning develops which seems to show gradual amelioration towards a clearly positive sense. This is sense 3 in the *OED*, which has seven sub-senses, covering such meanings as 'precise, particular, scrupulous, fastidious, fussy', which can be more or less positive or negative in different contexts, and eventually more positive senses including 'refined, cultured' and 'respectable, virtuous, decent'. It is not until sense 14 of the entry that we reach the PDE sense, 'agreeable, pleasant, satisfactory', first attested in 1747 in the phrase *nice white gloves*. Interestingly, the development of an ameliorated sense of *nice* seems to be unique to English. In modern French the word is restricted to regional use and retains the early meaning of 'foolish, ignorant', reflecting its Latin **etymon** *nescius* 'ignorant'. Cognates in related medieval languages, such as *necio* in Spanish and *nescio* in Italian, also have the sense 'foolish, ignorant'. Neither the PDE meaning nor any of the other meanings that emerge over the history of the word in English are found in any related language, thus illustrating the unpredictability of meaning change.

Pejoration (or deterioration or degeneration) is the opposite process, and describes the change from a neutral or positive meaning to a negative one, or from a positive meaning to a neutral one. This tendency is much more common than amelioration, and often accompanies narrowing, as when OE *stenc*, referring to a smell of any kind, narrowed and pejorated to refer only to extremely bad smells, the sense which survives in ModE *stench*.

The compound noun *cowboy* is an interesting, and relatively straightforward, example of pejoration. The earliest meaning of *cowboy* is predictable from its two elements: from the eighteenth century, it is attested with the neutral meaning 'a boy who tends cows'. It seems to broaden in meaning fairly quickly so that it can also refer to adult males who tend cows, and by the nineteenth century in the western USA it more commonly means 'a man employed to take care of cattle on a ranch'; this is the type of cowboy who appears in Hollywood films of the Western genre. By the twentieth century, *cowboy* shows negative meanings that have no association with cows. *OED* sense 3b is 'a boisterous or wild young man', the sense intended in an attestation from a 1959 London newspaper which explains that 'Coffee bar cowboys . . . are the teenagers with black jackets and fast motor cyclists who gather in cafés' (*News Chronicle*, 7 December 1959). An extension of this sense, which is perhaps more common in PDE, is the sub-sense 'a reckless or inconsiderate driver'. A further, and also very clearly negative, sense is attested from the 1970s, and shows the degree of pejoration that the word has undergone. The sixth edition of the *Oxford Advanced Learner's Dictionary* (2000) defines this sense as 'a dishonest person in business, especially someone who produces work of bad quality or charges too high a price'. The fact that this sense is well-established in PDE can be seen from newspaper headlines like 'Clamping down on claims firms' cowboy tactics' (*Express*, 18 April 2012) or a reference to 'business as usual in the Wild West of cosmetic surgery' in *The Times* (14 January 2014). As with the amelioration of *wicked*, the pejorated senses of *cowboy* have not replaced all of the earlier senses; rather the word has become a polyseme with three prototypical senses.

While the meaning of *nice* ameliorated from 'foolish' to 'pleasant', *silly*, the reflex of OE *(ge)sælig*, underwent pejoration in an opposite direction.[3] In Old English, *(ge)sælig* meant 'happy, blessed', but in PDE it has the meaning 'foolish, stupid'. A seminal study by Michael Samuels shows that its meaning went through several stages, which are illustrated in Figure 5.1 (Samuels 1972: 66–7). In the thirteenth century, the

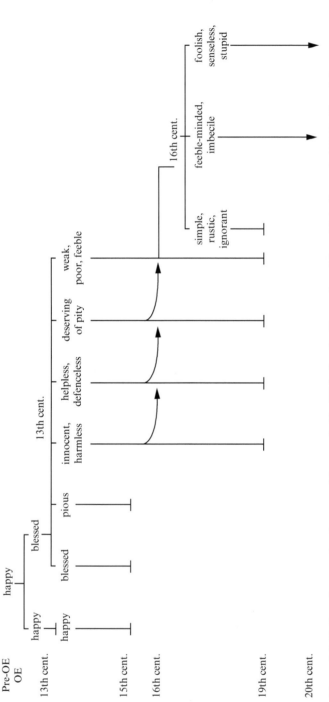

Figure 5.1 Dating of semantic changes of the word *silly*, OE *(ge)sælig*. (Reproduced from M. L. Samuels (1972), *Linguistic Evolution with Special Reference to English*, Cambridge: Cambridge University Press, 66.)

ME form of *silly* was highly polysemous, and the positive senses 'happy' and 'blessed' existed alongside neutral senses including 'innocent', and more negative senses like 'weak, poor, feeble'. By the sixteenth century the positive senses had become obsolete, and were replaced by negative senses such as 'ignorant' and 'feeble-minded', alongside the prevalent modern sense 'foolish, senseless, stupid', and by the nineteenth century the more neutral senses had also been lost. This example provides a clear illustration of the complex nature of semantic change. Although it is true to say that the meaning of *silly* has pejorated through time, it is not the case that a positive meaning has been replaced by a negative one in a single stage; the process of change has involved many other senses. Traugott (2012: 168) suggests that in cases of pejoration and amelioration 'the invited inferences are not only conceptually but also socially motivated'; in the case of *silly*, those considered blessed and innocent 'may be evaluated as ignorant or foolish' by people who are more worldly-wise than they are.

5.5.3 Metaphor and metonymy

The final two tendencies in semantic change are slightly different from the processes we have considered above, since they describe conceptual relations which trigger change, rather than being processes of change in themselves. The first of these is change involving metaphor, and the second change involving metonymy. These will be dealt with fully in Chapter 9, so are only mentioned briefly here.

Metaphor has traditionally been thought of as a figure of speech, by which one concept is described in terms of another: for example, in a famous scene in Shakespeare's *Romeo and Juliet*, Romeo says that '*Iuliet* is the sunne' (II, ii, 796). The target of this metaphor, the thing being described, is Juliet; the source, or the thing being used to refer to Juliet, is the sun. Metaphor scholars talk about the source being 'mapped' onto the target. Metaphor is based on a relationship of similarity between the two concepts, and therefore seems to be a matter of thought rather than simply a matter of language: in this example, Juliet is being described as the sun because Romeo perceives some kind of similarity between the two – both are radiant, and 'light up' their surroundings – so is linguistic evidence of the way he is thinking about her. Although this metaphor involves poetic language, metaphor is common in everyday speech as well, and there are lots of highly conventional metaphors that are used all the time and which are not thought of as involving special or unusual language. For example, we often refer to arguments as *battles* which can be *won* or *lost*; we *spend* or *borrow* time; we talk about ideas *hitting* us, and describe uncomfortable situations as *nightmares*.

Metonymy also involves a mapping between two concepts, but the source and target have a different kind of relationship, which is based on association rather than similarity. A monarch can be referred to as the *crown* or a scientist as a *brain* because in each case the source and target are concepts related in experience. There is no similarity between the queen and a crown, but the crown is an object that is recognisably associated with the queen. Similarly, a brain is only part of a scientist, but it is a salient part, because scientists are thought of as being clever. Metonymy is therefore described as having a referential function. Metonymies are at least as common as metaphors: it is highly conventional to talk about 'boiling the kettle', where *the kettle* stands for 'the water inside the kettle', or to refer to the intentions of ruling politicians as 'the UK's plans', where the country stands for the people governing the country.

Both metaphor and metonymy are important triggers for semantic change. If a word is often used metaphorically or metonymically, the metaphorical or metonymical sense can become so conventionalised that it is no longer regarded as figurative and becomes a new sense. There are many examples of this in the history of English. In ModE, *mouse* has become polysemous and can be used to refer to both a rodent and a computer device, presumably because the computer device looks (vaguely) similar to the rodent in size and shape. Other terms in computing also result from metaphor: we talk about *files, folders* and *windows*, and computers can become *infected* by *viruses*. All of these are the usual names for the concepts they denote.

Examples of change triggered by metonymy are also common. In OE and ME, *bath* referred to the act of bathing, as in PDE *have a bath*, or to liquid which had been prepared for someone's bath, as in *I ran a bath*. Both of these senses survive and are still common, but *bath* is now also used to refer to the vessel in which one bathes (also called the *bathtub*), so that it is unproblematic to talk about having a new *bath* installed in a house.

5.6 Grammaticalisation

So far we have been talking mainly about lexical change; that is, changes in the content words of the language. One area in the study of change where considerable progress has been made in recent years is **grammaticalisation**, which occurs when a word loses some of its semantic content and becomes part of the grammatical system. A more general term for this phenomenon is **bleaching**, and in older literature it is sometimes referred to as 'weakening' of meaning. This process can be exemplified by *nice*, used as an intensifier in the phrase *nice and* — , as in *we were nice and cosy by the fire*, attested from 1796 (*OED nice* 14b). A similar process has taken place in a large number of English adjectives and adverbs which originally referred to feelings of fear or wonder but are now used as intensifiers that strengthen the meaning of the words they modify but have little semantic content. Adverbs which have weakened in this way include *awesomely, awfully, dreadfully, fearfully, frightfully, marvellously, wonderfully* . . . no doubt you can think of others.

A classic example of grammaticalisation is the OE verb *gān*, which originally meant 'to move, walk'. It has retained this meaning in ModE *go*, but has also developed into an auxiliary verb expressing futurity, part of the grammatical system, as in *I'm going to leave next week*. The English modal auxiliaries, such as *may* and *must*, have also developed in this way. For example, the OE verb *cunnan* 'to know' has lost much of its semantic content and survives mainly as the auxiliary verb *can*, expressing the speaker's view of possibility.

An exciting outcome of research in this area is that general patterns in semantic change, such as the change from adverb to intensifier, are being detected. Further examples are discussed in Jucker and Taavitsainen (2013), including the development of discourse markers such as *well* in pragmatic functions like indicating a new turn in a conversation (138–43).

5.7 Why do words change meaning?

Observing how words change meaning is relatively straightforward, even if particular changes are difficult to interpret; it is possible to look at lots of examples of use from different periods and trace the emergence of new senses and the decline of earlier senses. As the examples above show, some words are highly polysemous, and it can be tricky to tease out the relationship between the senses and sub-senses in different periods, but modern technology allows us to search through large collections of data to find examples and identify patterns of collocation which might help us to notice changes in use. *Why* words change meaning is a more difficult question, though it is arguably an even more interesting one. Examples like those we have looked at in this chapter suggest that there are a number of possible reasons for semantic change, and these can interact in complex and unpredictable ways.

It is not always possible to account definitively for semantic change, but we can say that it tends to be the result of particular kinds of pressures on the language system. We can divide these pressures into two groups: those which come from outside the system, that is language-external pressures, and those which are internal to the system. We might also think about an intermediate category, which sits between the two: influence from languages other than English, which are internal in their effect but external in origin

5.7.1 External factors

Language-external pressures can include any changes in the social or cultural world which impact upon the language. For example, an object or concept which is new to a group of speakers might be named using an existing word in a new sense; a change in the use, nature or perception of an entity might lead to a change in the meaning of the label which refers to it; changing cultural ideas might be reflected in the meaning of the terminology used to discuss these ideas. Studying semantic change therefore often involves the study of non-linguistic history.

One of the most obvious language-external pressures for semantic change is technological change, which often necessitates new names for new objects or concepts. As we discussed in Chapter 2, new words can be introduced, but often existing forms are used with new senses. Many of the computing terms discussed in section 5.5.3, as well as other terms like *printer*, *hardware* and *monitor*, already existed in the language before they were adopted into the language of computing. *Hardware* was originally a general term for 'small metal objects', but narrowed to mean specifically '(metal) components of a device', and then narrowed further as computing advanced and a term was needed to refer to computer components. *Software* was then coined on the model of *hardware* to refer to non-physical operating systems, programs, etc., because *hard* and *soft* were already established opposites in other senses. In most of these cases, the earlier meanings are still commonly used, so each word has acquired an additional prototypical meaning. Sometimes, but not always, the newer sense becomes more frequently used than the earlier one: this may be the case for *hardware*, which is still used to mean 'iron-mongery' but more often refers to computing equipment. In some cases, earlier senses can be lost completely. For example, the earliest sense of the noun *computer* was 'a person who makes calculations (i.e. who computes)' (cf. the discussion of *typewriter* in section 2.5). It was also used to describe early devices that performed calculations, but as more sophisticated electronic equipment was developed the usual meaning of the term changed and the earlier senses have dropped out of use.

As we saw with the example of *gay* in section 5.2, changes in the social world can also impact upon the lexicon and result in semantic change. The compound noun *landlord* has extended its meaning as social structures have changed, and is no longer **transparent**. In its earliest use during the OE period, it refers to 'a lord or landowner who lets land to tenants'; it broadens in meaning around the sixteenth century to refer to someone who lets any kind of property, either land, a building or part of a building. Presumably this change happens as the letting of buildings becomes more common, and is less based on hierarchical social relationships: the meaning of *landlord* no longer necessarily involves either land or a lord. Around the same time, the word *landlady* is recorded, perhaps showing an increased role for women in such transactions. In modern times, both words commonly have a more specialised meaning, 'someone who lets a domestic dwelling (a house or flat) or rooms in a domestic dwelling' (*OED landlord*, noun 1), corresponding to new ways in which domestic housing is managed. Both words have also developed a second specialised sense in PDE, 'the owner or manager of a pub', and could change again in response to further social change.

Language-external pressures often account for cases in which the relationships between words and their referents have become **opaque** through time. For example, the highly polysemous form *iron* is used in PDE to refer to a golf club of a particular shape and to an implement used to press clothes, although these items are no longer made of iron. The semantic content of the senses of *iron* has shifted slightly as a result, but this is the result of technological change rather than anything inside the language system.

5.7.2 Internal factors: polysemy, homonymy, synonymy

In some cases, semantic change occurs without any obvious corresponding change in the external world. It is more difficult to account for this kind of change, and there is much less agreement among linguists about its causes, but in some cases pressure seems to come from within the language system. In order to account for the semantic changes that affect a single sense of a word, we need to remember that meanings do not exist in a vacuum, but form complex relationships with other meanings, both at the level of the word sense and beyond. Like the components of other aspects of language, such as phonology and syntax, meanings are part of a system, and need to function efficiently; confusion, redundancies or clashes within the system are inefficient, and can lead to shifts in one or more meanings. Both polysemy and homonymy can trigger semantic changes, since polysemous and homonymous words are single forms with two or more meanings, and are thus potentially ambiguous.

Synonymy, the opposite situation where two or more words share the same meaning, can also be a trigger for change. This focus on system implies an essentially structuralist view of meaning, as noted in Chapter 1 and described in section 3.2.2. Within this view we can explain the connections among meanings by visualising the lexicon metaphorically as a large space, and the meanings of words as covering an area of that space; if one area of the lexicon becomes overcrowded, or changes in some other way, regulation of the system (**systemic regulation**) can take place and meanings shift in their location or in the amount of space they occupy. An extended example of this phenomenon can be found in the discussion in section 7.4 of the realignment of the boundaries of colour terms in the history of English. In other theories of Semantics, particularly those focusing on the development of individual forms, different metaphors are employed, such as the metaphor of meanings radiating from a prototypical core or being linked together in a polysemous chain.

The cases of polysemy we have considered so far in this chapter, and throughout this book, show that for much, and perhaps even most, of the lexis of English, polysemy is the norm. In many cases, multiple meanings function alongside one another in a fairly stable way for long periods, even if individual meanings shift. However, if there is any chance of confusion or tension between senses this can lead to semantic change, often in the form of the loss of one or more senses. A classic example is the adjective *quaint*, which has the meaning 'attractively unusual or old-fashioned' in PDE (*Oxford Dictionaries Online*). *Quaint* is discussed by Samuels (1972: 76), and revisited by Durkin (2009: 228–31), who reconsiders Samuels' account in light of *OED3* revisions and finds it largely substantiated. Its history provides compelling evidence of the way a new sense can impact upon existing senses and lead to their obsolescence.

According to *OED3*, *quaint* was borrowed into English from French in several senses, and is attested first in the early thirteenth century. Between the thirteenth and the early nineteenth centuries, it had meanings describing people which relate to intelligence and skill; these range from 'wise, clever', for example (in *OED* citations) describing orators or craftsmen, to 'cunning, crafty', for example describing women or the devil. Related meanings which describe things, plans and schemes, such as 'skilfully made' 'cunning' and 'ingenious', are found from around the same time and slightly later, and in turn these senses give rise to meanings like 'attractive, beautiful, fashionable (of things)' and 'ingeniously elaborate, smart (of speech)'. It is also found from the fourteenth century onwards in the sense 'strange, unusual, unfamiliar'. Most of these meanings are attested until the late eighteenth or very early nineteenth century, but the emergence of a new meaning in the late eighteenth century appears to change the semantic profile of the word dramatically. The sense 'attractively or agreeably unusual in character or appearance; *esp*. pleasingly old-fashioned' is first attested in 1762 (*OED3* sense 9), and although it is uncertain why this sense develops at this time, it seems to replace all of the earlier senses within a generation. Although 'pleasingly old-fashioned' is not a negative meaning, 'old-fashioned' generally has negative connotations, adding a degree of pejoration to *quaint*, and this perhaps explains why it displaces the other senses. Any speaker who was aware of both positive and negative senses of *quaint* would presumably avoid using it with a positive sense in case this was interpreted as a negative sense: for example, if a phrase like *a quaint idea* is no longer unambiguously positive, it is not useful to anyone who intends a positive meaning. Speakers therefore seem to have avoided the positive senses entirely, leading to obsolescence. It is important to stress that a clash of this kind is only likely to happen if meanings can be confused in context, with the consequent risk of misunderstanding and communicative failure. When we looked at *wicked*, which can mean both 'bad, evil' and 'good', we saw that these senses were not likely to be confused because they are used by different speakers in different contexts.

Homonymy, the situation where a form has two or more etymologically unrelated meanings, can also act as a pressure for semantic change, leading to **homonymic clash** and the possibility that one or more senses can shift or die out. An example of this process is shown by the homonyms *ass* 'donkey' and *ass* 'posterior, buttocks'. *Ass* 'donkey' is a native OE word. In modern times the animal name *donkey* is a more usual term than *ass* in the usage of most British speakers, but in earlier times *ass* was dominant; *donkey* is not found in English until the late eighteenth century (*OED donkey*, noun 1a). The homonym *ass* 'posterior' is not attested in the *OED* until 1860, and is apparently a variant form of *arse*, reflecting a particular pronunciation of that word (*OED ass*, noun 2, 1a). Although the earliest attestation is in a British text, most of the early examples are in US English, and modern dictionaries generally consider *ass* to be US slang, with *arse* still the British equivalent.

The obsolescence of *ass* 'donkey' and its widespread replacement by *donkey* seems to be triggered by the spread of *ass* 'posterior' in the twentieth century. Speakers probably disliked the association of *ass* 'donkey' with its homonym, considered to be a vulgar term for a taboo body part, and preferred the alternative which already existed in the system. The tainting of one meaning by the other may also be reinforced by a remaining shared meaning, which adds to the lack of clear differentiation between the two: both *ass* 'donkey' and the variant forms *arse/ass* 'posterior' develop the meaning 'stupid person', as in *silly ass/ arse*.

The pressure for change exerted by synonymy also relates to the systemic nature of the lexicon. As we saw in Chapter 2, English has a high level of partial synonymy, but true or exact synonyms are rare because of the pressure towards efficiency in the system: there is no need for several forms with the same meaning. Where true synonymy arises, one of the words is likely to become obsolete or undergo a shift such as specialisation or pejoration. An example is OE *steorfan* 'to die', the etymon of ModE *starve*, which came into competition with *die* in early ME, a word of disputed etymology but most likely a loanword from Norse. *Starve* was already associated with death from two common causes, cold and hunger, and specialised in these directions, while *die* retained the general meaning. Another OE synonym *sweltan* (*OED swelt*, from the same root as *swelter*) specialised in a different direction, coming to mean 'faint or swoon, especially from heat'. *Starve* succeeded in the meaning 'die from lack of food', but 'die from cold' is restricted in later English to northern dialect use, while *swelt* has largely disappeared.

Temporary synonymy often arises in English through the introduction of foreign loanwords, especially those from French and Latin. In such cases the semantic effects can be considered an example of the intermediate category combining external and internal factors mentioned in section 5.7. An example from one of the periods of heavy borrowing is the verb *migrate*, first attested in the seventeenth century. *Migrate* is borrowed from classical Latin, where it has a range of senses such as 'move about, move from place to place, move residence', 'move or shift (belongings, etc.)', and 'pass into a new condition or form'. In the seventeenth and eighteenth centuries, it has many of these senses in English, but in PDE it is largely restricted to the more specialised senses, '(of an animal) to move from one region or habitat to another according to the seasons' and '(of a person) move to a new area or country'. It also has technical senses related to computing, but it is very rarely used with a general sense relating to movement, which is covered by a range of other words, such as *move* itself. Further discussion of the effects of synonymy on the lexicon can be found in Chapter 6.

5.7.3 Stylistic factors

As we also saw in Chapter 2 (e.g. section 2.3), the availability of synonyms increases stylistic choice for speakers and writers. Such choices can be motivated by factors as different as the desire to create greater impact and the need to avoid embarrassment. These factors are worth mentioning briefly here since they can also drive semantic change. The bleaching of meaning in words such as *terribly* or *awful* can be attributed initially to **overstatement** (**hyperbole** in classical rhetoric): if you say that an exam was *awful*, you are probably only saying that you didn't like it much, not that it filled you with a deep feeling of awe; when you claim that you are *starving*, you may be quite hungry but are not on the point of death. Likewise, you might use **understatement** (**litotes**) when you describe a quarrel as a *misunderstanding* or say that something is *not bad* when you are in fact extremely pleased with it. Similar effects can be obtained with **euphemism**, where an unpleasant or taboo topic is named by a word which disguises its unpleasant aspects. These are often words from the more formal Latin-derived lexis, for example *mortician* replacing *undertaker*. The classic example in English is words for 'toilet', where a new euphemism seems to be required by every generation, ranging from OE *gangpytt* 'going hole' to modern *smallest room* (see Fischer 2004). An opposite effect is created by **dysphemism**, where the seriousness of a topic is diminished by treating it with lexical disrespect, as in expressions for dying such as *kick the bucket* or *push up the daisies*. All of these can be taken as examples of the human capacity to manipulate language in order to achieve a desired purpose.

5.8 Conclusion

In this chapter we have looked at a number of complex word histories, which show some of the ways in which lexical meanings typically change over time. We have seen the inherent fuzziness of the semantic level of language; at any one time most words have a range of connected meanings which are difficult to separate neatly and sometimes also vary from speaker to speaker. This means that semantic change itself is rarely neat, and usually involves more than simply the shift from a single 'old' meaning to a single 'new' meaning. Much more often, one or more meanings declines or drops out of use over time, or additional new meanings emerge from existing senses, perhaps changing the prototypical use of the word. Because polysemy is so common, the tendencies we have observed in semantic change – widening and narrowing, amelioration and pejoration, changes triggered by metaphor and metonymy – are best thought of as tendencies which affect one or more senses of a word, rather than that word as a whole.

The question of why words change meaning is tricky, and there is no single answer, although we can observe typical language-external and language-internal triggers. The examples we have looked at in this chapter show that every case of semantic change is different, involving pressures of different kinds, so that extra-linguistic and intra-linguistic factors often interact. For example, the emergence of the new dominant sense of *gay*, 'homosexual', and the corresponding decline of the earlier established sense 'happy', involved both language-internal and language-external factors. Initial pressure for the emergence of a new sense was language-external, since it related to the new need for a term in changing social circumstances. The subsequent decline of the sense *gay* 'happy' can be attributed to language-internal pressure, because it was triggered by adjustments in the language system to accommodate the rise of *gay* 'homosexual'.

Exercises

1. Find some examples of the use of *literally* in writing or speech and decide which meaning is intended. If you have access to English speakers of different ages, get their reactions to your examples and assess how acceptable the intensifier meaning is and whether there is evidence of generational change.
2. In section 5.5.1 we looked at how the meaning of *bird* had broadened. ME *fowl* (OE *fugol*) has undergone the opposite kind of change, narrowing. Use the *OED* to make an analysis of the semantic development of *fowl*, comparing it to the development of *bird*. If you have time, you could also include *chick* and *chicken* in your analysis.
3. Use the internet or some of the corpora mentioned in section 4.5 to make an assessment of the currency and meaning of the word *sweetmeat* in PDE.
4. Collect some additional examples of computer terminology and find out what their origins are and whether they show evidence of semantic change.

Further reading

Allan (2012) discusses some of the issues involved in using the *OED* to track semantic change. Useful summaries of lexical change with interesting examples can be found in Durkin (2009, chapter 8), and Minkova and Stockwell (2009, chapter 9). Geeraerts (2010, 1.3) discusses the development of theories of change, as do Traugott and Dasher (2005, chapter 2). Robinson (2012a) is a more detailed account of the past and present meanings of *gay*, and Robinson (2012b) demonstrates another semantic change in action by analysing *skinny*. Crystal (2014, chapter 5) discusses the *HTOED toilet* category. For work in Pragmatics on invited inferencing and grammaticalisation, see Traugott and Dasher (2005) and Jucker and Taavitsainen (2013).

Notes

1. Hansard Parliamentary Proceedings, HL Deb 21 November 1979, vol. 403 cc171. Available via the Historic Hansard website: http://hansard.millbanksystems.com/.
2. HC Deb 22 July 1980, vol. 989 cc300.
3. (*ge*) is an optional prefix in OE and doesn't affect the meaning of the word here. It is generally ignored in alphabetical listings of OE words. Its ME reflex is *i-* or *y-*; the earliest attestations of the word appear in the *OED* under *i-sele*.

6 Larger categories

6.1 Introduction

In Chapters 4 and 5, we saw how much we can learn about the development of individual words by using the *OED*. As with most dictionaries, the *OED* is organised alphabetically, proceeding steadily from A–Z. However, this is not the only way to organise information. We can envisage a dictionary organised by parts of speech, or affixes, or etymologies, though none of these might be very practical. We can also envisage one organised by meaning – what is usually called a thesaurus, from a Greek word meaning a 'storehouse' or 'treasury'. The best-known of these for English is *Roget*, first published in 1852 and frequently revised since then. As the various editions cover a period of over 150 years, *Roget* has some intrinsic interest for historical linguists; however, for more specifically historical information, we will depend in this chapter mainly on the *HTOED* (2009), which is available as a printed book, online from the University of Glasgow, and as a component of the *OED Online* website. Two points need to be borne in mind when using this resource:

- *HTOED* is based on the second edition of the *OED*, not the online version which includes *OED3* entries. Where entries have been revised for *OED3* after the publication of *HTOED*, dates, semantic category references and other information may differ between the print and online versions. In this book, we will refer to the print edition.
- Coverage in the print *HTOED* and the Glasgow online version is fuller than in the *OED Online* version (or indeed any edition of the *OED*). This is because the *OED* omits all the OE words which are not recorded after 1150, whereas *HTOED* includes the contents of *TOE* (2000), thus covering the complete recorded vocabulary of OE.

Details of the availability of these thesauruses are given at the end of this book (see pp. 191–2). If you want to delve even further into the past, a fascinating book is *A Dictionary of Selected Synonyms in the Principal Indo-European Languages* (ed. Carl Darling Buck), first published in 1949 and reprinted in 1988. Although called a dictionary, the book is organised like a thesaurus and contains lists of words in ancient and modern languages for core concepts such as Sun and Moon (1988: 52). What all these books have in common is that they give us a completely different perspective on the lexicon, unlocking semantic information which is concealed by the structure of alphabetical dictionaries. They do this by focusing on the connections between words, as revealed by relationships such as synonymy, hyponymy, meronymy and antonymy (for these terms, see Chapter 3). At the same time, as we shall see in this chapter and in Chapters 7 and 8, they are a rich source of information on how cultures develop over the years.

6.2 A brief history of thesauruses

Few people nowadays have any difficulty in using an alphabetical dictionary; putting words in alphabetical order is a skill we develop in childhood. Tackling a thesaurus is less straightforward, since each one will have a different plan of classification, reflecting the views of its authors and the times in which they lived. For this reason, most thesauruses will help their users by providing both a synopsis of the structure and an alphabetical index.

Alphabetical order seems so obvious to us that it may come as a surprise to learn that the earliest wordbooks were semantically organised. Scholars have traced such books as far back as the Akkadian Empire and Ancient China, and they are found in England from the eighth century onwards, the most famous being one by the great Anglo-Saxon scholar Ælfric. Their primary purpose was the teaching of Latin, and they include words listed under such useful topics as the body and its parts, precious stones, medicinal herbs, and natural kinds such as animals, birds, fish and plants. Production of such lists continued throughout the Middle Ages, and it is not until 1604 that we find the first alphabetical English–English dictionary, Robert Cawdrey's *A Table Alphabeticall, Conteyning and Teaching the True Writing, and Understanding of Hard Usuall English Words*. According to its preface, these words were 'gathered for the benefit & helpe of Ladies, Gentlewomen, or any other unskilfull persons', thus reminding us of how many 'hard words' entered English during this period (see the discussion of 'inkhorn terms' in section 2.4). Cawdrey apparently felt that alphabetical order was so novel that it needed to be explained in detail, writing:

> If thou be desirous (gentle Reader) rightly and readily to vnderstand, and
> to profit by this Table, and such like, then thou must learne the Alphabet,
> to wit, the order of the Letters as they stand, perfecty [sic] without booke,
> and where euery Letter standeth: as *b* neere the beginning, *n* about the
> middest, and *t* toward the end. Nowe if the word, which thou art desirous
> to finde, begin with *a* then looke in the beginning of this Table, but if with
> *v* looke towards the end. Againe, if thy word beginne with *ca* looke in the
> beginning of the letter *c* but if with *cu* then looke toward the end of that
> letter. And so of all the rest. &c.

His efforts bore fruit, since alphabetical dictionaries flourished from then
on, while production of thesauruses slumped, with the notable exceptions of *An Essay towards a Real Character, and a Philosophical Language* by
John Wilkins, published in 1668, and *Roget* in 1852. The word *thesaurus*
appears in the titles of works from many publishing houses nowadays,
but most of these are alphabetically organised dictionaries of synonyms
without a conceptual structure.

Both Wilkins and Roget were scientists and both had grand ambi-
tions. They aimed first to classify the 'things and notions' which exist in
the outside world, and then to insert the words used to describe them
into their classifications. They thus imposed a 'top-down' classification
on the lexicon, allowing the conceptual fields to establish the lexical
fields. Wilkins went even further by devising his 'philosophical language', which was intended to enable representation in symbolic form
of all words in all languages, thus eliminating the need for translation
and improving understanding among people.

The *Historical Thesaurus of English* (*HTE*) project, which forms the
basis of *HTOED*, was founded by Professor Michael Samuels in 1965,
with a view to providing a new, and novel, resource for researching the
history and development of the English lexicon. He believed that we
could not fully explain why words came into the language, or died out,
or developed new meanings:

> [...] until it is possible to study simultaneously *all* the forms involved in
> a complex series of semantic shifts and replacements. The required data
> exist in multivolume historical dictionaries like the *OED*, but they cannot
> be utilised because the presentation is alphabetical, not notional. The
> need is for a historical *thesaurus* which will bring together under single
> heads all the words, current or obsolete (and all the obsolete meanings of
> words still current) that have ever been used to express single and related
> notions. (Samuels 1972: 180)

With this objective in mind, Samuels and his team set to work,
extracting information from historical dictionaries and recording it on

paper slips. Once this was done they sorted the slips according to the meanings of the words and gradually built up a classification, proceeding from the most specific meanings to the most general. In contrast to the work of Wilkins and Roget, such a classification can be described as 'bottom-up', since the starting point is the words themselves rather than a predefined view of the universe. Only when this manual stage was complete was the work transferred to an electronic database, which generated both the printed text and the online versions.

6.3 The structure of thesauruses

The concept of synonymy is essential to the structure of any thesaurus, though sometimes it is very loosely applied. Whatever the overall plan of a particular thesaurus, words of approximately similar meaning will be grouped together in synonym sets, which generally consist of both good (prototypical) and less good examples of the central concept. These sets may be paired with sets of antonyms and will often be linked to sets of more or less specific meaning by the hierarchical relationships of hyponymy and meronymy.

Thus, if you look up the concept of 'hat' in *HTOED* (see Figure 6.1), you will find a list of words ranging from *hat* itself, listed with its OE form *hæt* to show that it has been current since OE, to more recent equivalents, such as the slang term *lid* or the dialectal *nudger*. If you look further down the column, you will find words and phrases

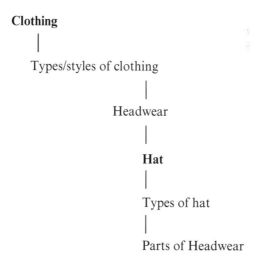

Clothing

|

Types/styles of clothing

|

Headwear

|

Hat

|

Types of hat

|

Parts of Headwear

Figure 6.1 The position of the category *Hat* in the *HTOED* hierarchy

for different kinds of hat, grouped by characteristics such as shape (*bowler*), material (*straw hat*) or purpose (*sun-hat*). These expressions are all hyponyms of *hat*. Still further down, you will find words for parts of a hat, meronyms of *hat*, such as *brim, ear-flap, peak*. If you now find *hat* again and search back through the column, you will find that the *Hat* category has a hyponymic relationship with a more general superordinate category, *Headwear*, and with the still more general *Clothing*. Hats have always been an important part of our apparel and the concept is highly **lexicalised** in English; that is, it has a large vocabulary allowing for a good deal of discrimination among various aspects of the concept. The vocabulary also shows considerable innovation and obsolescence in response to changing fashions, materials, technology, and so on; the category is well worth a look. A less important or more recent concept such as 'bathing dress' has a much smaller and less detailed vocabulary.

The structure described above essentially consists of two relationships: 'less specific than', the relationship of a superordinate to a hyponym or meronym, and 'more specific than', the relationship of a hyponym or meronym to a superordinate. In Chapter 3, we applied these terms to individual words, but here they are applied to categories of synonymous words. As Geeraerts writes:

> [. . .] why should semantic categories have different characteristics when they are found within the structure of a single word, or when they are found across different words, within the vocabulary as a whole? The patterns of thought at work in both cases remain the same, and semantic categories remain semantic categories, whether they have an infralexical or a supralexical status. (2010: 203)

As we saw in the *Hat* example above, such relationships are recursive in that a category can simultaneously be in a hyponymic relationship to a more general term, as *Hat* is to *Headwear*, and in a superordinate relationship to a more specific term, as *Hat* is to *sun-hat*. Categories such as *Sun-hat* and *Bowler hat*, which are at the same level in the hierarchy, i.e. are co-ordinate with one another, have a relationship of co-hyponymy.

Meronymy (the part–whole relationship) can be subsumed within the general hyponymy relationship, since, like hyponyms, meronyms differ from their superordinate by an additional component of meaning. Antonymous categories, differing only in the component of [NOT], as in *Happiness/Unhappiness*, can also be fitted into this structure, but the varying nature of antonymy makes this problematic (see section 3.2.2.1). Superficially, there is a clear opposition between categories like *Love* and *Hatred*, yet a sentence like 'I don't love her but I don't hate her' makes perfect sense. What we have here is rather a cline of meaning running from *Love* at one pole through weaker notions of *Liking* and *Disliking* to *Hatred*, *Loathing* and *Disgust* at the other. Some categories simply have no antonymic relationships: what is the opposite of *Anger* or *Friendship*, other than the absence of these qualities, or indeed of *Hat?* Roget set great store by antonymy as an organising principle in his thesaurus, but sometimes struggled to make it work. For example, he contrasts category 228 *Dressing* with 229 *Uncovering*, but, while the former contains lists of terms for various items of clothing, the latter has only general terms for the concept, plus a category for *Stripper* that includes dancers, nudists and people like shearers who strip hair from animals. Murphy (2003: 113) points out that similar problems occur in the electronic WordNet thesaurus, where antonymy is also an organising principle and where terms like *unangry* and *thoughtless* are offered as not very satisfactory antonyms of *angry* and *contemplative* in order to fill **lexical gaps**.

6.3.1 Basic level and other categories

Early work on the structure of categories and lexical fields concentrated on the relationships described above. Although the idea of superordinate and hyponymous levels remains important in any work of lexical analysis, more recent work in Cognitive Semantics has introduced a category of a different kind, the **basic level category** (see **categorisation**), which identifies the level people find most useful in dealing with the world around them, and which thus may tell us more about the mental processes involved in categorisation. As Taylor writes:

> There is ... a level of categorization which is cognitively and linguistically more salient than the others. This is the **basic level** of categorization – the level at which (in the absence of reasons to the contrary) people normally conceptualize and name things. (2003a: 50; see also Geeraerts 2010: 199–201)

Members of such categories have a large number of features in common and share few features with members of other categories, thus enabling easy identification of their referents: few people, for example, would have any difficulty in picking out a hat, a jumper and a shirt (all basic level categories) from a collection of garments, or any difficulty in naming them. However, these categories also exhibit **prototype effects**, such as degrees of membership (some members are better examples than others) and fuzzy edges, shading into neighbouring categories (see section 3.3 on fuzzy sets). Basic level categories are learned earliest,

when we're growing up and sorting out the world. If a child points to
a dog and says 'What's that?' the carer is likely to respond with a basic
term, 'It's a dog', not 'It's a mammal' (a superordinate) nor 'It's a King
Charles spaniel' (a hyponym). This response helps the child to recognise and internalise the features that lead to objects being designated
as members of a set, in this case the set of dogs as opposed to the set
of cats or rabbits. Within Cognitive Semantics, the set of categories or
concepts we store in our minds can be considered as underlying our
mental lexicon, the stock of words that we know. When we come across
new items in the outside world, we match them against these categories
and decide whether they are sufficiently like the prototypical members
to be admitted to the category and denoted by the category name (of
course, we do not necessarily do this consciously).

In English at least, basic level categories tend to be named by relatively short, single words; a large number of these are of native (OE)
origin rather than more complex borrowed words. Such words are
more efficient – if we talk about something often, it's more economical to use a brief, readily understood expression. In this respect, basic
level categories contrast with higher and lower level categories, which
are sometimes named by single words, but often by compound terms
or phrases. If superordinate categories are labelled by single words,
these are often rather strange: collective terms like *headwear* and *hardware*, which are singular nouns despite the fact that they refer to large
numbers of things; technical words like *sibling* or *mammal*; latinate terms
like *canine* or *umbelliferous*; or phrases like *domestic appliances* or *white
goods*. Shops and catalogues are a rich source of the latter. Sometimes
the superordinate category can have the same name as the basic level
category, for example *Man* 'mankind' and *Man* 'male human being'. If
this becomes confusing, or otherwise unacceptable, a new superordinate may take over, as *Humankind* has tended to do for this particular
category in recent years.

At the lower levels, hyponymic categories are usually named with
phrases or compounds which pick out their distinguishing features.
Having surveyed the terms for different kinds of dresses, we might
set up a category *Dresses worn at particular times of day*, which would
include *day-dress*, *evening-dress* and *night-dress*. As historical linguists,
however, we might notice that in the eighteenth century *night-gown*
was a synonym for *evening-dress*, and didn't develop the meaning 'dress
to be worn in bed' until the nineteenth century. We might therefore
decide to subdivide the category further in order to provide homes
for both meanings. The hyponymic level is the most flexible and
open-ended level of categorisation and easily absorbs new members,

often in response to cultural changes; the category *Weatherproof jacket*, for example, developed during the twentieth century to cover terms such as *anorak, cagoule* and *windcheater* when these became fashionable. Sometimes a hyponymic category can achieve basic level status because of its cultural importance or **salience**, as may be happening to the category *Jeans*. Although technically a hyponym of *Trousers*, the word *jeans*, first recorded in the mid-nineteenth century, is the term most likely to be used when referring to that particular garment and has hyponyms of its own, such as *designer jeans, skinny jeans, Levis, bootlegs, flares, parallel legs, drainpipes, worn-in, ripped, baggy* and *faded jeans* (with thanks to the students who supplied these and other examples).

If you're doing lexical analysis of a set of related terms, the basic level categories are a good place to start. One way of identifying them is by a drawing test. If I ask a group of people to make a line-drawing of a table or a tree or a sword, the results (give or take the ability of the artist) will be pretty similar and easily identified by others as the objects in question. However, if the task is to draw a piece of furniture or a plant or a weapon, people may draw completely different objects: a chair or a wardrobe; a bush or a daffodil; a gun or a dagger. If the task is to draw a coffee table or a plane tree or a claymore, the artists may have more difficulty, perhaps because their encyclopedic knowledge doesn't extend to the distinguishing features of these objects; we may have read about claymores in historical novels, but know only that they are a kind of sword. For more familiar objects like the coffee table, we may resort to including the distinguishing feature, for example by putting a coffee cup on the table rather than drawing the table alone. On this basis, at least for depictable concrete objects, we can say that *Table, Tree* and *Sword* are basic level categories while *Furniture, Plant* and *Weapon* are superordinate, and *Coffee table, Plane tree* and *Claymore* are hyponymous. The fact that jeans would be quite difficult to distinguish from other kinds of trousers in a drawing may raise a question about whether they constitute a basic category. For basic level abstract categories, such as *Anger* or *Fear*, we have to resort to other means, such as listing the characteristics of a person suffering from these emotions (a stereotype: see section 3.3). Just as we couldn't draw 'furniture', so we couldn't make a similar list for the superordinate category *Emotion*.

6.3.2 Folk and expert categories

One reason why English is short of convincing names for superordinate categories may simply be that we have relatively little need for them in the discourse of everyday life. Many superordinate terms, such as *mammal* or *umbelliferous*, are, or were originally, part of the language of scientific taxonomies, coined by experts as headings for categories based on systematic analysis of items in the real world. *Mammal*, for example, defined by the *OED* as 'An animal of the vertebrate class Mammalia, the members of which are characterized by having mammary glands that secrete milk to feed the young', is first recorded in 1813. *Umbelliferous* first appears in 1662 in the work of John Ray, who used it to classify plants such as hemlock or elder which have a mass of small flowers on a single branching stalk. Ray was a pioneer of botanical classification and influenced broader theories of classification through his co-operation with John Wilkins (see section 6.1). Because they are devised by people with specialised knowledge and expertise, such systems are called **expert taxonomies**, and a category like *Mammal* is an expert category. The role of the expert is to devise rules for membership of the category, which results in Aristotelian categories where membership is on a 'yes' or 'no' basis without any concept of prototypicality (see section 3.3). In such classifications, there is no doubt about whether penguins and emus belong to the class of birds, despite the fact that they lack some of the qualities of prototypical birds such as shape and small size, as long as they meet the scientific criteria for that class. If they did not, a new class would have to be set up.

Expert taxonomies are contrasted with **folk taxonomies**, which, like basic level categories, are grounded in the perceptions and priorities of ordinary language users, how important things are to them, and how things function in their world. Such taxonomies are of particular interest to sociologists and anthropologists because of what they reveal about societies. For example, as we will see in Chapter 8, classifications of kinship terms based on social obligations rather than biological facts occur in many societies around the world and determine how people behave towards one another.

Folk taxonomies, and their relationship to expert taxonomies, are also of interest to historical linguists, both because they may change over the years in line with society's knowledge, and because such changes may result in linguistic change. Any student of physiology in medieval Europe, for example, has to take account of the theory of the four cardinal humours, bodily fluids which were thought to determine a person's temperament and cause illness when out of balance. Lexical categories reflecting these ideas will be found in the languages of cultures subscribing to this theory. They may survive long after the theory itself has been discredited, as in English words describing different temperaments, such as *sanguine, melancholic, choleric* and *phlegmatic* (see further Geeraerts 2010: 251–2). Similarly, folk taxonomies are among the earliest detectable in English for categories such as Animals and Plants. Animals are classified according to whether they are wild or domesticated or available for hunting, plants according to whether they are edible or useful in some other way, for instance in making fabrics or as an ingredient in medicine. These categories cut across the expert taxonomies of later periods. Some of them, such as *Wild animal* and *Weed*, persist to this day, and others have been added, such as *Pet animal* or *Garden plant*, both first recorded in the lexicon in the eighteenth century. Such classifications reflect social rather than scientific reality: pets and garden plants, for example, indicate an increasingly prosperous society, where such items could be afforded. Even scientific categories can be influenced by culture: chimpanzees and other higher primates are very close to human beings genetically, and it might be logical to put us all in a single scientific category, but this would probably not be socially acceptable.

Much of the work on taxonomy has been done in areas where science has made most progress in the last few hundred years, producing ever more detailed and sophisticated analyses of the natural world. In modern societies, where many people have some degree of scientific education, speakers may know and operate both folk and scientific taxonomies. The *OED* defines *fruit* scientifically as: 'the edible product of a plant or tree, consisting of the seed and its envelope, *esp.* the latter when it is of a juicy pulpy nature, as in the apple, orange, plum, etc.', and adds a helpful note pointing to a folk taxonomy: 'As denoting an article of food, the word is popularly extended to include certain vegetable products that resemble "fruits" in their qualities, e.g. the stalks of rhubarb' (*OED fruit*, noun 2). Thus, although we know intellectually that rhubarb is not a fruit (because it doesn't have seeds), we don't have any problem in classifying it as a fruit for practical purposes, such as finding it in a supermarket, because it is used in sweet dishes like other fruits. (See also the discussion of *tomato* in section 3.3.1.)

6.4 Using *HTOED*

We have looked at various sections from *HTOED* in this book, and seen how helpful it can be in tracing lexical change and offering us clues to social and cultural change. *HTOED* is a unique resource: it is the first and only comprehensive historical thesaurus for English and, as far as we know, for any other language, although others may follow for languages which have resources comparable to the *OED*, such as Dutch and Scots. This section will look in more detail at the structure of *HTOED* and at some of the kinds of information that can be extracted from it.

First level		
01 The world	02 The mind	03 Society
Second level		
01.01 The earth	02.01 Mental capacity	03.01 Society/the community
01.02 Life	02.02 Emotion	03.02 Inhabiting/dwelling
01.03 Physical sensibility	02.03 Philosophy	03.03 Armed hostility
01.04 Matter	02.04 Aesthetics	03.04 Authority
01.05 Existence	02.05 Will	03.05 Morality
01.06 Relative properties	02.06 Refusal/denial	03.06 Education
01.07 The supernatural	02.07 Having/possession	03.07 Faith
	02.08 Language	03.08 Communication
		03.09 Travel/travelling
		03.10 Occupation/work
		03.11 Leisure

Figure 6.2 Top-level categories in *HTOED*

6.4.1 The structure of HTOED

Overall, *HTOED* contains nearly 800,000 word senses arranged in approximately 225,000 semantic categories. There are twelve possible levels of classification (from general to specific), represented by increasingly long number strings, though many sections don't use so many levels. Compared with other thesauruses such as *Roget*, the *HTOED* system differentiates more finely among semantically related words and makes their relationships more explicit through its category headings. As shown in Figure 6.2, there are three major divisions at the first level, followed by twenty-six second-level categories. The first major section, 01. *The World*, contains categories for the words describing objects and events in the material universe. In historical terms, this starting point is based on the assumption that categorising the world and our interaction with it is a primary concern for human beings and their languages. Next comes 02. *The Mind*, since, as we see in many places in this book, we express abstract ideas such as 'thinking' through metaphorical transfer from the vocabulary of material existence. The final major division, 03. *Society*, reflects the increasingly complex development of human social organisation, especially in more recent years; although Section 01 is by far the largest of the three, Section 03 shows the highest degree of lexical innovation and semantic change.

Second-level categories have some of the characteristics of lexical

03.02.07.03.09.07.02 (n.) *Sofa/couch*
cribb OE · hlinbed OE · hobanca OE · reclinatory
1412/20–*a*1633 · couch *c*1450– · crabat 1483 · day-bed 1594– ·
squab 1664– · repose 1701 · settee 1716– · sofa 1717– ·
sopha 1728–1832 · duchesse 1794– · chaise-longue 1800– ·
sultane 1803 · lounge 1830– · dormeuse 1865 · long chair
1891– · canapé 1892; 1955 · Berbice 1951; 1959 · lounger
1969– · takht 1979–   **01** *in Eastern countries* sofa 1625– ·
sopha *c*1637–1808   **02** *for two persons* confidante/
confidente 1794; 1925– · causeuse 1844– · sociable 1851– ·
conversation chair 1861 · tête-à-tête 1864– · cosy 1876– ·
love-seat 1904– · two-seater 1973–   **03** *for reclining at*
meals bur þrybeddod OE · dining-bed 1581 · triclinium
1646– (*Roman Antiquity*) · feast-bed *a*1661 · supper-bed
*a*1661 · mensal bed 1675 · table-couch 1877   **04** *sun*
lounger sun bed 1967– · sun lounger 1972– · sun lounge
1979 (*US*)   **04.01** *for artificial sunbathing* sun bed 1980–
05 *ottoman* ottoman 1806– · pouf 1884– · box-ottoman
1912   **06** *other sofas/couches* bed-loft 1606 · divan 1702– ·
bergère 1762– · stibadium 1840 · Davenport/davenport
1898– (*N. Amer.*) · Chesterfield 1900– · (Madame) Récamier
1924– · contour couch 1952– · tuxedo (style) sofa 1961– ·
futon(g) 1972–   **07** *part of sofa* sofa-back 1878– · settee
1891

Figure 6.3 *HTOED* category 03.02.07.03.09.07.02 *Sofa/couch*

fields, but are much broader in conception than the lexical fields of
classical theory (see section 3.2.3) in that they cover the vocabulary
associated with a field as well as the network of sense relationships
within it. They thus have more resemblance to the encyclopedic view
of meaning developed in Cognitive Semantics, and the notion of the
domain.

Level 2 is followed by 354 categories at level 3, and by increasing
numbers at lower levels. Even level 3 is too large to show here, but it
can be seen in the printed volume or on the *HTE* website. Basic level
categories can occur at any level of the hierarchy depending on how
complicated its structure is. How it all works can best be explained by
the example from the printed book in Figure 6.3. If you are using the
version linked to the *OED Online*, find *sofa* in the *OED* and click on the
link on the right to *Thesaurus* to find the complete category. The num-
bering system, however, is not represented in the *OED*.

Figure 6.3 shows all the nouns recorded for the concept of a sofa or

Level 1	03 Society
[...]	
Level 2	03.02 Inhabiting/dwelling
[...]	
Level 3	03.02.07 Inhabited place
[...]	
Level 4	03.02.07.03 A building
[...]	
Level 5	03.02.07.03.09 Furniture
[...]	
Level 6	03.02.07.03.09.07 Seat.
[...]	
Level 7	03.02.07.03.09.07.01 Chair
	03.02.07.03.09.07.02 Sofa/couch
	03.02.07.03.09.07.03 Bench
	03.02.07.03.09.07.04 Stool

Figure 6.4 The place of 03.02.07.03.09.07.02 *Sofa/couch* in the *HTOED* hierarchy

couch in the history of English, starting with the oldest words from OE. It should be remembered that these forms represent one specific meaning of each word, since other meanings of polysemous forms, whether in current use or obsolete, will be recorded in the appropriate categories elsewhere in the thesaurus. The form *illustrious*, for example, appears in *Reputation* in its modern meaning of 'renowned, famous', but also in two other categories on account of its obsolete meanings, the literal one 'bright, lustrous' in *Light* and another figurative one, 'evident, obvious', in *Communication*. *Couch* appears in 03.02.07.03.09.07.02 in its modern meaning, but also elsewhere in 03.02.07.03.09 meaning 'bed' and 'tablecloth', and in several other places in *HTOED*.

Figure 6.4 shows the category's place in the structure as a whole; [...] indicates a category which has been omitted because it is not relevant to the present discussion. The highest-level superordinate category of *sofa* is 03 *Society*, but its actual place is in a level seven category 03.02.07.03.09.07.02 *Sofa/couch*, which is in a subordinate relationship with all the categories above it and is co-ordinate with categories for other kinds of furniture at the same level as itself. Each of the intermediate levels represents a more specific concept than the preceding one. Thus, 03.02 *Inhabiting/dwelling* is a particular aspect of social behaviour. 03.02.07 *Inhabited place* can be seen as part of the general concept of *Inhabiting/dwelling, A building* is part of this place, and *Furniture* is part of a building. *Seat* is a type of *Furniture*, while *Chair*, *Sofa/couch*, *Bench* and *Stool* are hyponyms of *Seat* and co-hyponyms of one another. From these headings, we can build something like a definition by working our way upwards: 'a sofa is a kind of seat, which is a kind of furniture, which is part of a building, which is part of an inhabited place, which is part of the activity of dwelling, which is a social activity'. By doing this, we are unpacking the process by which the meanings were classified in the first place.

In addition to the seven main levels, there is also the possibility of five levels of sub-categories for even more specific types of sofas and couches. There are examples of these in Figure 6.3, including 04 *sun lounger* at level 8, and, even more specific, 04.01 *for artificial sunbathing* at level 9, an abbreviated heading which in full would read *sun lounger for artificial sunbathing*. People can find the long strings of numbers rather off-putting (when *HTOED* was published, one reviewer compared them to telephone numbers), but they are the most economical way of representing and retrieving the taxonomic relationships in the thesaurus structure. In this example, the main relationship is hyponymy, with the discriminating features based on place and purpose: types of sofa *in Eastern countries, for two persons, for reclining at meals.*

Like the polycentric lexical categories described in section 3.3.2, complex structures such as the one shown above can be described as family resemblance categories: the meanings of the various members of the category are related, but in a number of different ways which are made clear by the intervening links.

6.4.2 *Inside* HTOED *categories*

Within each category and sub-category of *HTOED*, we find lists of synonyms in chronological order. OE words are simply labelled 'OE', but from ME onwards, the first and last recorded dates of use are given from the *OED*; where a word is still current, as *sofa* is, the first date is followed by a dash and no end date. Where a word is rare, or there is a long gap between recorded uses, a semi-colon replaces the dash between dates. Thus in sub-category 02 *for two persons* in Figure 6.3, the entry '*confidante/confidente* 1794; 1925–' tells us that the word has two spellings, and that it was recorded in 1794 and then from 1925 onwards. Categories are further divided by part of speech, usually in the order noun, adjective, adverb, verb. *HTOED* mainly includes words from these major word classes, which have lexical meaning, but not words with grammatical meaning like conjunctions or pronouns. Some semanticists believe that a word's part of speech is irrelevant to synonymy, and that all words for a particular concept should be presented together in a single list. However, after some experimentation, the *HTE* team decided that, given the amount of data and the complexity of the taxonomy, the extra degree of separation afforded by the part-of-speech arrangement would be most convenient for users; this is consistent with the practice in most thesauruses. Some labels indicating restricted use are included, for example '03 *triclinium* 1646–' is labelled 'Roman Antiquity' to indicate that it is used only in historical contexts, while 'N. Amer.' after 06 *Davenport* tells us that the expression is found largely in North American usage.

The fact that *HTOED* entries are accompanied by their dates of use makes it possible for the researcher to see which words were available to speakers and writers at any particular point in the history of the language, and, equally important, which were not (though the dates can only be taken as approximate evidence; see further the discussion in Chapter 4). The *OED* can then be consulted for further information about the use of particular words. For example, many of the words in our *Sofa/couch* category date from the mid-seventeenth century or later and would not have been available in Shakespeare's time. According to the *OED*, however, he was the first person to use *day bed*, when Buckingham said of Richard 'He is not lulling on a lewd day bed' (*Richard III*, 3, vii, 72, *OED Online*, quoted from the First Quarto edition of Shakespeare and dated 1597).[1] In addition to its literary role when examining an author's choice of words, knowledge of the availability of words is useful if you are searching historical texts electronically; there is no point in looking for the word *sofa* when searching a corpus of medieval texts or a catalogue of sixteenth century books, but it might be productive to include the word *reclinatory*, current in those periods, as a search term.

Examining words organised in lexical sets can start us thinking about the linguistic or cultural reasons why words might have entered or disappeared from the language or changed their meanings. An example from the *Sofa/couch* set is *canapé*, recorded in 1890, 1908 and 1955, meaning 'A piece of bread or toast, etc., on which small savouries are served' (*OED* noun 1), and in 1892 and 1955 with the meaning 'sofa' (*OED* noun 2). A check with *HTOED* shows that the first meaning of *canapé* has no synonyms in English other than the more specific *angels/ devils on horseback*, which suggests that the word filled a gap in the language when such snacks became popular, so that it is now the accepted word for the concept. On the other hand, *sofa* and many of its synonyms were already established in English by the time *canapé* appeared, with the result that it never passed into general use. These deductions are supported by the *OED* citations: sense 1 appears in the everyday contexts of a cookery book, a newspaper and a novel, whereas sense 2 is restricted to specialist books about furniture and in one case is obviously used as a French word. This example illustrates how much can be teased out about words by working back and forth between the *OED* and *HTOED*. It also demonstrates the role of serendipity in lexical analysis: the starting point for the analyst here was simply the observation that *canapé* was an odd word to find in a list of terms for 'sofa', and should be investigated further.

Sofa and its co-hyponymous categories *Chair, Bench* and *Stool* are basic level categories in the Furniture group, that is categories which people discriminate amongst without much difficulty, drawing on components of meaning such as [+BACK] and [+FOR MORE THAN ONE PERSON]. Establishing meanings for these terms for earlier periods may be less straightforward because of linguistic and cultural changes. According to the *OED*, the original meaning of the word *couch* was 'A frame or structure, with what is spread over it (or simply a layer of some soft substance), on which to lie down for rest or sleep; a bed', first recorded in 1340 (*OED* noun 1a). The meaning more familiar to us, 'an article of furniture for reclining or sitting on' (noun 3a), is first recorded around 1500. On the *OED* evidence, prototype split seems to have taken place somewhere between 1450 and 1550. After that, as the *OED* notes, the earlier meaning is found mainly 'in literary use, a general or vague term, implying that on which one sleeps, whether in ordinary language a *bed* or not', and the last citation is 1859. Sense 3a, on the other hand, has continued in use, and given rise to new meanings and expressions, such as the *psychiatrist's couch* (first recorded in 1952) and *couch potato* (first recorded in 1979). Historical linguists have to be aware of the potential for ambiguity and misinterpretation of textual evidence during periods of overlap of two closely related meanings such as these.

6.4.3 Concrete and abstract categories

Complex taxonomies like *Furniture*, with many layers of nested meanings, are typical of the vocabulary of concrete objects. By contrast, the lexis of abstract qualities and mental processes is usually less hierarchical in structure and shows more variety in its organisational criteria. Category 02.02.01 *Angry*, for example, which derives from 02 *The Mind* and 02.02 *Emotion*, has five subordinate categories at the next level down:

Manifestation of Anger, Furious Anger, Indignation, Irritation and *Irascibility.* *Furious Anger, Indignation* and *Irritation* could be categorised as types of anger, but have an additional component of [+/-STRENGTH] of feeling. *Manifestation of Anger* and *Irascibility* (proneness to anger) have no obvious hyponymous relationship to the superordinate *Anger* but are included on the basis of their semantic association with the central concept of the domain.

If you read through this section in *HTOED*, you will also see a range of minor headings. Some are rare like *[furious] at evening,* which has a single exponent, the OE poetic compound *æfengrom,* or *[irritating] in minor way,* covering *pin-pricking* (square brackets enclose words which have to be supplied by the reader from the heading of the superordinate category; see section 6.4.1). Others are recurrent and characteristic of adjectival meanings, for example *affected by X, becoming X, capable of X, characterised by X, causing X,* where X is the feeling in question. You may also notice that, in common with other well-established abstract categories, those in *Anger* often contain a much larger selection of synonyms than we find in more concrete categories. There are a variety of reasons for this situation. Concepts like 'anger' or 'thought' or 'contempt' are less subject to cultural change than a concept like 'furniture', and, at least for later stages of the language, meanings in concrete categories tend to be more clear-cut, especially in those such as *Minerals* or *Plants* where there has been input from expert taxonomies. The boundaries of both the synonym categories and the synonyms themselves are thus inherently fuzzier in abstract categories, leading to a greater potential for overlap both semantically and chronologically, and hence in some cases to semantic change. A short example of a fairly typical verb category is given in Figure 6.5.

02.01.13.03 (vt.) *Hold an opinion*

ween<(ge)wenan OE–c1570; 1721 (*Scots*) ·
think<(ge)þencan OE– · believe 1297– · judge 1297– ·
hold *a*1300– · suppose 1340–1658 · take 1380–1642 ·
conceive *c*1380–1651 · feel 1382–1544 · suppone *c*1500–1597 ·
esteem 1548–1765 · argue 1548– · opinion 1555– ·
meditate 1585–1609 · intend 1586(2) · opine 1611– ·
opinionate 1621– · opiniate 1624–1656 · state 1671 · doom
1742 · calculate 1830– (*US colloq.*) · consider 1830–

Figure 6.5 *HTOED* category 02.01.13.03 verb transitive *Hold an opinion*

Category 02.01.13.03, the transitive verbal category *Hold an opinion*, is part of 02.01.13.03 *Expressed belief, opinion*, and can be tracked back to 02.01.13 *Belief* and ultimately to 02 *The Mind*. Most of its synonyms will be familiar to modern English speakers, but some have disappeared or changed their meanings. Of the two OE verbs, *think* (OE *þencan*) has persisted in this and many other meanings, while *ween* (OE *wenan*) has virtually disappeared from the language in all its meanings. The reason for this could be to do with its form rather than its meaning: two common forms of its past tense and past participle from ME onwards were *went*, which could be confused with the past tense of *to go*, and *wend*, which coincides with both present and past tense forms of the verb *to wend*, which survives marginally in the phrase *to wend one's way*. If this is so, then what we have here is a case of homonymic clash (see section 5.7.2), where the accidental falling together of forms creates ambiguity and may lead to the disappearance of at least one of them.

Believe (OE *belyfan*) also dates back to OE, usually in religious contexts with the intransitive meaning of 'have trust or faith in a god'. It gradually diversified into more general meanings like this one, while also retaining its original meaning. *Hold* (OE *healdan*) was also well-established in OE in a variety of meanings, while *judge* entered English from French a little later with a range of legal and general meanings. Perhaps because these words were well-established, other borrowings had a comparatively short life, although *suppose, conceive, esteem* and *meditate* all survive in other categories where they have a more central role, such as 02.01.13.04 *Supposition, surmise*, and 02.01.06.03 *Continued thinking, reflection, contemplation*. *Opine* is the only really successful borrowing in EModE, although there are other short-lived forms of verbs close to the well-established noun *opinion*. These examples point to the fact that there had been little, if any, change in the underlying concept of 'having an opinion'; this is also borne out by the fact that only two new ways of expressing it, one an American colloquialism and the other a somewhat rare use of *consider*, are recorded in ME.

6.5 Conclusion

We began this chapter by quoting Samuels' reasons for initiating the *HTE* project. We then demonstrated the various kinds of information that can be collected by examining the English lexicon within such a framework, and how this information can be combined with that available for individual words from the more detailed entries in the *OED*. We suggested ways in which changes in the lexicon thus revealed may be interpreted. At a more general level, we stressed the importance of categorisation in human thinking, and the contribution of views of categorisation developed in Cognitive Semantics to historical lexical analysis.

Samuels concluded his discussion of the need for a historical thesaurus by writing:

> The production of such a thesaurus is arduous. Every attested meaning, past and present, must be semantically analysed and classified, and this can be achieved only by conventional methods, not by computer. It is at present being attempted for English only, and, from experience so far gained, will be a lengthy task. (1972: 180)

He was certainly right on the last point, as the following statistics on the Glasgow *HTE* website reveal:

> The *Thesaurus* project itself formally began on 15 January 1965 at an address to the Philological Society in London, where Professor Michael Samuels announced that the work would be undertaken by himself and his colleagues at Glasgow, and the production of version 1 of the *Thesaurus* ended at the final launch party on 22 October 2009; this first stage of the project therefore consumed 44 years, 9 months and 1 week exactly (or 16,351 days) ... Overall, the *Thesaurus* is the work of over 230 people, taking approximately 320,000 person-hours to complete – the equivalent of 176 years of solid work for one person. (http://historicalthesaurus.arts.gla.ac.uk/stats-and-figures/)

Along the way, the project generated a separate *TOE* ([1995] 2000, ed. Jane Roberts and Christian Kay) as well as numerous theses and research papers. It is now generating new projects, notably 'Mapping Metaphor' with the Historical Thesaurus and SAMUELS (Semantic Annotation and Mark-Up for Enhancing Lexical Searches), more fully described in Chapter 10. These exploit both the power of Samuels' original insight and the results that can be achieved by harnessing that insight to the power of the computer.

Exercises

1. Look through the *HTOED* noun category *Headwear* (01.02.10.02.03 in the print edition). Try to classify some of the criteria for the names of the various kinds of hats listed there, such as particular shapes, uses, materials, influences from individuals or artistic contexts or foreign cultures. In cultural terms, how do these sources correlate with the dates at which the words are first recorded in English? Further information about the words and their origins is available in the *OED*.

03.02.07.03.09.07.03 (*n.*) *Bench*

bencþel OE · formelle OE · bench<benc OE- · benking
*c*1200 · benk *c*1200–*c*1440 · bink *c*1200–1603 (*Scots & northern
dial.*); 1855– (*Scots & northern dial.*) · bank 1205–*a*1680 · form
1387– · sede 1552 · siege 1560 (*Scots*); *a*1614 (*Scots*) **01** *settle*
langsettle 1352/3–1855 (*northern dial., also Dict.*) · settle
1553– · by-settle 1602 · settle-chair 1688 · settle-bench
1741 **02** *ale-/mead-bench* beorsetl OE · ealubenc OE ·
medubenc OE · mead-bench 1860 (*History*) **03** *to sit on
at meals* meat-form *a*1400 **04** *at fireside* ingle-bench
1853; 1881 **05** *little bench* benchlet 1865; 1884 **06** *other
types of bench* rout-seat 1836/7– · banquette 1851– ·
rusbank 1880– (*S. Afr.*) · park bench 1906– **07** *specific
benches* penniless bench 1560/1– · log 1609; 1639

Figure 6.6 *HTOED* category *Bench* 03.02.07.03.09.07.03

2. Above is the *HTOED* category *Bench* 03.02.07.03.09.07.03 (Figure 6.6).
Using the analysis of *Sofa/couch* above as a guide, make an analysis of
this category.
3. Below is a paragraph from the opening chapter of Charles Dickens'
novel *Bleak House*, published in parts from 1852–3. It describes a foggy
day on the River Thames in London. Make a thesaurus-style classification of the major parts of speech in the text (nouns, verbs, adjectives, adverbs). Check the meanings of any words you are unsure of
and note the reasons: are they, for example, technical or obsolete?
Give your categories headings such as *Weather* or *Shipping*. What
level are these at (superordinate, basic, hyponymic)? Finally discuss
your results with fellow students; compare the problems you've
encountered and whether your decisions agree (but don't worry if
you don't agree or if some of the words don't fit in anywhere!).

Fog everywhere. Fog up the river, where it flows among green
aits and meadows; fog down the river, where it rolls defiled among
the tiers of shipping, and the waterside pollutions of a great (and
dirty) city. Fog on the Essex marshes, fog on the Kentish heights.
Fog creeping into the cabooses of collier-brigs; fog lying out on
the yards, and hovering in the rigging of great ships; fog droop-
ing on the gunwales of barges and small boats. Fog in the eyes
and throats of ancient Greenwich pensioners, wheezing by the

firesides of their wards; fog in the stem and bowl of the afternoon pipe of the wrathful skipper, down in his close cabin; fog cruelly pinching the toes and fingers of his shivering little 'prentice boy on deck. Chance people on the bridges peeping over the parapets into a nether sky of fog, with fog all round them, as if they were up in a balloon, and hanging in the misty clouds. (Charles Dickens, *Bleak House* [1853: chapter 1])

Further reading

A good deal of information about the history and development of the *HTE* project is available at http://www.glasgow.ac.uk/thesaurus – spend some time browsing the site and finding out more about this remarkable work.

A general overview of modern and historical thesauruses can be found in Kay and Alexander (forthcoming 2015) and Kay (2015). Crystal (2014) offers an introduction to a selection of *HTOED* categories. For a more detailed discussion of the examples from *HTOED* and their cultural implications, see Kay and Wotherspoon 2005. Geeraerts (1997: 32–47) has a detailed historical discussion of Dutch terms for leggings, which defines the available terms componentially and compares their use; see also Taylor (2003a: 53–5). O'Hare (2004) discusses a project to devise a folk classification for the *HTOED Plants* category, comparing it with Linnaean scientific classification. The papers by Alexander, Kay, Wild and Wotherspoon in Adams (2010) describe various aspects of the creation and applications of the *HTE* project. They are available on the *HTE* website together with a longer list of publications making use of the project in various ways. See: http://historicalthesaurus.arts.gla.ac.uk/publications-and-bibliography/

Note

1. The First Folio edition of 1623 has *Loue-Bed* [love-bed] in place of *day bed*, also a first recorded use.

7 English colour terms: A case study

C. P. Biggam

7.1 Introduction

In Chapter 6, attention was drawn to the importance of basic level categories: that is, those that are especially cognitively salient, are learned first by children, and generally evoke a high level of agreement across speakers. These include categories of animals like *Dog* and *Cat*, objects like *Chair, Table, Hat* and *Trousers*, and abstractions such as *Anger* and *Fear*. Basic level categories are also important in the way we think and talk about colours, a rich and extensive area of the lexicon. This chapter deals with the development of the English colour lexicon and shows in depth how the techniques of historical linguistics can be applied to one area of our vocabulary. It begins by discussing the particular techniques and problems of Historical Colour Semantics.

Nothing can be taken for granted in colour studies because, although we tend to believe that our own colour system is the only sensible and possible one, a quick look at other languages of the world shows that there are many different ways to classify colours. Some societies consider green and blue to be different shades of the same colour, for example, and others have to consider the brightness, dryness, shape or size of objects before they can choose the appropriate colour term to describe them. Various unexpected aspects of colour semantics like these can be found in the historical records of English, showing that not only have the words used for colours often changed over the centuries, but so has the way in which English speakers have used those words.

7.2 How to describe colour

When the need arises to describe a colour, English speakers normally use a commonly occurring term such as *blue* or *green* and, if necessary, qualify it by a term such as *pale, bright, dark* or *dull*. The speaker can thus reduce the basic category of, for example, BLUE to a section of BLUE which may be referred to with phrases such as *dark blue* or *dull blue*.[1] These smaller areas of hue, such as that denoted by *dull blue*, can be even further reduced by additional qualifiers which are not specific to colour, producing longer phrases such as *very dark blue* or *slightly dull blue*. In all these cases, the speaker has taken a principal colour term (*blue*), usually referred to as a **basic colour term** or **BCT**, and has 'zoomed in' on increasingly precise areas of the cognitive category (**basic colour category** or **BCC**) that it names. This process is similar to the profiling of domains we observed in section 3.4.

English speakers (and others) also use **non-basic colour terms**, which are often the same as, or derived from, words for gems, fruit, flowers or other objects which are considered typical examples of the colour, for example *emerald*, *orange* and *rose*. Such terms are particularly prevalent in fields such as advertising, fashion and poetry. A phrase such as *dark blue* is somewhat utilitarian; it offers a helpful description of the colour but is a little vague and definitely unexciting. In the world of advertising, there is a need to catch the eye of potential customers, to intrigue them, and to make them look at the product more closely. Similarly, in creative literature the writer is often keen to catch the reader's attention and focus his or her imagination by the use of what may be called 'fancy' colour terms such as *taupe*, *burgundy*, *tangerine* and *terracotta*. The advertising industry in particular also makes use of evocative expressions, often conveying an indeterminate colour sense, which may encourage feelings such as nostalgia or sophistication in a potential purchaser. Such phrases are often highly imaginative, for example *Paris mist*, *highland falls*, *April glow* and many more.

At the other end of the imagination scale are the colour descriptions found in fields such as Vision Science, Psychology, pigment manufacture, textile dyeing and others, in which the above approaches would be hopelessly subjective. Everyday terms such as *red* and *pale blue* lack the precision needed in such work, and fancy terms are often unclear as to hue. These research fields and occupations require exactitude, so they resort to precisely defined names (sometimes specific to their subject), to codes or numbers on a colour chart, or to accurate measurements of the **hue** wavelength and other elements of colour.

Leaving aside these highly codified colour descriptors and the more manufactured colour expressions of advertisers, how can the colour terms of ordinary English be described? To answer this question, we must consider those constituent parts of colour which play a significant role in English vocabulary. There is no doubt about the most important element. In ModE, the word *colour* is used principally (and almost exclusively) of hues, that is the range of observed impressions on the visible part of the electromagnetic spectrum. English speakers use BCTs such as *red, green, yellow* and *blue* to denote these hues, as well as a range of non-basic terms such as *turquoise, scarlet, violet* and *crimson.* For the majority of English speakers, the words *colour* and *hue* are synonyms, but in the technical language of colour studies *colour* denotes all the elements which combine to create a particular colour experience, including hue.

Apart from hue, a colour can be described by means of its **tone**, the amount of black or white which is perceived as being involved with a hue in a visual impression. This sounds like the mixing of a paint colour and, although we know that the colours of many other things have not been mixed literally, we tend to interpret colours intuitively in this way. A hue containing a noticeable white element is usually described as *pale, whitish* or *light*, and a hue with a black element is described as *dark* or *blackish*. The tone range can also operate independently of hue, when it is known as the **achromatic** range (meaning literally 'without hue'). This range has three principal categories, which in English are labelled *black, white* and *grey.*

Colours can also be described by the purity of their hues. If we look at a hue, for example red, and ask whether it looks greyish to any degree, we may decide that, far from looking greyish, it can be described as pure red or the reddest possible red. Such a colour is an example of a fully-saturated hue which is at the vivid end of the **saturation** scale. If this red hue were combined with a certain amount of grey, it would look duller, perhaps just slightly duller than vivid red, or maybe so grey that the red hue is only just perceived. English speakers tend to call a vivid or saturated hue *bright*, as in 'She painted her room a bright green', but this can be confused with another aspect of colour, called **brightness**.

In Colour Studies, brightness refers to the amount of light involved in a colour impression. This may affect the appearance of an object which *produces* light, such as the sun or an electric light bulb, or it may refer to *reflected* light from an object with a shiny surface, or it may simply be an impression of a pale (but not necessarily reflective) colour viewed in a well-lit environment. You can experiment with various objects to see how different lighting conditions apparently change the colour of an object when viewed, for example, at night, in sunshine, at dusk, or in artificial light. Similarly, a colour on a matt surface looks different from the same colour on a shiny surface. In English we describe such visual impressions by the use of words like *shiny, dazzling, glowing* and *dim.* Other aspects, both visual and non-visual, such as texture, shape, lustre, moisture and softness, also affect a colour impression, and some of these play a significant role in colour naming in other languages (or in scientific research), but they are rarely considered relevant to colour descriptions by English speakers.

7.3 What are basic colour terms?

As we have seen in section 7.2, English has both basic and non-basic colour terms. There are eleven ModE BCTs: *black, white, red, green, yellow, blue, brown, grey, purple, orange* and *pink*. Earlier phases of English had fewer BCTs. In ME the BCTs were: *blak, whit, red, grene, yelwe, bleu, broun* and *grei*, with a developing BCT *purpur(e)*. ME had no basic terms, therefore, for the BCCs of PURPLE, ORANGE and PINK. In OE the basic terms were: *blæc* (or *sweart*, which survives in ModE as *swarthy*), *hwit, read, grene, geolo* and *graeg*, with developing BCTs *haewe(n)* (usually meaning 'blue' or 'greyish blue') and *brun*. OE, therefore, had no fully developed BCTs to denote the categories BLUE, BROWN, PURPLE, ORANGE or PINK. OE and ME had various non-basic terms and descriptive phrases for these categories, but no BCTs. So what makes some colour terms basic and why is it important to recognise them?

A BCT is a colour term which is commonly used in both speech and writing, and which is known by every adult native speaker, but this definition could also be true of several non-basic terms. There are other tests a colour term must pass before it can be considered a BCT. For example, it must not be a hyponym of another colour word, as ModE *emerald, olive* and *verdant* are hyponyms of the BCT *green*, which denotes the whole BCC of GREEN (see section 3.2.2.1 on hyponymy). Another important test for basicness in Colour Semantics is contextual restriction. A BCT must not be largely confined to a particular context such as hair, skin or an animal's coat. A simple test is to take a doubtful term, such as *brunette* (a human hair colour) or *swarthy* (a skin colour) and use them of other things, for example *a brunette book* or *a swarthy cupboard*. A native speaker of English will reject such phrases, and it soon becomes clear that these words cannot be freely used of every appropriately coloured object, so they must be non-basic. In some cases, the above considerations may still leave doubts about the basic status of certain English colour terms, suggesting the need for further tests (see Biggam 2012, chapter 3 for further tests appropriate to English). Some examples of further basicness tests appropriate for historical studies are as follows: BCTs are more likely than non-basic terms to occur frequently in texts; they are more common in colloquial expressions such as sayings, and in metaphors and similes; and there are likely to be morphological variants for BCTs, just as *black* has the variants *blacken* and *blackish*. All these factors indicate that BCCs, as denoted by BCTs, have psychological salience over non-basics in the field of colour.

So why is it important to know the BCTs of a language? Their significance is that BCTs are the linguistic labels for the basic cognitive categories of colour (BCCs) which are used by a particular speech community. The BCCs are the principal divisions of the colour space and can function as abstract concepts among a particular group of people; to take one example, the group may have a concept of RED which operates quite independently of specific red objects. (This is why contextual restriction disqualifies a colour term from having basic status.)

You may wonder why the BCTs of a speech community are worth researching, since everyone with normal vision knows the visible hues. In fact, the basic categories differ in both number and nature between groups and in many cases even between individual speakers of the same language; for example, there may be differences between the young and the old, between men and women, and between monolinguals and bilinguals. In addition, as we have seen, BCCs also differ between the various periods of a society's history, as shown by their changing BCTs. Speakers of some languages (including OE and ME) interpret some or all of the purple, pink, orange or brown hues as areas of their red category, rather than as categories in their own right. Similarly, speakers of some languages regard yellow and green (and other combinations) as areas of a single category. Basic categories such as these, which seem so extensive to ModE speakers, are referred to as **macro-categories** or **composite categories**. Although macro-categories may seem quite alien to speakers of ModE, they were present in older forms of English and their speakers did not feel the need to have eleven BCTs denoting eleven basic categories as in ModE. We will now consider how and when the basic categories evolved in English.

7.4 The evolution of basic colour categories

Historical colour semanticists have a useful resource in what is usually referred to as the **evolutionary sequence**. Based on some earlier work, it appeared in its more modern form in a highly influential book published in 1969, *Basic Color Terms: Their Universality and Evolution*, by Brent Berlin and Paul Kay (see 1969: 4 for the original evolutionary sequence). Aspects of the sequence have always been controversial, and it has been revised and discussed many times since that date. References in this chapter will be to the current version as it appears in Kay and Maffi (1999: 748) and Paul Kay et al. (2009: 11).

The sequence claims to display the order in which BCCs may

develop in various languages, as revealed by their BCTs. The controversy mentioned above resulted from early claims that the sequence represents a **linguistic universal**, that is a feature that we can expect to find in all languages. Its current version, however, is intended to show the acquisition of basic categories by those languages studied in the World Color Survey, a research project at the University of California at Berkeley, which investigated the colour systems of 110 languages from around the world (see Paul Kay et al. 2009 and www1.icsi.berkeley.edu/wcs/). Even though there remain many languages whose BCCs have not yet been investigated, there is now a great deal of data on this subject, since there have been other multi-language projects, such as Robert MacLaury's Mesoamerican Colour Survey (MacLaury 1997), and countless studies of individual languages and language families.

Findings from these studies strongly suggest that, although there are differences in the numbers and extent of basic categories in various languages, the historical order of acquisition of the categories is remarkably consistent. There is a small number of different trajectories (routes) which individual languages have taken along the sequence but, when compared with the theoretically possible number of trajectories, the actual number used is minimal. This suggests that, rather than having no guidance at all on the early history of colour category acquisition, researchers are justified in considering the trajectories on the sequence as being by far the most likely routes taken by communities of speakers in the cognitive development of their colour systems. Let us now consider these most likely routes.

The two earliest categories acquired involve, firstly, white and the so-called 'warm' hues such as red and yellow, and, secondly, black and the 'cool' hues such as green and blue. Because the sequence is concerned only with hues and achromatics (white, black and grey), there is currently no facility for accommodating tone, saturation or brightness in the sequence. These two earliest categories are simply labelled 'W/R/Y' (white/red/yellow) and 'Bk/G/Bu' (black/green/ blue), often referred to as *macro-white* and *macro-black*. It seems highly likely, however, that these two concepts represent the opposition of categories such as LIGHT/BRIGHT/PALE/WHITE/WARM, and DARK/ DULL/BLACK/COOL, probably best summarised as brightness versus darkness, and based on the prototypes of 'day' and 'night'. As shown below, macro-white at this stage (Stage I of the sequence) involves the so-called 'warm' colours (red and yellow) and those colours closely related to them such as pink and orange, while macro-black involves green, blue and sometimes grey and violet. The classic example of a

Stage I	Stage II
W/R/Y	W
Bk/G/Bu	R/Y
	Bk/G/Bu

Figure 7.1 Stages I and II in the evolutionary sequence

Stage I language is Dani, spoken in Indonesian New Guinea (Biggam 2012: 74). Apart from some apparently rare exceptions, a Stage I language can accommodate all colour impressions in these two basic categories.

The evidence shows that, when the first entirely chromatic (hue-based) category is developed at Stage II of the sequence, it is most likely to be a macro-category containing red, yellow and usually other warm hues. It will no longer include white, but brightness may still be involved, as this new macro-red category is likely to be based on the prototype of 'fire'. An example of a Stage II language is Ejagham, spoken in the West African countries of Nigeria and Cameroon (Paul Kay et al. 2009: 227–8). The sequence encodes the macro-red category as R/Y (red/yellow), now cognitively separate from the category encoded W (white), as shown in Figure 7.1.[2]

A speech community which has developed a macro-red category will as a result have reduced the extent of the pre-existing macro-white category, necessitating a realignment of category boundaries. In other words, colours which initially would have been included in the earlier W/R/Y category, and which could therefore be referred to using the same BCT, will be referred to by the new terms instead.

If a community develops further basic categories over Stages III and IV of the sequence, they are most likely to involve an emphasis on green, yellow or grue. The term *grue* is simply a convenient way of referring to a macro-category consisting of GREEN+BLUE and sometimes +GREY as well. There are three possibilities at this stage for the BCTs that are likely to emerge. Some communities evolve a separate category of YELLOW (Y) at Stage III, having separated it cognitively from MACRO-RED (R/Y), as shown in Figure 7.2.

The Kwerba language of Irian Jaya (Indonesia), when it was investigated in 1978, was in transition from Stage II to Stage III (option 1), with

Stage II	Stage III (option 1)
W	W
R/Y	R
BK/G/Bu	Y
	BK/G/Bu

Figure 7.2 Stages II and III, first option

Stage II	Stage III (option 2)
W	W
R/Y	R/Y
Bk/G/Bu	G/Bu
	Bk

Figure 7.3 Stages II and III, second option

basic categories which can be coded as W, R and Bk/G/Bu and a yellow category which was basic for the majority of the community but not all of them (Paul Kay et al. 2009: 341–3).

Other speech communities evolve a grue category (G/Bu) at Stage III, having separated it from MACRO-BLACK (Bk/G/Bu), as shown in Figure 7.3. The Chácobo language of Bolivia is a good example (Paul Kay et al. 2009: 167–8).

Yet others evolve an unusual macro-category consisting of YELLOW+GRUE (Y/G/Bu) (Stage III, option 3), as recorded for the Karajá language of Brazil (Paul Kay et al. 2009: 305–7).

The three options for Stage III may change in different ways if speakers of those languages experience a need to add a further colour category, thus developing a Stage IV system. The Stage IV options are shown in Figure 7.4. Those communities with a yellow category may develop either a green (G) or a grue (G/Bu) category from their macro-black category (Bk/G/Bu).

The Ifugao language of the Philippines is an example of Stage IV (option 1) with two BCTs for GREEN (Paul Kay et al. 2009: 279–83).

Stage III (option 1)	Stage IV (option 1)	**OR**	Stage IV (option 2)
W	W		W
R	R		R
Y	Y		Y
Bk/G/Bu	G		G/Bu
	Bk/Bu		Bk

Figure 7.4 Alternative developments at Stage IV (option 1)

Stage III (option 2)	Stage IV (option 2)
W	W
R/Y	R
G/Bu	Y
Bk	G/Bu
	Bk

Figure 7.5 Development at Stage IV (option 2)

Stage IV (option 2) is recorded for the Zapotec language of Mexico, which has a BCT for GRUE (Paul Kay et al. 2009: 579–81).

Those communities which developed a grue category at Stage III develop a new yellow (Y) category at Stage IV by separating it from their macro-red (R/Y) category, thus reaching Stage IV (option 2) by a different route, as shown in Figure 7.5.

The rare languages with a yellow+grue (Y/G/Bu) category at Stage III either develop separate yellow (Y) and grue (G/Bu) categories at Stage IV (option 2 again), or they develop a new blue (Bu) category while retaining YELLOW+GREEN. The latter situation can be seen in the Cree language of Canada (Paul Kay et al. 2009: 201–6).

All the World Color Survey languages judged to be at Stage V, the final stage in the current sequence, have separate basic categories for WHITE, BLACK, RED, YELLOW, GREEN and BLUE, as do ME and ModE. The brown, purple, orange, pink and grey categories, which appeared at Stages VI and VII of the earlier versions of the sequence, are now considered to be less predictable than the other categories. If developed at all, they emerge at various stages of the sequence, as will be shown below for English.

7.5 The development of colour terms in English

In this section we'll apply the evolutionary sequence to developments in the three main periods in the history of English. In addition to the *OED* and *HTOED*, this section uses evidence from the period dictionaries: the *DOE* (in progress, letters A–G available), the *MED*, the *AND*, a dictionary of Anglo-French, and the *DSL*. These are described in section 4.4 and details of how to access them are given in the References section (pp. 191–2). Because of the nature of colour, the earliest sense of each colour term recorded is usually an adjective (though they can all be used as nouns as well).

7.5.1 Old English (OE: 700–1150)

The value of the evolutionary sequence to historical semanticists is that its general principles (see section 7.4), as opposed to its details, provide a set of implications and a relative chronology for the development of basic categories which may or may not be universal, but which are clearly extremely widespread. In other words, there is a strong likelihood that, for example, a language with a BCT denoting GREEN must have developed a basic category for RED at an earlier date. The earlier basic categories evolved over many years, even centuries; several of the OE categories were inherited from the language's ancestors, such as **proto-Indo-European** and **proto-Germanic** (Biggam 2010: 234–52).

Judging as best we can from the surviving records, it appears that OE had six BCCs: WHITE/BRIGHT, BLACK/DARK, RED+, YELLOW, GREEN and GREY. It had thus reached Stage IV in the evolutionary sequence, with an additional category of GREY. It has five fewer basic categories than ModE, but in addition the *content* of the categories differs from that of the modern language. The white category is not restricted to one end of the achromatic scale but also includes types of brightness (see section 7.2), and similarly the black category includes darkness. The red category is denoted here as RED+ because it includes at least some shades of purple, pink, orange and brown in addition to red. GREY includes not only achromatic shades but also various dull hues (Biggam 1998: 86–9). OE also appears to have had some relatively salient terms for the concepts of BLUE and BROWN but these were almost certainly not *basic* categories until the ME period. So what were the BCTs which labelled the OE BCCs?

Several of the OE BCTs will look familiar to speakers of ModE: WHITE/BRIGHT was denoted by *hwit* (ModE *white*); RED+ by *read* (*red*); YELLOW by *geolu* (*yellow*); GREEN by *grene* (*green*); and GREY by *græg* (*grey*). However, the OE colour words do not necessarily denote entirely familiar colour categories, since at least *hwit*, *read* and *græg* cannot always be accurately translated by *white*, *red* and *grey*. Also, the black/dark category was named by two principal terms which appear to have been in competition. The older term *sweart* (ModE *swarthy*) is cognate with other Germanic terms for BLACK, such as Modern German *schwarz*, but OE *blæc* (ModE *black*) was at least equally salient and, judging by later developments, was probably taking over the pre-eminent position formerly held by *sweart*.

Although OE shows signs of having incipient blue and brown categories they do not appear to have developed a basic status. The principal term for BLUE was *hæwen*, but this word appears to have been strongly associated with grey (Biggam 1997: 128–9). OE *brun*, the principal term for BROWN, has long caused astonishment among students of the language since it can be glossed as 'dark' as well as 'brown', and was used to translate Latin terms meaning 'black', 'purple', 'red' and 'dun' (*DOE brun*, adj. 1).

Most difficult of all to understand is the use of *brun* in poetry to mean (apparently) 'shining' or 'gleaming' of metalwork such as swords and helmets (*DOE brun*, adj. 3). Over the years, scholars have struggled to explain how a word could mean both 'dark' and 'gleaming'; some of the resulting suggestions show how colour terms must be studied in their cultural context, in this case considering aspects of Anglo-Saxon social and military life. One explanation of the contradictory meanings of *brun* was offered by Tremaine (1969). He suggested that early medieval weapons were literally dark in tone because of a surface treatment known as 'browning', which involves allowing a thin layer of rust to develop and then polishing the metal to create a brownish colour. This technique has been used in modern times to prevent the sun glinting off the barrels of firearms, thus revealing one's presence to the enemy; such a use seems unlikely in the Anglo-Saxon context, which involved the proud display of elite gear such as swords and helmets.

Another suggestion concerns the process used in ironworking, which involves heating the metal and quenching it in water (Walker 1952). The blacksmith must choose the right moment to quench a sword-blade or it may not have the correct hardness and flexibility. That right moment is determined by the changing colour of the metal in the fire:

a brown colour indicates the correct temperature. A further explanation, made by the present author, relies on Colour Semantics. I have suggested that *brun*, and related words in other languages, had their origin in one of the several ancient terms connected with fire. With this history, the word could easily indicate both darkness and brightness, depending on context, since fire involves both the brightness of flames and the darkness of scorched and burnt material. Such a combination of different semantic features is typical of the early macro-categories (for a fuller discussion of *brun*, see Biggam 2010: 256–9).

Although OE had fewer BCTs than ModE, lacking basic categories for BLUE, BROWN, PURPLE, ORANGE and PINK, that does not mean Anglo-Saxons found it impossible to refer to these hues. They could use non-basic terms and expressions, compound terms, and phrases constructed from other basics or non-basics (such as *geoluread* 'yellow-red'), as well as descriptions and comparisons with referents such as blood, dyes, flowers and more (for example, *geole crog* 'saffron yellow' and *rosen* 'made of roses, rose-coloured').

It is possible to predict that OE would have developed a purple category after the blue and brown categories. This is because there are several surviving colour words which, at least sometimes, appear to indicate a purple hue, whereas the scarcity of expressions for ORANGE and PINK suggests a lower salience for those categories. The following terms are among those which researchers have suggested can at least partly denote purple: *basu, brunbasu, felleread* (an error for *pelleread?*), *hæw-mænged, pællen, scirbasu, purpuren* and *purpul*. This collection of non-basic colour terms, some closely connected with textiles, can be interpreted as an awakening interest in a colour which had probably been considered either a type of blue (violet shades) or of red (red-purple shades). However, although it may seem obvious to us that OE *purpuren* was destined to become a BCT for PURPLE at some future date, this was by no means guaranteed, since the term principally referred not to a colour but to an expensive textile known in Latin as *purpura*, which was produced in several colours.

7.5.2 Middle English (ME: 1150–1500)

As we saw in Chapter 2, the principal lexical difference between OE and ME was the considerable vocabulary adopted from or via French after the Norman Conquest of 1066. In spite of the prestige of Anglo-French, the six BCTs already established in OE survived with little more than relatively minor changes in pronunciation, spelling and meaning, evolving into the ME words *whit, blak, red, yelwe, grene* and *grei*. These spellings are used as headwords in the *MED*; ME spelling was extremely variable (see section 2.3) and a range of other spellings can be found in the sources.

ME speakers had a tendency to separate the hue element of colour from the tone, saturation and brightness elements whereas OE speakers had tended to combine them in the semantics of each colour term. The dominance of hue in certain ME terms, especially in BCTs, was at least encouraged by certain cultural innovations of the later Middle Ages such as banners, livery, and the display of heraldry on coats-of-arms, all of which encouraged the development and use of strong dyes and paints. Cognitively, a tendency to regard white, black and grey as additional hues probably began in this period, thus weakening the involvement of these three categories with brightness, darkness and dull hues respectively (there were plenty of non-basic terms to deal with these concepts). The ModE speaker would, however, still notice some differences from his or her own basic categories. For example, ME had no basic categories for PURPLE, PINK and ORANGE, so it is likely that ME *red*, and probably *yelwe* too, could indicate an orange hue, while *red* could also still refer to some purples and to pink.

During the ME period, a basic category for BLUE developed, with considerable help from French. French had a colour term *bleu* which indicated unnatural skin colour such as the paleness of a sick, wounded or elderly person, and the blueness of bruising. For reasons which are not fully apparent, English speakers found no use for the 'pale' sense of this word, but adopted it to indicate BLUE in preference to the OE word *hæwen*. Even though *hæwen* could denote very blue things such as blue gemstones and woad (a blue dye), its ME descendant *haue* was narrowed to indicate a bluish or grey colour, most often in connection with textiles. It was eventually lost to southern English, but survived for longer in northern England and even longer in Scotland, where it denoted bluish, leaden, dull, pale and greenish colours into the twentieth century, functioning as a hyponym of *blue* (*DSL*, *haw* adj.). *Hæwen* is a clear example of how speakers of the same language in geographical proximity do not necessarily have identical colour semantics.

The second salient but not basic colour term of OE (*brun*) eventually evolved into the brown BCT in ME. There was no competition with French terms in this case since Anglo-French *brun* was very similar in pronunciation, written form and meaning. It had a primary sense of 'dark, brown' and a sub-sense of 'shining, burnished' (*AND brun*, adj. 1 and 3). It is noteworthy that the same senses of 'dark' and 'shining' discussed above occurred in both the OE and Anglo-French words.

BCTs for purple, orange and pink seem not to have emerged during this period. ME had a colour term *purple*, but it did not become basic until EModE. It also had a noun *orange* referring to the fruit or the tree, but no adjectival colour usage is recorded. It is difficult to determine the situation concerning PINK. There was certainly no BCT, but there are several non-basic ME terms which could be interpreted as 'pale red' or 'pink', many of which have the rose as their prototype. The rose in question is *Rosa canina* L., variously called the 'wild-', 'hedge-' or 'dog-rose', the flower of which is usually a shade of pink (although it can also be white). ME 'rose' words often have primary or secondary senses referring to 'oil of roses' (also known as 'attar of roses'), an oil distilled from rose petals, and chiefly used in making perfumes. Thus there are ME terms such as *rosen* 'made of or consisting of roses; rose-coloured, rosy' (*MED* adj. a and b) and *roset* 'made of a distillation of red or white roses', also used as a noun denoting 'rose-colour' (*MED* adj. a and noun d). Other adjectives which can function as colour terms in this category are *rosi* 'rose-coloured, rosy' and *roseat* 'roseate, rosy' (*MED*).

7.5.3 Modern English (ModE 1500–)

From EModE onwards, the colour vocabulary of English increased enormously, as a glance at the *HTOED* colour categories reveals. Travellers to the New World discovered dyes such as logwood and some types of cochineal, while Renaissance artists experimented with pigments to introduce new effects to their paintings. Much later, synthetic dyes were introduced, beginning with so-called 'mauveine', a purple shade, in 1856. In the same century, the development of industrial processes capable of producing identical items which could only be distinguished by their colours encouraged the proliferation of colour terms to identify and market such products. The twentieth century saw the rise of the mass fashion industry with its regular announcements of 'this year's colours'. In periods like the 1960s, colour, especially vivid hues, seemed to dominate the cultural scene. All of these factors motivated the coining of new colour terms. The burgeoning of the interior décor industry, which has a never-ending supply of subtle mixes of hues and tones, also brought colour to the forefront of modern minds, resulting in a torrent of new colour words and phrases. It has been estimated that Modern British English has at least 8,000 colour terms (Kornerup and Wanscher 1978: 140).

    We have seen that ME speakers probably had eight basic colour categories; the remaining basic categories of PURPLE, ORANGE and PINK developed in ModE. After an erratic development from a textile term to a generally red term, ModE *purple* took on its familiar sense of a hue range at the intersection of red and blue from about the fifteenth century. However, it takes time for a speech community to develop an abstract basic category after the earliest recognition of a particular colour sense, so the emergence of *purple* as an English BCT would have happened later. The adjective *purple* developed from the OE noun *purpure*, referring to expensive and prestigious cloth (not always purple in colour) and the clothing made from it. The first recorded occurrence of *purple* in an adjectival colour sense is 1415, but its early use is restricted to textiles. However, the amethyst gemstone is described as having 'a purpill colour' in a text dating to sometime before 1500, indicating a loosening of the contextual restriction to textiles and dyes (*OED purple*, adj. 2a).

ModE *orange* developed a colour sense from its ME meanings of the orange fruit and tree. The earliest recorded colour sense of the adjective is from 1532 (*OED orange*, adj. a) but, as with *purple*, its development towards basic status would have taken time. The last basic category to develop among English speakers was PINK. The earliest recorded colour use of the adjective *pink* dates to 1607 (*OED pink*, adj.[2] II. 2a), and, once again, it would have required time to become a BCT. Indeed, for some (British) English speakers, it may still be considered a pale red, not quite basic.

Colour terms and concepts in English are not restricted to purely descriptive uses: they also have metaphorical, contrastive and symbolic roles in the language, such as the use of red to indicate importance in written texts. They feature in similes, for example *as white as a sheet*, usually said of a terrified, ill or shocked person's face. The phrase evokes a white exemplar, a sheet, which in an ideal world should be spotlessly clean and crisp. Its referent, a person's face, cannot literally be such a pure colour; the meaning is something like 'a face much paler than normal for a white person'. The use of the white BCT creates a compact expression packed with cultural, non-literal and contrastive meaning.

Colour terms often take on metaphorical meanings which operate in particular societies to convey a strength of meaning which the standard word for the concept may lack. Thus a person may be called *yellow*, which implies cowardice in many varieties of English, and is somehow more damning than the straightforward word *cowardly*. Similarly, feeling *blue* seems more depressing than simply feeling *sad*. Most of these metaphorical uses of colour terms involve BCTs, as their long history in the language has allowed their meanings to develop and change.

7.6 The changing nature of a basic category: BLUE

A BCC has not only at least one BCT but also several non-basic terms indicating only parts of the category or the use of that colour in only a particular type of context. This means that, even if the BCTs of two languages are easily translatable, the composition, nature and extent of their categories are likely to be different. It is important to be aware that ModE and earlier English had markedly different categories, and this difference has implications for our understanding of historical records and our appreciation of older literature. The adjectives of the blue category throughout the history of English provide an interesting example.

OE included the following adjectives which denoted a simple blue or partly blue meaning: *blæwen, glæsen, hæwen* and *wæden* (Biggam 1997). *Blæwen* probably denoted a dark blue in the context of textiles and dyes, *wæden* was used in the same context, and *glæsen* is likely to have denoted a pale blue shade, especially used of eyes. The principal blue term, *hæwen*, appears in several compounds, such as *blæhæwen* 'dark blue, dark grey', *grenehæwen* 'greenish blue, greenish grey' and *swearthæwen* 'dark blue', allowing reference to a variety of shades involving blue.

The blue category in ME was influenced by French more than any other colour category, and its vocabulary changed completely. Other categories usually acquired a large number of new colour terms from French (and some from Latin) while also retaining many English words. Even though we must make allowance for the smaller number of records surviving from Anglo-Saxon England, it seems apparent that the number of colour terms increased considerably in ME. The ME adjectives denoting simple blue or partly blue meanings are: *azure* (*asur*), *blae/blo, blue* (*bleu*), *glawke* (*glauk*), *haw* (*haue*), *inde, perse, plunket, sapphire* (*saphir*), *sapphirine* (*saphirine*), *venet, violet* and *wachet* (*HTOED, MED* headwords are given in brackets where their spelling differs). These words covered a wide range of meanings. For example, a vivid, strong blue could be *saphir* or *saphirine*; a pale blue could be *wachet*; a dull, greyish blue could be *perse* or *plunket*; and a livid blue (often referring to bruising) could be *blo* or, in the north of England or Scotland, *blae* or *haw*. In surviving ME records, the contexts of several blue terms appear to be dominated by descriptions of clothes, textiles and dyes, especially *inde, plunket* and *wachet*. The principal blue term, *blue* (*bleu*), could be qualified by other terms, such as *bright* (bright or vivid), *dep* (deep, intense), *inde* (dark), *light* (bright), *sad* (dark) and *violet* (purplish), but they did not usually form compound terms, as had been the case with OE *hæwen*.

In ModE, the BCT *blue* is the superordinate of a veritable army of terms which have been used or are still used for blues in the modern period; a mere selection is given here. Simple terms include *sapphiric* (vivid/fully-saturated), *cyaneous, cobalt, lazuline* (dark, strong), *azurine, periwinkle* (pale), *cerulean, lazure* (pale and bright), *turquoise, aquamarine* (greenish), *gunpowder, Silurian* (greyish), *hyacinthine, violaceous, lavender* (purplish). Colour phrases and compound terms abound, including *electric blue, powder-blue, coal-blue, lead-blue, sky-blue, indigo-blue*, many of these terms can be further qualified by words such as *dark* and *pale* (see section 7.2). However, not content with these verbal riches, the fashion and paint industries invent fanciful words and phrases to name each shade, often replacing them regularly as they become well known. Blue examples, taken at random from paint charts, include *forget-me-not, king-fisher, Oxford blue, Indian Ocean, Cambria, sea satin, moon shadow, Trafalgar* and *porcelain blue*.

7.7 Summary

Leaving aside the non-basic colour terms and concentrating on hues, we can summarise the major changes to colour categories and terms that have taken place in English as follows.

The basic (cognitive) colour categories (BCCs) of OE, ME and ModE are:

OE: (1) WHITE/BRIGHT, (2) BLACK/DARK, (3) RED+, (4) YELLOW, (5) GREEN, (6) GREY

ME: (1) WHITE, (2) BLACK, (3) RED+, (4) YELLOW, (5) GREEN, (6) GREY, (7) BLUE, (8) BROWN

ModE: (1) WHITE, (2) BLACK, (3) RED, (4) YELLOW, (5) GREEN, (6) GREY, (7) BLUE, (8) BROWN, (9) PURPLE, (10) ORANGE, (11) PINK

The BCTs of OE, ME and ModE are:

OE: *hwit, blæc/(sweart), read, geolu, grene, græg*
ME: *whit, blak, red, yelwe, grene, grei, bleu, broun*
ModE: *white, black, red, yellow, green, grey, blue, brown, purple, orange, pink*

7.8 Conclusion

Colour is an integral feature of our world, and is deeply engrained and widely applied in the cognition and language of English speakers. However, as this chapter has shown, English BCCs and BCTs have changed over the centuries and non-basic colour vocabulary has grown. These changes inevitably affect how the modern reader understands historical texts. For example, he or she must consider how much of the modern concept of PINK lies behind earlier uses of words meaning 'red', 'pale red', or 'the colour of the rose'; whether an earlier use of a 'grey' word could mean 'dull blue' or 'dull green' rather than 'grey'; and whether an earlier use of a 'brown' word could mean 'shining, flashing' rather than 'brown'. Such possibilities also have implications for the meanings of other contemporary colour terms, since a society's conceptualisation and naming of colour constitutes an interlocking and interdependent system: where one category changes, others must change to accommodate it. However, bearing in mind the differences of colour usage among contemporary speakers, Colour Semantics can often provide the modern reader with insights into the age, gender, linguistic expertise or locality of an earlier writer. The potential of Colour Semantics for providing cultural glimpses into past societies is only beginning to be explored.

Exercises

1. The colour adjective *pink* is problematic in many ways, including its derivation. Use the *OED* or an etymological dictionary to examine the candidates for its origin, and decide which you think is most likely.
2. Make an examination of the *HTOED* adjective category *Blue* (01.04.09.07.06 in the print edition). For a selection of words, consider such factors as the dates when the words are first recorded, their origin, their referents in the external world and any contextual restrictions they may have. Further information about the words and their origins is available in the *OED*.
3. Use the *OED* to find metaphorical uses of the English BCTs. What are the earliest uses you can find? Have these uses survived into ModE? When have new uses entered the language, and can they be related to cultural developments at the time?
4. Use the resources at your disposal to try to establish when *purple* became a BCT in English. You may find the information about spelling variants and etymology at the head of the *OED* entry useful, especially if you plan to use other resources.

Further reading

Biggam (2010) offers further information on topics covered in this chapter, while Biggam (2012) is the most comprehensive account of Historical Colour Semantics available. Burnley (1976) and Biggam (1993) deal with aspects of colour in ME. Three chapters in Anderson et al. (2014) use *HTOED* to examine the development of colour, especially in metaphor: Alexander and Kay; Anderson and Bramwell; and Hamilton. There is also a keynote chapter by Biggam on the history of colours.

There is a section on OE colour terms in the online package *Learning with the Online Thesaurus of Old English*, available at http://www.gla.ac.uk/schools/critical/research/fundedresearchprojects/learningwiththeonlinethesaurusofoldenglish/

For quick reference, a handy dictionary of OE is *A Concise Anglo-Saxon Dictionary* ([1894] 1960, ed. J. R. Clark Hall).

Notes

1. Small capitals are used throughout this chapter to indicate semantic categories (as opposed to words or phrases). This convention is usually followed in Colour Studies.
2. The category codes used in the current evolutionary sequence are the following: W (white), Bk (black), R (red), Y (yellow), G (green) and Bu (blue). Macro-categories are shown by linking these codes with forward slashes, as in W/R/Y (macro-white). Roman numerals are used to identify stages in the sequence.

8 Language and culture

8.1 Introduction

Throughout this book, we have stressed the importance of the links between language and the culture in which it is used. In section 3.4, we noted the emphasis in Cognitive Semantics on studying the meanings of words in the context of the knowledge and beliefs of speakers, and we will explore this idea further below. In Chapter 6, we traced the development of the category *Sofa/couch* in English, and saw that it was often difficult in early texts to tell whether the item in question was intended for lying or sitting on. If we had looked further into the material culture of the time, we would have discovered that few people in the medieval period possessed either beds or sofas as we understand these objects nowadays. Most of them slept on simple straw pallets, perhaps with a cloth covering, and sat on wooden stools or benches, while a lucky few had structures covered with fabric and cushions on which to recline. A domestic revolution took place in the seventeenth century when upholstery was invented in France, leading to much more comfortable furniture. This invention coincided with an improvement in living conditions in Britain, where the increasingly prosperous middle classes were able to afford both better furniture and houses big enough to have separate rooms for sleeping and daytime activities. Items for sleeping and sitting on became more clearly differentiated, as did the vocabulary used to describe them.

Sometimes words can be linked to the activities of individuals rather than to general social developments, most obviously in eponymous terms such as *cardigan*, bearing the name of the Earl of Cardigan, who is reputed to have worn such a garment in the cold conditions of the Crimean War of 1855, or the verb *to boycott*, derived from the name of Charles Boycott, an Irish landlord who was ostracised. An interesting, if less direct, example is the word *vest*. In the sense of a garment worn by men beneath their coats or jackets, it is first recorded in Samuel Pepys' diary of 8 October 1666; he writes: 'The King hath yesterday in council, declared his resolution of setting a fashion for clothes ... It will be a vest, I know not well how. But it is to teach the nobility thrift' (*OED vest*, noun 3a, 3b). The desire for thrift was apparently a reaction to the recent Great Fire of London, which had caused considerable distress among the population. A week later, Pepys revealed that the garment Charles II recommended was '. . . a long Cassocke close to the body, of black cloth and pinked with white silk under it, and a coat over it, and the legs ruffled with black riband like a pigeon's leg' (*OED vest*, noun 3b). This may not sound like a recipe for thrift, but was presumably intended to decrease the amount of heating required by increasing the amount of clothing worn. Over the years, Charles II's 'long Cassocke' has morphed into the shorter garment now called a *waistcoat* in British English but still referred to as a *vest* in America.

Other words may give us insight into social attitudes. On the face of it, we might expect the terms *right-handed* and *left-handed* to have developed along similar lines as referring to equivalent parts of the body, but this is far from being the case. If we work our way through *right-handed* in the *OED*, we find it developing meanings such as 'skilful, dexterous' (1b) or 'good, worthy, favourable' (2), while *right hand* is used in phrases like *right-hand man* (an essential assistant), and even *right-hand error* (one which is well-motivated). Synonyms for *right hand* in *HTOED* suggest vigorous and aggressive activity: *sword-hand, pistol-hand, spear-hand, whip-hand*. *Left-handed*, by contrast, develops a greater range of meanings, all negative: 'crippled, defective' (2a), 'awkward, clumsy' (2b), 'underhand' (2c), 'doubtful, questionable' (3), 'ill-omened, inauspicious, sinister' (4), all first recorded in the seventeenth century, and even a 'left-handed marriage' (5), which is in some way legally questionable. Synonyms for *left hand* cover a less aggressive range of activities in warfare and horsemanship than those for *right hand*: *bridle-hand, bow-hand, buckler-hand, rein-hand, shield-hand*. There is no discredit in these – they simply designate actions, such as holding a shield while wielding a sword with the right hand, which would usually be carried out left-handed by a right-handed person. The senses of *left-handed*, however, reflect both the difficulties of a left-handed person operating in a right-handed world, and the suspicion with which people who differ from the majority are often regarded (with apologies to any left-handed readers!). For example, the Devil is often depicted as left-handed, and people who spill salt sometimes throw a pinch over their left shoulder in order to placate him. The fact that these senses are largely obsolete nowadays, except in occasional phrases like *left-handed compliment* (which may well be an insult), can be taken by historical linguists as indicating changing social contexts.

8.2 Linguistics and anthropology

Two names which stand out in any discussion of language and culture are those of the American linguistic anthropologists Edward Sapir (1884–1939) and Benjamin Lee Whorf (1897–1941). Both men studied American Indian languages, as did many of their contemporaries. They were struck by how different these languages were from familiar European languages, and spent much time discussing the extent to which speakers are influenced by language in the way they perceive the world. The theory which developed from these discussions is generally referred to as the **Sapir-Whorf Hypothesis**, but it is important to note that this title was given to their work by later writers, not by the two men themselves, whose ideas differed from one another. Both men also changed their views on the language–culture relationship in the course of their lifetimes. In its most extreme form, the Sapir-Whorf Hypothesis can be summarised in Sapir's words:

> In a sense, the network of cultural patterns of a civilization is indexed in the language which expresses that civilization . . . the 'real world' is to a large extent unconsciously built up on the language habits of the group. No two languages are ever sufficiently similar to be considered as representing the same social reality. The worlds in which different societies live are distinct worlds, not merely the same world with different labels attached. (Sapir 1929: 209, cited in Salzmann 1993: 153)

The above view of the relationship between language and culture, described by Whorf as **linguistic determinism**, claims that language imposes categories on the world; as we grow up and learn our native language, we learn these categories and this influences how we think and make judgements about the world. A less extreme form of the hypothesis, which Whorf called **linguistic relativity**, made the weaker claim that languages classify experience in different ways, and therefore reflect the world-views of their speakers, but do not determine the way we think. This weaker relationship can most easily be seen in the vocabulary of a language, though the concept can be extended to grammar, as in the example of pronouns of address below. Most linguists nowadays would accept some version of this weaker view, although there is still considerable debate about the interpretation of the hypothesis, and the link between language and culture in general.

8.3 Pronouns of address

Sapir and Whorf drew their data from contemporary languages, but their work is also relevant in diachronic linguistics since different historical stages of a language can be compared in the same way as different languages. An example from European languages to illustrate this point is the way in which people are addressed. Many European languages make or have made a distinction similar to English *thou/you* or French *tu/vous* (referred to as T/V systems), where the plural pronoun (V) is used in more formal situations to address individual people. In general, the plural (polite) V form indicates respect and is used to address individual strangers or older people or people perceived as having superior social status. The singular (familiar) T form is used to address people regarded as of lower status than oneself, such as children or servants, or to equals such as siblings, or close friends.

The T/V system also affected the form of the verb in earlier English, distinguishing *thou hast* in the second person singular from *you have* in the plural. Introduced as a result of French influence in the thirteenth century (see section 2.3), the system broke down relatively early in ModE. In Shakespeare's plays, for example, it can be quite difficult to interpret: in some places it is used conventionally as described above, and in others it is deliberately breached in order to indicate changing relationships among characters. A good example is Act III, scene iv of *Hamlet*, where Gertrude is talking to her son in her private chamber about his unacceptable behaviour. The basis of his discontent is that Gertrude has married her brother-in-law (referred to as 'thy Father' in line 2), whom Hamlet suspects of having killed her first husband, his birth father.

1. *Hamlet:*   Now Mother, what's the matter?
2. *Gertrude:*   *Hamlet,* **thou** hast thy Father much offended.
3. *Hamlet:*   Mother, **you** haue my Father much offended.
4. *Gertrude:*   Come, come, **you** answer with an idle tongue.
5. *Hamlet:*   Go, go, **you** question with an idle tongue.
6. *Gertrude:*   Why how now *Hamlet?*
7. *Hamlet:*   Whats the matter now?
8. *Gertrude:*   Haue **you** forgot me?
9. *Hamlet:*   No by the Rood, not so:
10.   **You** are the Queene, your Husbands Brothers wife,
11.   But would **you** were not so. **You** are my Mother.
12. *Gertrude:*   Nay, then Ile set those to **you** that can speake.

13. *Hamlet*:   Come, come, and sit **you** downe, **you** shall not boudge
              [budge]:
14.   **You** go not till I set **you** vp a glasse,
15.   Where **you** may see the inmost part of **you**?
16. *Gertrude*: What wilt **thou** do? **thou** wilt not murther me?
17.   Helpe, helpe, hoa.

Hamlet, III, iv, 2385–2402

Gertrude begins by addressing Hamlet as *thou*, the normal form from parent to child. When he responds aggressively, she switches in line 4 to *you*, presumably as a sign of anger. Further threats produce a switch back to *thou* at the end of the extract, either to remind Hamlet that she is his mother (and the queen) or because she fears that she is at his mercy. Hamlet uses the respectful *you* throughout the conversation, perhaps inviting a contrast between his formal politeness and the content of what he says. A more explicit example of an inappropriate form being used insultingly in Shakespeare occurs in Act III, scene ii of *Twelfth Night*, where Sir Toby Belch advises Sir Andrew Aguecheek to use *thou* as an insult to his rival in love, saying: 'if thou thou'st him some thrice, it shall not be amisse' (1423–4). It is also noteworthy that Sir Toby addresses Sir Andrew as *thou*, while Sir Andrew uses the polite V form in addressing him. The two are equals in terms of social status, but not in their level of respect for one another.

From the seventeenth century onwards, the polite *you* became the normal pronoun of address in English regardless of the addressee, although *thou* lingered on in dialects and was adopted as the usage of Quakers. Other European languages, such as Spanish, Dutch and Swedish, retained the distinction much longer, but showed signs of breakdown in the twentieth century. Interestingly, however, the familiar T form became the general term of address for these languages. Can we deduce anything from this situation? If the structure of a language influences how we think, then people who make the T/V distinction presumably grow up with a greater sense of social difference: some people are more deserving of respect than others. Conversely, English-speakers, who mostly have been liberated from this system, might be expected to be more egalitarian in their attitudes. Here you can perhaps begin to see one of the arguments against the stronger version of the hypothesis emerging. If language imposes a fixed grid of categories on our perception of the world, then logically that system could never change in the lifetime of an individual. We'd be locked into our respectful attitudes by the categories of our language. This is plainly not the case; social and political revolutions take place without reference to linguistics, and British society is probably less egalitarian than some societies which retained the T/V distinction longer.

Nevertheless, it is perfectly plausible to argue that social change in a particular historical context is reflected in language. It is possible that in seventeenth-century Britain, in the wake of the Civil War and the brief abolition of the monarchy, there was a desire to extend respect more widely by using V forms; in a socially confused situation, it is probably safer to offer too much respect rather than too little. Conversely, in twentieth-century Europe, where democracy had extended much further, there may have been a wish to recognise equality by extending the friendly T form to everyone regardless of their status; it may be no accident that one of the places where this change seemed to happen most quickly was in post-Franco Spain, following a political revolution. For English speakers, without the T/V distinction, other ways of democratising the language have to be sought, for example in the use of first names or nicknames rather than titles and surnames among people who are virtually strangers. Older speakers, in Britain at least, may find this disconcerting, for example when being addressed by a health worker or a younger person whom they have never met before, since it implies a familiarity which they feel does not exist.

What concerns English-speaking society nowadays, perhaps, is not so much rank as age. We have an ever-increasing range of words to denote people of different ages, such as *teenager*, *pre-teenager* and *tweenager*, all first recorded in the 1940s, when we also find the American *bobby-soxer* used of teenage girls. At the other end of the scale are the less-than-respectful *wrinkly* and *crumbly* for an old person, dating to the 1970s. Until the 1940s, although there were words referring to adolescence, the condition of being a teenager apparently lacked social significance: you were either a child or an adult and that was that. For a variety of reasons, older children began to have more status in society and a new word was coined to refer to them. Youngsters in the 10–12-year age-group were then perceived as forming a special class of incipient teenagers, and words such as *tweenager* and *pre-teenager* came into use. People had no difficulty in recognising these new categories of human beings or in learning new words to refer to them. The framework within which we assign meanings to words is constantly developing as society changes.

8.4 Kinship

One of the things that surprised and inspired anthropological linguists was the varied internal structure of apparently equivalent domains in the world's languages. An early and enduring interest has been colour terminology, where, as we saw in section 7.4, the number of BCCs recognised by a language varies from two to eleven. This doesn't mean that eyesight varies around the world, or that some people are more capable of perceiving certain colours than others, but rather that BCCs reflect the lifestyles of communities. We also saw, in section 7.5, that the number of BCCs in English has increased over the years so that a speaker of ModE recognises more BCCs than a speaker of OE or ME. Here too we can see a connection between the way people live and the concepts encoded in their language.

Another area of enduring interest for both anthropologists and linguists is kinship terminology, the language used to describe relationships among members of a family group. Just as, from the standpoint of a modern European language, it seems obvious that yellow, green and blue are distinct colours, so it may seem obvious that relationships such as mother, father, uncle and cousin are so clear-cut that any language is bound to have equivalent terms for them. However, this is far from being the case. Both synchronically and diachronically, even where superficially equivalent terms exist, closer examination may show that their meanings are subtly or strikingly different. This point can be demonstrated by an extract from Jane Austen's *Pride and Prejudice*, published in 1813. Mr Darcy has written to his sister, Georgiana, to tell her that he is engaged to Elizabeth Bennet. The story continues:

> The joy which Miss Darcy expressed on receiving similar information, was as sincere as her brother's in sending it. Four sides of paper were insufficient to contain all her delight, and all her earnest desire of being loved by her **sister**. (Jane Austen, *Pride and Prejudice*, 1813: chapter 60)

You might read quickly through this passage without noticing anything strange, or you might stop and wonder why Georgiana was calling Elizabeth, who is clearly going to be what nowadays we would call her *sister-in-law*, her sister. In fact, a glance at the *OED* shows that this usage was quite common at the time: sisters-in-law and brothers-in-law were often not distinguished linguistically from full brothers and sisters. The *OED* definition of *sister* reads: 'A female in relationship to another person or persons having the same parents . . . Sometimes loosely used in the sense of *half-sister* and in that of *sister-in-law*' (*sister*, noun 1a). This usage can be explained by social conditions at the time. People tended to live in larger groups than we do nowadays, and unmarried women usually lived with their parents. If, as in Georgiana Darcy's case, her parents were dead, a young woman might live with the family of a brother or a married sister or aunt (presumably because she needed a male relative to protect her). There was no need to distinguish between sisters and sisters-in-law in the family circle, so the term *sister* tended to be used for both relationships. An equivalent situation may arise nowadays with step-sisters or half-sisters. If you live in a family which combines two existing families and perhaps adds a third one, then you may have sisters who are related to you through only one parent. However, you may not feel the need to make this distinction clear in the dealings of everyday life.

If we go back to the *OED*, we can find similar complexity in other terms which we may think of as perfectly straightforward, such as *nephew* and *niece*, now usually restricted to the children of someone's brother or sister. Over time and in different locations, *nephew* has referred to a grandson (*OED* 2a) and a niece (2b), while *niece* has been used for a range of relatives, especially a cousin (1a), a grand-daughter (1c), or a male relative, especially a nephew (2). Both words entered Middle English from French with multiple meanings, and can be traced back to its parent language, Latin, where their principal meaning was a descendant, more specifically a grandson or granddaughter. Their development in English may have been affected by the fact that OE already had cognate words for these concepts, *(ge)nefa* 'nephew' (*OED neve*, noun 1) and *nefene* or *nift* 'niece' (*OED nift*, noun), both primarily used for the child of a brother or sister, though occasionally for a grandchild. The narrowing of *nephew* and *niece* to the modern meaning may reflect an increasingly complex religious and legal framework in relation both to permitted marriages and to the inheritance of property, which made precise knowledge of certain relationships more important.

OE also had native compound words for these relationships:

Nephew: *broþorsunu, sweostorsunu*
Niece: *broþordohtor*

These can be translated fairly obviously as 'brother's son', 'sister's son', and 'brother's daughter'. Although only one word for 'niece' survives, we can guess that there might also have been a word for 'sister's daughter', and thanks to the transparency of OE compounds, we can work out that it might have been **sweostordohtor*. It may be an accident of history that no such word survives, or it may reflect something about the relative importance of these relationships within the Anglo-Saxon family structure. We also find a word *sweostorbearn* 'sister's child, nephew', but no **broþorbearn*. Interestingly, some of these words survive longer in Scots and northern dialects of English than they do in southern English. The *DSL* records *britherdochter* (brother's daughter, niece, the equivalent of *broþordohtor*) and *britherson* (brother's son, nephew, the equivalent of *broþorsunu*) into the seventeenth century. It also has examples of two of the forms we noted as missing from OE: *sisterdouchtar* (niece, the equivalent of **sweostordohtor*) and *broderbarn/britherbarn* (brother's child, the equivalent of **broþorbearn*). Examples like these could be taken as evidence of the existence of such words in at least some varieties of OE, but such assumptions have to be made with caution. Both the OE and the early Scots record have large gaps in chronological and geographical coverage and in the kinds of texts represented. Many of the OE words are recorded only once, often in glossaries explaining words in Latin texts, and may not have been in general use; others may have disappeared without being recorded. Nevertheless, it can be worth checking regional dictionaries for apparently 'missing' words.

OE also had four words for the concepts of uncle and aunt:

Uncle: *eam* 'uncle, mother's brother', *fædera* 'father's brother'
Aunt: *modrige* 'mother's sister', *faþu* 'father's sister'

The OE word *eam* can refer to an uncle on either side of the family, but many scholars believe that it originally designated a maternal uncle, and thus made a pair with the surviving word for a paternal uncle, *fædera* (see Fischer 2002, 2006). In many societies, including early Germanic society, there was a special bond between a boy and his mother's brother, who might play a part in his upbringing, and hence a distinct word for this relationship emerged. Although a boy's primary relationship was with his father's family, his bond with his maternal uncles formed a useful link with his mother's family. It may be because of the importance of this meaning that *eam* developed a more general meaning, covering all uncles. It survives into ME as *eme*, but the citations from about the mid-fourteenth century are restricted to Scottish and northern English uses.

It should be clear from these examples that a key factor in the OE system was the side of the family to which your relative belonged. Kinship imposed strong obligations in Anglo-Saxon society and law. For example, if one of your kinsmen was attacked, you had an obligation to go to his aid. If he committed an offence such as murder and was obliged to pay compensation to his victim's family, his relatives had to help him to pay it, and those on the father's side had to pay more. Terms distinguishing relatives on the two sides of the family were common in the Germanic languages and still survive in some of them, such as the Scandinavian languages; they disappeared earlier in Latin and therefore are not found in its direct descendants, such as French and Spanish. So why do they not survive in English? The answer, as so often when English develops in unexpected ways, is the Norman Conquest of 1066, when the French legal system was imposed along with terminology denoting relationships which were important within it. New kinship terms recorded in English, mainly in the late thirteenth century, by which time the French legal system had become established, include *aunt, uncle, cousin, spouse*, and the *in-law* terms, such as *brother-in-law*. An important social factor here is the Norman system of primogeniture, whereby property passes to the oldest son rather than being divided among all the children as in Anglo-Saxon times. The key line of descent is thus from father to son, with the linguistic effect that there is no longer any great need for terms which distinguish, for example, maternal and paternal uncles, leading to the obsolescence of such terms. Primogeniture helps to preserve large estates intact, but also has its disadvantages. The plots of many English novels revolve around the problems of families without a male heir, of daughters whose marriage prospects are blighted by lack of a dowry, and of younger sons who have to make their own way in the world.

8.4.1 Recent changes

As a glance at its *OED* entry shows, *cousin* is another word which has meant many things in the course of its history. For people in much of the English-speaking world today, it refers to the children of an aunt or uncle, who are strictly speaking our first cousins. We may also apply it more vaguely to children of more distant relatives, who may be our second or third cousins, or to the children of our first cousins, who are technically our first cousins once removed. When confronted with this system, and invited to name, say, a second cousin once removed, many people nowadays simply give up. They are suffering from what is sometimes known as **fade-out**: our knowledge of the system fades as the information it contains loses importance. We may never have met our second or third cousins, and may feel no obligation towards them as we might towards closer relatives. *Cousin* in English could thus be described as a fuzzy category with a clear core (the prototypical first cousin) and a less clear periphery containing the much less prototypical second, third and removed cousins.

Another example of recent change is the word *family* itself, first recorded around 1400 but uncommon until the sixteenth century. Initially it referred to the servants of a household or the retinue of a nobleman (*OED* 1a, 1b). From there its meaning developed to include parents and children as well as servants, and then to what we would now regard as its prototypical meaning: 'The group of persons consisting of the parents and their children, whether actually living together or not' (*OED* 3a). In the twentieth century, two other expressions come into use: *nuclear family* (first recorded in 1924), usually denoting only parents and children, and *extended family* (first recorded in 1942), covering these and a wider range of people, such as aunts, uncles and grandparents. The concept of an extended family isn't new in Britain; as we saw in section 8.4, people in the nineteenth century lived in larger groups, as did people in earlier periods. However, since this situation applied to everyone, there was no need to distinguish two types of family; the single word *family* would suffice. Two factors may have contributed to changing the situation. The first was industrialisation, beginning in the late eighteenth century, and the resulting break-up of larger family groups as people left their farms and moved to towns. In more recent times, this trend has been accelerated by increased prosperity – better housing, more education, more financial independence, especially for women and young adults – which can lead to people living in smaller units and depending as much on friends and colleagues as on family. The second factor is immigration to Britain from areas such as the Caribbean and the Indian subcontinent where the extended family is prototypical. If you look at the quotations for *extended family* and *nuclear family* in the *OED*, you'll see that their early uses are as technical terms in Sociology and Anthropology, referring to overseas cultures, and it is not until the 1960s that they are applied to indigenous British society and pass into more general use. The only synonym for either of these terms, *joint family* for *extended family*, first recorded in 1876, seems to have remained as a technical term of Anthropology.

In one sense, then, the kinship system in ModE has become simpler than its OE equivalent. However, at the same time relationships within the nuclear family are becoming more complicated because the nuclear family itself is less stable. Changing social attitudes are reflected in new words and phrases for concepts which were previously unknown, or at least unremarkable. A selection of recent hyponyms includes: *single parent, lone parent, single parent family, birth mother, birth partner, working mother, absent father, weekend father* (who is there only at weekends). Other terms have been adopted from the jargon of Psychology, for example *mother-substitute* (1943) or *sibling* (1903), which supplies a gap for a term covering both brother and sister. It will be interesting to see what happens to these words over the course of time. Some of them may become obsolete; at the moment we feel the need to comment on different kinds of parents or mothers, but in the longer term we may feel that the distinctions are not worth making. If new meanings for words like *partner* (of someone in a social relationship) are accepted, then older words like *husband* and *wife* may also become obsolete. At the same time, we may need a new word for a business partner if the social usage causes ambiguity. Just as after the Norman Conquest, so in recent history new terminology has developed in response to changes in society.

8.5 Time

For the historical linguist, the realisation that certain concepts are not lexicalised in a language may be just as interesting as the study of those that are. A case in point is the domain of time in English, which has become considerably more complicated in structure over the years. In ModE we have a variety of systems which we use to divide this domain into smaller units, also referred to as domains or sometimes as sub-domains. In other words, we profile this domain in different ways according to various models or schemas, depending on which aspects of it we want to emphasise (on domains, profiling and schemas, see section 3.4). For the domain as a whole, we employ a bounding schema which divides time into manageable chunks that make sense over a human lifespan. These are often presented in order, for example in a sequencing schema, here in descending order of size: *year, month, week, day, hour, minute, second.* The list is by no means complete; we could add terms at either end, such as *century* or *microsecond.* This particular system enables us to pinpoint moments in time with the degree of precision our culture demands, as in 'The ceremony took place at 11.30 on Thursday, 27 June 2013'. Note that even here there are ambiguities and omissions: we have not specified whether the ceremony happened in the morning or evening – perhaps we felt that this could be left to the context, or that 11.30 in the morning was a more likely time for such an event. Nor have we stated that 27 June occurs in week twenty-six of the year, since this information is not usually considered relevant.

If you look up time in *TOE*, you will find words for *year, month, week, day,* which are themselves all of OE origin. There are two words for hour, *hwil* 'while' and *tid* 'tide', which also have more general meanings, but the word *hour* itself comes from French and is first recorded in 1250. Of the concepts of minute (first recorded *a.*1393) and second (not recorded until 1588), there is no trace. However, there is a well-developed system of terms for church hours, the times of services such as Matins and Vespers which took place at appointed hours throughout the day (and night). We thus begin to build a picture of a society where small units of time were unimportant, but time mediated by religion had a key role. There were no mechanical clocks in Anglo-Saxon England, although we find references to sundials and to clocks that worked by measuring the burning of a candle or the dripping of water through a spout. The word *clock,* however, derives from the OE word for a bell;

these would have been rung to mark the church hours, and thus would have given a sense of time passing.

One fact that may surprise us is that the day was not neatly divided into twenty-four equally-sized hours. For ordinary people, as opposed to churchmen influenced by Latin culture, the word *dæg* 'day' referred primarily to the daylight hours, and *niht* 'night' to the hours of darkness. These periods of daylight and darkness were each divided into twelve units, which thus varied in length according to the season. Hence we find an OE word *winterstund* 'winter hour' referring to the shorter daylight hours during that season. For a largely agricultural society, and one with only rudimentary forms of artificial lighting, the daylight hours, when work could be done and people could move around in safety, were of crucial importance. This point is reinforced by the fact that there is a well-developed vocabulary for key times in the day, such as cock-crow, dawn, morning, sunset, twilight and evening.

In ME, the domain of the week can be profiled as seven consecutive days, in the same kind of sequencing schema as the months of year. Such sequencing can be reflected in dictionary definitions, such as the *OED*'s definition of *February*: 'The second month of the year . . . falling between January and March', which makes sense only in the context of the sequence as a whole. Until quite recently, the first day of the week in diaries and calendars was Sunday, but in our more secular age Monday is usually placed first. (A Sunday start, however, is the only way of making sense of the German word for Wednesday, *Mittwoch* 'middle of the week'.) There is also a vaguer system, which we might describe as a folk schema, which is related to the way people live and distinguishes weekdays, on which people work, and weekends, a time of leisure, normally covering Saturday and Sunday. We draw on these profiles in utterances like:

1. Thank goodness it's Friday (rather than Monday or Tuesday).
2. I've got the Monday-morning blues.

In order to interpret these utterances we use our store of knowledge about the cultural context: many people stop work on Fridays and generally greet the beginning of the weekend with pleasure; on Mondays, they begin work again and may feel depressed as a consequence. In fact, this system of weeks and weekends is relatively recent. The practice of giving working people Saturday afternoon as a holiday dates in Britain to the mid-nineteenth century; in 1879 the word *week-end* was still sufficiently novel for the linguistic journal *Notes and Queries* to offer a very specific definition of what was apparently then a regional term:

'In Staffordshire, if a person leaves home at the end of his week's work on the Saturday afternoon to spend the evening of Saturday and the following Sunday with friends at a distance, he is said to be spending his *week-end* at So-and-so' (*OED week-end*, noun 1a). Before this pattern developed, non-working days consisted principally of religious observance on Sundays and holy days (from which ModE *holiday* derives), although they could include quite a lot of pleasure as well. In our own time, this profile of the week may be changing again because increasing numbers of people work shifts rather than a regular five-day week.

The domain of the year can be profiled in various ways, such as twelve months or four seasons. In both of these schemas, the Anglo-Saxon system was in a transitional state. While the names of the days of the week in OE are familiar to us (*sunnandæg, monandæg, tiwesdæg, wodnesdæg, þunresdæg, frigedæg, sæterdæg*), the names of the months offer a choice between a formal Latin-based system from which ModE names derive, and an older Germanic system based on the activities and ceremonies of the rural year. A selection of the OE words is given in Figure 8.1; others can be found in *TOE* or *HTOED*. A quotation from the headword information for *October* in the *OED* describes this bilingual situation:

January: *ianuarius, se æftera geola* (second month of yule)

February: *februarius, solmonaþ* (muddy month)

March: *martius, hlyda* (noisy month)

April: *aprelis, eastermonaþ* (Easter month)

May: *maius, þrimilcemonaþ* (three milk month)

June: *iunius, midsumermonaþ* (midsummer month)

July: *iulius, mædmonaþ* (meadow month)

August: *agustus, hærfest* (harvest)

September: *september, hærfestmonaþ* (harvest month)

October: *october, winterfylleþ* (month of the first full moon of winter)

November: *nouember, blotmonaþ* (month of sacrifice)

December: *december, se ærra geola* (first month of yule)

Figure 8.1 OE words for months

On ðam teoðan monðe on geare bíð   xxxi daga; þone mon   nemneð
In the tenth month of the year are 31 days; the month is named
in Leden Octember, ond on ure geðeode   Winterfylleð.
in Latin October, and in our language Winterfylleð.

Old English Martyrology

Some of the connections to agricultural life in the OE names for
months are clear, others less so since the reasons for the names may not
be obvious. OE *sol* means 'mud', which is often a feature of the English
countryside in February, so February is the 'muddy month'. The name
for March derives from OE *hlyd* 'sound, noise', so may refer to the
strong winds and storms of that month. May is a time when there is
plenty of grass in the fields and cattle can be milked three times daily,
while July refers more generally to meadows. August and September
are the months of *hærfest* 'harvest', a word which has narrowed to refer
only to the activity in later English. *Blot* is the OE word for 'sacrifice',
so the name *blotmonaþ* may refer to ceremonies which took place during
November. It may also be more generally associated with OE *blod*
'blood'. In Dutch, where a Germanic system of month names is preserved in dialects, November is *slachtmaand*, the month when animals
were slaughtered to provide food for winter. Different activities are
profiled in other Dutch months: February is *sprokkelmaand*, the month
for gathering wood, and July is *hooimaand*, the month for making hay, a
meaning which may be implicit in the OE *mædmonaþ*.[1]

Other OE names highlight important points of the year, both religious
and secular: June is *midsumermonaþ*, and *midwintermonaþ* is an alternative
name for December. October heralds the start of winter with the first
full moon of the season. Yule, the winter festival which later developed
into Christmas, was spread over two months, hence the phrases *se ærra
geola* and *se æftera geola* naming January and December. April references
the festival of Easter, while September can also be called *haligmonaþ*
'holy month', possibly referring to rituals associated with harvest.

Nowadays we are accustomed to the idea of four equally-sized
seasons: Spring, Summer, Autumn, Winter, though we may not be
entirely certain where each one begins and ends. Does Winter cover
November, December and January (more common in the UK), for
example, or December, January and February (common in the USA)?
Try a straw poll of your friends. In OE we find the remains of an older
two-season system consisting simply of *winter* 'winter', beginning in
October (as evidenced in the name *Winterfylleð*), and *sumor* 'summer',
starting around April. Both are ancient core vocabulary words; *winter*
probably comes from an Indo-European word meaning 'wet', and

summer from one meaning 'half' in reference to a half-year. The Anglo-Saxons used expressions referring to the other two seasons, but none of them seems to have been fully established as season names. Those referring to Autumn centre on the idea of harvest, including *hærfest* itself and compounds such as *hærfesttid* 'harvest-tide' and *riptima* 'reaping time'. Those for Spring, such as *lenctentima* 'lenten-time', are associated with the religious festivals of Lent and Easter. *Autumn* is first recorded as a season name in Chaucer's work in the fourteenth century, and in the sixteenth century we find occurrences of the words *Spring* and *Fall*, developing from two key events of these periods, the springing or bursting forth of new leaves and later their descent from the trees.

The two-season year persisted into early ME, as shown, for example, in the thirteenth-century lyric 'Sumer is icumen in', which reads:

> Sumer is icumen in –
> Llude sing! cuccu,
> Groweth sed and bloweth med
> And springth the wude nu –
> Sing! cuccu.
> Awe bleteth after lomb,
> Lhouth after calve cu.

(Davies 1966: 52)

[Summer has come in. Loudly sing! cuckoo. The seed grows and the meadow flowers, And now the wood bursts forth. Sing! cuckoo. The ewe bleats for her lamb. The cow lows for her calf.]

Most of the phenomena associated here with Summer, such as cuckoos, new growth and young animals, would be associated with Spring once the four-season system was fully established.

8.6 Conclusion

The purpose of this chapter has been to illustrate the interrelationship between language and culture, and to show how the study of culture can sometimes be used to elucidate problems of meaning and vice versa. As Taylor writes, 'The acceptability – and interpretability – of linguistic expressions depends, very often, on the activation of knowledge about the world' (2003a: 87). Such knowledge can be more essential, and more difficult to acquire, if the world we are studying is different from the one in which we live. Time and kinship may seem like relatively stable concepts but in fact are subject to change in tandem with social conditions; in OE we have the opportunity to see some of these changes in progress and to think about the reasons for them. We can also track such changes in more recent periods. The entry for *time* and its associated phrases and compounds was revised by the *OED* in 2012 and produced numerous new expressions reflecting nineteenth- and twentieth-century life and technology: *time capsule, time constraint, time difference, time pressure*, and many more. If you want to find out more about how languages change, it's interesting to work through these expressions and try to relate them to what you know about the social developments which may have produced them.

Exercises

1. People interested in Anglo-Saxon life and language may like to look at the package *Learning with the Online Thesaurus of Old English*, available at http://www.gla.ac.uk/schools/critical/research/funded researchprojects/learningwiththeonlinethesaurusofoldenglish/

   In addition to sections on Families and Time, which give more information on these subjects than has been possible here, there are units on Clothing, Colour, Death, Farming, Food and drink, Landscape, Plants, and the Universe.

2. The new baby's name is:

   George (first name) Philip Arthur (middle names) Smith (last name).

   Do you know any synonyms for terms like 'first name'? What terms would you use to describe your own name? Check for historical synonyms in *HTOED* to see if any changes reflect social factors.

3. As we saw in Chapter 5, meanings often weaken over the years as a result of overstatement. In Time, these include expressions like 'I won't be a *second*' and 'It took me *ages*', which aren't usually taken at face value. There are also many words like *soon* (OE *sona*), which originally meant 'immediately' but now refers to a vaguer future time. Think of some other Time expressions with vague meanings and use the *OED* to examine when and why they changed. Is such weakening a result of social change, or could it be attributed to something else, such as human nature?

4. An alternative folk schema for profiling the day is based on concepts such as morning, afternoon and evening, largely defined by recurrent factors in people's lifestyles, such as meal times, homework time, leisure time, bedtime. Make a plan of a typical day in your life using such terms, and check their historical development in the *OED*. Note any information you find about when particular meals such as dinner or supper were eaten in earlier periods.

5. Make the analysis of recent Time expressions in the *OED* mentioned at the end of section 8.6.

Further reading

For more detail on ways of addressing people, see Jucker and Taavitsainen (2013, especially chapter 5). Wild (2010) discusses the language used to refer to young people. Most Semantics textbooks will contain some discussion of the Sapir-Whorf Hypothesis; for a fuller treatment, see Lucy (1992). Pinker (1994) and McWhorter (2014) have a negative view of the hypothesis while Deutscher (2011) views it positively. Whorf's key papers can be found in Whorf (1956). Goody (1983) offers an interesting overview of the development of the family and related terminology. For studies of kinship in English and Scots, see Fischer (2002) and (2006), and Kay (2013). On the seasons in earlier English, see Earl Anderson (1997) and (2003), and Fischer (1994).

Note

1. With thanks to Janneke Mol for providing the Dutch examples.

9 Metaphor and metonymy

9.1 Introduction

In Chapter 5 we discussed tendencies in semantic change, including two of the most important triggers for change, metaphor and metonymy. In this chapter we will look at these in more detail, and think about their importance as linguistic phenomena which are basic to the way people think. Within Cognitive Semantics, metaphor and metonymy have been very widely studied, particularly since the publication of Lakoff and Johnson's influential book *Metaphors We Live By* ([1980] 2003). This book sparked off a new wave of research with a particular focus, and revitalised some very old and long-running debates about the nature of metaphor. It also paved the way for increased attention to metonymy as an equally important and pervasive feature of language. Most importantly for our purposes, attention has been given to the importance of metaphor and metonymy as triggers of semantic change and polysemy.

9.2 Metaphor in language and thought

Most definitions of metaphor treat it as a linguistic device, a 'figure of speech', which is something special and different from 'normal' language. Literary texts and especially poetry are often thought of as being particularly rich in metaphor, which might show the creativity of the speaker or writer. Aristotle's comment about metaphor in his fourth-century BC work the *Poetics*, which is quoted in all the standard textbooks, expresses this idea:

> The greatest thing by far is to be a master of metaphor. It is the one thing that cannot be learned from others; and it is a sign of genius, since a good metaphor implies an intuitive perception of the similarity of dissimilars. (Quoted in Richards 1936: 89)

Aristotle clearly treats metaphor (or at least, successful metaphor) as something special and unusual, and something that not all writers or speakers are good at. Many particularly famous quotations from literature include the kind of metaphor that Aristotle seems to have in mind. Some of Shakespeare's well-known lines provide examples, including the following spoken by the philosophising Jaques in *As You Like It*:

> All the world's a stage,
> And all the men and women, meerely Players
>
> (*As You Like It*, II, vii, 1118–1119)

The **target** or **tenor** of this metaphor – the thing being discussed – is the world, and the **source** or **vehicle** is the theatrical stage. In the second part of the quotation, the metaphor is extended, so that an aspect of the theatre, the actors, is used to talk about an aspect of the world, people. (In this particular example of metaphor, the sources and targets are both named explicitly, though this is not necessarily the case.) The metaphor is effective because it seems novel and striking (although it wasn't original in Shakespeare's time), and it presents a different way of thinking about its target. Jaques goes on to say more about the **entailments** of the metaphor, the characteristics of the source domain (the theatre) that are 'projected' or **mapped** onto aspects of the target domain (life):

> All the world's a stage,
> And all the men and women, meerely Players;
> They have their *Exits* and their Entrances,
> And one man in his time playes many parts,
> His Acts being seuen ages.
>
> (*As You Like It*, II, vii, 1118–1122)

We can set out these entailments or correspondences between the source and target in the mapping. It is conventional to express the mapping as a statement in small capital letters, in this case something like THE WORLD IS A THEATRE or LIFE IS A THEATRICAL PERFORMANCE.

Source: THE THEATRE	Target: LIFE
the stage	the world
actors ('players')	people
entrances and exits (on stage)	births and deaths
theatrical parts	'roles' in life (baby, schoolchild, lover, etc.)
acts in a play	periods in life (infancy, childhood, adolescence, etc.)

Examples like 'All the world's a stage' seem to bear out views like that of the nineteenth-century scholar and encyclopedia writer Abraham Rees, who considered figurative language as a type of ornamentation. Although he does not name metaphor here, it seems to be the focus of his comments:

> Figures contribute to the beauty and grace of style, by enriching the language, and rendering it more copious; by bestowing dignity upon style; by giving us the pleasure of enjoying two objects presented together to our view without confusion; the principal idea, which is the subject of the discourse, along with its accessory, which gives it the figurative dress; and by giving us frequently a much clearer and more striking view of the principal object, than we could have if it were expressed in simple terms, and divested of its accessory idea. (Rees 1819, unpaginated)

A similar view is echoed by more modern sources; for example, the definition of metaphor in the *Oxford Advanced Learner's Dictionary* is 'a word or phrase used in an imaginative way . . . to make the description more powerful'.

'All the world's a stage' tends to strike us as a classic example, the kind of metaphor that we think of as typical. In recent times, though, the focus of the study of metaphor within Cognitive Semantics has shifted away from literary, poetic language and towards more everyday language, which has been shown to include a great deal of metaphor of a different nature. If we look closely at another type of text we can see the evidence of this. The following is a fairly standard UK fire safety notice which gives instructions about what to do in the event of a fire. As you read through, look for any words or phrases which might not be strictly literal:

If you discover a fire:
Raise the alarm by breaking the glass of the nearest fire alarm point. Assume you are the first person to see the fire or smoke. The alarm points are situated as shown on the accompanying plan for your building.

Call the emergency services. To call for the assistance of the Fire Brigade, Police or an ambulance, dial 4444 on any University telephone extension. This will reach the Security Staff who will send for, and direct, the appropriate emergency services. In the event of difficulties call the emergency services direct by dialling 9-999. If you have time still try to inform the Security Staff, but the priority is safe evacuation once an alarm has sounded and the Fire Brigade have been summoned. If there is any element of risk to the person close the door and evacuate the building.

This text is obviously very much more mundane than the Shakespeare quotation above, and is designed to give clear information in a simple, straightforward way. It is not the kind of thing we associate with figurative language and certainly does not contain original, thought-provoking metaphor. Nevertheless, it does provide several examples of a different kind of metaphor. You may have noticed the following:

- In the phrase *raise the alarm*, no physical movement is involved; compare *raise your arm*. The meaning of *raise* can therefore be considered metaphorical here.
- In the phrase *in the event of difficulties*, the preposition *in* is used in a metaphorical way, since no physical containment is involved; compare *in the box*.
- Another common phrase later in the text is *if you have time*. Again, *have* here has a metaphorical meaning; compare *if you have any money*, where *have* involves literal physical possession.

These are all common, unexceptional expressions that we are used to seeing; they do not stand out, and you may not have thought of them as metaphorical before. (There are other words and phrases in the text that might also be considered non-literal, and we will come back to some of these later, in section 9.3 on metonymy.) However, these three examples are enough to show that conventional metaphor is a pervasive feature of all types of language, which speakers and writers use and encounter all the time, often without noticing it. The literary critic I. A. Richards famously referred to metaphor as 'the omnipresent principle of language' (1936: 92). Lakoff and Johnson's *Metaphors We Live By* ([1980] 2003) developed this point at greater length, and provided very detailed evidence of the conventional metaphors that are embedded in language. Although it has been around for many years now, it is essential reading for anyone coming to the field for the first time.

As well as this, the evidence of the fire safety notice suggests that metaphor is not simply a decorative figure which can be used to 'dress' some types of text, something which is different from 'ordinary' language and can be easily replaced by a simpler literal equivalent. In each case, it is difficult to see how the metaphor could have been avoided, at least without substantial rephrasing. It is possible to talk about *sounding* or *setting off* an alarm, although arguably neither conveys exactly the same sense since they don't imply alerting others to the same extent. The phrase *to have time* is absolutely the standard way to talk about time, though, and can't be replaced with another verb without some awkwardness. Similarly, it is usual to find metaphorical uses of *in* in phrases like this one, both *in* expressions like *in the event of (fire, rain, a crisis, war*, etc.) and *in* other non-literal uses including *in fact, in trouble, in the news, in a panic*. None of these strikes us as special or unusual linguistically, but rather they are embedded in the way we speak and write. I. A. Richards recognised this, and, like later scholars including Lakoff and Johnson, he suggested that metaphor is not simply a matter of language:

> The traditional theory ... made metaphor seem to be a verbal matter, a shifting and displacement of words, whereas fundamentally it is a borrowing between and intercourse of *thoughts*, a transaction between contexts. *Thought* is metaphoric, and proceeds by comparison, and the metaphors of language derive therefrom. To improve the theory of metaphor we must remember this. (1936: 94)

In other words, linguistic metaphor – the type of metaphor that we find expressed in spoken and written language – is the product of the way we think, though not necessarily of our conscious thought. For example, we conceptualise time, an abstract relation, as if it were a physical substance which we can manipulate, so that it makes sense to us to talk about *having, using* and *borrowing* time. Similarly, we use *in* in metaphorical expressions (as in the text) because we think of abstract events and situations as if they were physical containers: we can be *in a job, in conversation with* someone, or even *trapped in a relationship* or *struggling to get out of debt*. Lakoff and Johnson term examples like TIME IS A PHYSICAL SUBSTANCE and STATES ARE CONTAINERS **conceptual metaphors**, since they are not one-off words or phrases but systematic 'ways of thinking' that are reflected in many different expressions including these ones.[1]

In its title and its premise, Lakoff and Johnson's book also engaged with a central question in the discussion of metaphor: do metaphors die? That is to say, when a linguistic metaphor becomes so conventional that people no longer recognise it as metaphorical, has the meaning become literal? One approach would be to treat examples like those in the fire drill text as simply polysemous, and to reserve the term 'metaphor' for cases that are noticeable and striking. Lakoff and Johnson reject this view, and argue that conceptual metaphors cannot be regarded as dead because of their importance to the way we think; this is the sense in which they are 'metaphors we live by'. Other scholars have also observed that thinking of **conventional metaphors** as 'dead' is unhelpful because sometimes they can come 'alive' again if our attention is drawn to them. For example, it is conventional to refer to intelligent people as being *sharp*. Although this sense can be found alongside the sense 'pointed' from OE onwards, and so might not be an obvious example of a 'live' metaphor, playful use of the word in this sense in the phrase *so sharp she might cut herself* draws attention to its metaphorical nature. To acknowledge this kind of possibility, Cornelia Müller (2008) suggests that it is more helpful to think of metaphor on a scale from 'sleeping' to 'waking'; others have used related terms like 'dormant' (Perelman and Olbrechts-Tyteca 1969).

We might want to create a separate category for words that have metaphorically **motivated** meanings from a historical point of view, but which no longer retain a corresponding literal sense. For example, the adjective *ardent* 'passionate' was borrowed into English from French and is ultimately from Latin *ardentem* 'burning, in flame'. It was borrowed in the ME period with the literal and metaphorical senses that are found in both French and Latin, but the literal sense was always much less frequent in English, and only the metaphorical one survives in the present day. Interestingly, the same conceptual metaphor exists across the history of English in a number of linguistic metaphors, which have been well documented. Amongst many studies, Kövecses gives several modern examples in a discussion of the mapping EMOTION IS FIRE/HEAT (Kövecses 2000: 75), and Gevaert looks at evidence in OE in an examination of the target ANGER (Gevaert 2002). In ModE there are words that retain both source and target senses: *burning* can mean both 'in flame' and 'passionate', and *icy* is an antonym in both senses, meaning 'frozen, of low temperature' and 'passionless'. Even in cases like *ardent*, the term 'dead' is not necessarily helpful, since the meaning 'passionate' may still be perceived as metaphorical by speakers who know the etymology of the word. A more neutral label is *historical metaphor*. (See Allan [2013] for a more detailed discussion.)

To historical semanticists, the issue of metaphor death is interesting, but the question of whether highly conventional metaphors become literal perhaps does not present a difficulty which we need to resolve here. Our major concerns are in the semantic histories of words, the principles and processes by which word meanings change, and the nature of polysemy. This means that conventional metaphor is of particular interest to us, since it involves metaphor as a trigger for **metaphorical polysemy** – polysemy in which one meaning has developed from another metaphorically and both survive. We can regard the question of whether the senses of a word should be regarded as synchronically literal or metaphorical as a terminological one and leave it to one side here.

9.3 Another kind of mapping: Metonymy

Alongside metaphor, there is another trigger for semantic change which involves a mapping from source to target, and this is metonymy. The major difference between metaphor and metonymy is the kind of link between source and target. Compare the following pairs of examples:

1. She's a real Jackson Pollock
2. I just bought a Jackson Pollock
3. Every child is a blank canvas
4. We spent the night under canvas

In each pair, the first example ((1) and (3)) contains a metaphor, while the second ((2) and (4)) shows metonymy. Metaphor is often described as a cross-domain mapping, where aspects of the source domain are projected onto aspects of the target domain; the mapping is usually motivated by some kind of perceived similarity between source and target, though this isn't always straightforward. In (1), the source *Jackson Pollock* is mapped onto the target *she*, presumably because of some similarity between the artistic styles of the two. This might not be a compliment, since Jackson Pollock is associated with 'action painting', where paint is splashed or smeared onto a large canvas in a spontaneous and imprecise way that is not universally appreciated! In (3), *every child* is described as *a blank canvas*, and this is a more complex mapping based on similarity that is itself metaphorical. Blank canvases are designed to be turned into pictures of some kind when they are painted on, in the same way that some people believe children's characters (metaphorically, the 'pictures' they become) are shaped or determined by the experiences that they are exposed to. (Note that it is difficult to describe the metaphor without using other metaphors here.) Again, we can set out the entailments of the metaphor as follows:

Source domain: ART	Target domain: RAISING CHILDREN
canvas	child
paint	experiences
artist	adult(s)
finished painting	experienced/educated child

If we compare these two examples to (2) and (4), we can see that these work in quite a different way. Metonymy involves mapping within a domain, which means that metonymy tends to involve a source and a target that are closely related in experience, and has a 'referring function' rather than indicating any kind of similarity between the two; in other words, the source 'stands in for' the target as a way of referring to it. The link between the source and target in a metonymy is therefore often described as a relationship of contiguity (involving concepts that are metaphorically 'next to' one another) rather than a relationship of similarity. In (2), *Jackson Pollock* means 'a painting by Jackson Pollock'. Since Jackson Pollock is an artist, both he and the painting can be said to belong to the same conceptual domain (or area of experience) – art; unlike in (1), no comparison is being made between Jackson Pollock and the painting, but rather the most salient feature of the painting, the artist who painted it, is used to refer to it. The mapping here can be described as PRODUCER FOR PRODUCT, and this is a common pattern of metonymy. We can refer to artworks of all kinds by their artists or creators, e.g. *a Dickens* for 'a novel by Dickens' or *the latest James Cameron* for 'the latest film directed by the director James Cameron'. We can also name other kinds of objects by the individuals or companies who invented or made them: *a Dyson* can mean 'a vacuum cleaner made by Dyson', and *Nikes* often means 'trainers made by the brand Nike'.

The other example, (4), shows a different pattern of metonymy, MATERIAL FOR OBJECT, and in this case the target, a tent, is referred to by the material it is made of, canvas. This is a particularly interesting example because it shows the way that metonymical senses of words can be subject to further semantic change: canvas tents are fairly old-fashioned now, and many tents are made of different materials, but *canvas* in the expression *under canvas* has widened semantically so that it can refer to tents made of other materials as well. There are many other examples. A *glass* can mean 'a drinking vessel made of glass', but it is also possible to talk about *plastic glasses* (the kind that are often used outdoors, for example at music festivals). If we go back to the fire safety notice, we can find a different type of metonymy there. The notice instructs readers to call *the emergency services, the Fire Brigade* and *the police*, and later refers to *the Security Staff*. In each case the institution stands for an individual or group of individuals that represent this institution. We might regard these as examples of the metonymical pattern INSTI-TUTION FOR PERSON. As with the conventional metaphors discussed earlier, this is absolutely typical and unremarkable, and it is easy to think of similar examples: newspapers often report what *the government* or *the BBC* said, or the way *Starbucks* or *Amazon* treat customers. A related but slightly different example in the text is *ambulance*, where the vehicle stands for the paramedics who drive the ambulance.

All of these examples show that metonymy is just as common a feature of language as metaphor, and some scholars have argued that it may be even more fundamental to the way we think and therefore even more pervasive in language (see for example Niemeier 2000 for a discussion). Because metonymy is a mapping between two concepts linked by experience, some linguistic metonymies are highly context-dependent and created spontaneously or 'on the fly'. A famous and much-discussed example is found in a sentence that might be said by a waiter in a café: *The ham sandwich is getting restless at table 20* (Nunberg 1978: 22). *The ham sandwich* refers here to a café customer who ordered a ham sandwich; for waiting staff, whose main function is to serve food to tables, the particular item that has been ordered by each customer is their most relevant feature in this situation, and so it is meaningful to refer to customers in these terms. (Taylor 2003b: 325 looks at a similar example.) Because this use of *ham sandwich* is rooted in such a specific context, and only makes sense in that context, it is unlikely that the meaning 'customer' would become conventional. However, metonymical meanings that are less contextually restricted are also common, and often become highly conventional, giving rise to **metonymical polysemy**. The compounds *football*, *basketball* and *baseball* all refer both to the games (e.g. *I like football*), individual matches or tournaments (e.g. *Did you see the football?*) and the objects that are used in the games (e.g. *I kicked the football*). Somewhat counter-intuitively, in each case the 'game' meaning appears to be earlier than the 'ball' meaning, although it perhaps makes sense that a need arose for a label to name the particular type of ball used in each game after the game itself was established.

In some cases, like the MATERIAL FOR OBJECT examples *canvas* and *glass*, the direction of the mapping is easy to establish, but in others it seems less obvious which meaning is the source and which is the target. Is the fruit *orange* called after its colour, or does the colour term come from the fruit? Are *waltz* and *polka* terms for dances that were extended metonymically to name types of music associated with these dances, or vice versa? Chapter 7 answers the first question: like many other colour terms, *orange* named the object first and was used as a colour term later. The *OED* gives us different answers for *waltz*, which is recorded earliest in English with the meaning 'dance', and *polka*, which is recorded earliest in English with reference to a piece of music (though with a complicated history that is unclear about whether the 'dance' meaning might have been earlier etymologically). In cases like these, we must examine the historical evidence, though that will not always provide a clear answer. In fact, we will see the same difficulty when we examine some metaphorical mappings, and this may not be surprising; if metaphor and metonymy are fundamental to the way we think, there may not always be a time delay between the emergence of source and target meanings that shows up in the historical record.

9.4 Metaphor and motivation

An obvious question to ask when we are considering metaphor and metonymy as triggers for semantic change is what motivates mappings: why do particular metaphors and metonymies arise, and what makes some sources 'suitable'? These are difficult questions which cannot be answered definitively, but there seem to be some commonalities across metaphorical and metonymical mappings that give us at least a starting point from which to explore and explain the issue of motivation. Again, we will concentrate on conventional metaphor and metonymy here, and we can identify some patterns that might be more evident in these kinds of mappings. We will consider metaphor first, and go on to look at metonymy.

The nature of the sources and targets of metaphorical mappings seems to support the idea that people think metaphorically, and linguistic metaphor is the product of this metaphorical thinking. As we have discussed already, metaphor is often described as a relationship of similarity between source and target, and for one type of metaphor this is fairly straightforward: **image metaphors** arise from visible similarities, for example similarities of shape or size (or both). The computer *mouse* was so called from the time of its invention in the 1960s because it is very approximately the same shape and size as a real mouse, and the cable that links it to a computer keyboard or screen resembles a tail, though modern wireless versions do not have this feature. A bunch of bananas has been called a *hand* of bananas since the late nineteenth century because of a similarity in shape, with fingers mapping onto the individual bananas, although this is a relatively rare usage outside the banana-growing industry. Of course, in reality the resemblance between the two is only partial, since *hands* of bananas are significantly bigger and have a variable number of 'fingers' (technically between eight and twenty), but they have enough in common visually for the mapping to be recognisable, even for speakers who have not encountered this meaning before. Some image metaphors are based on much more schematic similarities. We refer to the parts of some tall or upright structures in terms of the body, including the *head* and *foot* of a mountain, the *arm* of a mechanical crane, and the *shoulders* of a wine bottle. Again, this type of mapping has a long history in English, with *head* used for a wide range of entities including topographical features from the OE period onwards. In these examples, as in all image metaphors, the sources and targets are both concrete entities. As well as this, in each case the source of the metaphor is something common and familiar, and this is typical of all kinds of conventional metaphor and explains why some concepts are the sources for large numbers of metaphors. The body seems to be a particularly important source, and you will be able to think of lots of other examples: the *face* of a clock or watch (attested from the seventeenth century onwards, several centuries after *face* is borrowed from French around the early fourteenth century), the *nose* of a wedge of cheese (much more recent, and not recorded as a specific sense in the *OED*), the *mouth* of a cave (found from OE onwards), and so on.

If we look at another type of metaphor, we can see that in some cases metaphors are motivated by a kind of similarity, but one that is less obvious and more subjective. In English, and in many other languages, it is common to refer to people by animal names to indicate some aspect of their personality or habits. For example, a messy person might be called a *pig*, a playful or cheeky child told they are a *(cheeky) monkey*, or someone foolish referred to as a *(silly) ass*. Animal metaphors of this kind seem to have become common from the late ME period onwards. There are some even earlier examples: *wolf* is attested in OE (in the form *wulf*) as both a term for the animal and with the sense 'A person or being having the character of a wolf; one of a cruel, ferocious, or rapacious disposition' (*OED* noun 5a). In each of these cases, some salient feature of the animal's behaviour is compared to an aspect of the human's behaviour, and therefore motivates the metaphor, but there is not necessarily a factual basis for the comparison. For example, *cougar* has very recently started to be used to mean 'An older woman seeking a sexual relationship with a younger man' (*Oxford Dictionaries Online*). There are long discussions on the internet about the nature and behaviour of human *cougars*, but it is difficult to see any objective justification for the mapping. Male cougars rather than females are in control of selecting mates, and males breed with a large number of females across a territory, so have a wider range of mates. There is no evidence that female cougars breed with younger mates. What seems much more relevant is a perceived similarity between women and cougars which is based on an interpretation of animal behaviour in terms of human behaviour: the salient feature of big cats in general appears to be the way they hunt, and this is paralleled with the practice of actively 'hunting' for sexual partners. Human sexual behaviour is often metaphorised in terms of animal behaviour, so that *on the prowl* can mean 'seeking sexual conquests' (for example, in a bar or nightclub), and (usually) men who have exploitative sexual relationships of various kinds are called *sexual predators*. At the same time, women are often associated with cats – think of expressions like *sex kitten* and the recent coinage *tiger mother*. All of these factors feed into the mapping, so that established associations between humans and animals lay the foundations for the metaphor. It is still not entirely clear why the cougar rather than another big cat is the specific source, but this may be partly explained by the fact that many other big cats are already identified with other human characteristics and so are blocked as sources: for example, a *lion* is brave or powerful, while a *tiger* is fierce and aggressive. These established notions are based on the features of each animal's behaviour that are salient for humans, though this is not necessarily objective or accurate. Animal metaphors show very clearly the way in which cultural conceptions and associations inform metaphorical mappings, and we often need to take account of the time and place that a linguistic metaphor emerges to explain the perceived connection between its source and target. The role of culture in metaphorical mappings is something that has also been explored in detail in relation to the way anger is expressed in English (Geeraerts and Grondelaers 1995).

The idea that metaphor is based on a similarity between source and target becomes still more problematic when we consider other instances which involve abstract entities, and particularly the kind of highly conventional metaphors that are embedded in language below the level of consciousness. Research has shown that, usually (though not always), metaphorical mappings of this kind have concrete sources and abstract targets, and again this relates to the idea that metaphor is a matter of thought rather than simply a linguistic figure: we use metaphor to help us think and talk about what is difficult to comprehend, often unconsciously. In section 9.2 we looked at the metaphor TIME IS A PHYSICAL SUBSTANCE, which accounts for expressions like *to have, borrow* and *save time*; we could add many others to this list, including *make* or *find time* and *run out of time*. Time is an abstract concept, defined in the *Encyclopaedia Britannica* as 'a continuum that lacks spatial dimensions'. Conceptualising time as if it were a physical substance makes it possible for us to think and talk about it, since we are familiar with objects and substances that we can feel and touch, and we understand how these can be manipulated and divided. We also looked at the CONTAINER metaphor evidenced in the expression *in the event of difficulties*, and in other expressions like *in trouble, in danger*, and *in a hurry*. Both of these groups of examples are **ontological metaphors**, metaphors in which the targets – abstract states, processes or relations – are 'seen as' physical entities with substance that can be manipulated. Can we make sense of either of these groups of examples in terms of similarity? Is there something similar about time and physical substances, or about abstract states and physical containers? We might argue that we perceive some kind of similarity between them, but this seems dependent on the metaphors themselves. Cognitive linguists suggest that conceptual metaphors of this kind are not the products of similarity, but rather have an experiential basis; they are motivated by basic human experiences, which are mapped onto abstract concepts and 'structure our experience' of these concepts (Lakoff and Johnson 2003: 3). As physical beings, we are most able to understand other physical entities, so we think and talk about the non-physical in those terms. Again, as we saw with image metaphors above, this suggests that some concepts recur as sources for conceptual metaphor because they are familiar. Kövecses (2010: 17–31) identifies a number of common source domains (and also target domains), including the human body, cooking and food, heat and cold, and light and darkness: these are all unavoidable aspects of being human from very early on, and this is why they are a core part of our metaphorical system, reflected in the linguistic metaphors we use. In some cases there also seems to be a metonymical basis for particular metaphorical mappings that relates to these bodily experiences. We discussed the example of *ardent* in section 9.2 and saw that there are other linguistic metaphors that reflect the same mapping between temperature and emotion, such as *burning* desire, a *warm* smile or reception, and *cold* or *icy* meaning 'lacking emotion, unfriendly'. Scholars including Grady (1997) have argued that there is a physiological basis to this mapping, since we tend to experience warmth alongside some emotions. For example, when we feel affectionate we often get physically close to another person, and when we get angry we flush and feel hotter. This metonymical link motivates a metaphorical one, since physical temperature is not involved in the experiences or emotions named by these expressions. Kövecses (2010) includes some helpful explanation about the different kinds of motivation for metaphor, including this one.

The historical picture for highly conventional metaphors is often complicated and difficult, and in at least some cases it is hard to find evidence that the meaning we would assume to be literal is attested earlier than the metaphorical meaning. We suggested above that in expressions like *have time* and *in trouble*, the verb *have* and the preposition *in* have metaphorical senses which contrast with their literal senses 'to hold in the hand' and 'physically positioned inside'. In fact, it is probably impossible to prove that these literal senses are earlier in English, since both words, which are native, have had a complex range of concrete and abstract senses since they were first attested. In cases like these, we can try to trace etymologies further back to find evidence of earliest senses in Germanic, or even in Indo-European, but this does not always take us any further: cognate forms in related languages show a similar picture of polysemy. A comparable example is the verb *to see*, which has two main meanings in PDE: 'to perceive physically with the eyes', as in *I can see a ship*, and 'to understand mentally', as in *I see the problem*. The polysemy of *see* and other perception verbs has been discussed at length in a number of studies, including one which is notable in its focus on word histories, Eve Sweetser's *From Etymology to Pragmatics*. Sweetser examines a range of perception verbs with mental senses in PDE, and observes that 'There is a set of basic Indo-European roots which seem to have referred to vision as far back as their history can be traced' (1990: 33). However, for many of the examples she considers, mental senses seem to be attested just as early, though the evidence is difficult to assess with certainty (Allan 2008: 51–8 discusses this in more detail). In cases like these, intuition strongly favours the idea that physical, concrete senses are likely to be earlier, and this is certainly what has traditionally been assumed by linguists and lexicographers. In the etymology section of the *OED2* entry for *to have* (which was not revised for *OED3* at the time of publication of this book), there is a section on 'signification', which begins with the following comment:

> From a primitive sense 'to hold (in hand)', *have* has passed naturally into that of 'hold in possession,' 'possess,' and has thence been extended to express a more general class of relations, of which 'possession' is one type, some of which are very vague and intangible.

The entry is structured with this 'primitive' sense first to reflect the assumed semantic development of the word, even though the etymon in Germanic is already polysemous. The sense development of linguistic metaphors which do show a delay between source and target meanings supports the idea that concrete > abstract is a general principle, so perhaps gives a more sound basis for assuming that direction of sense development where there is no clear evidence. And we might also conjecture that if we really do think metaphorically, and if metaphor does enable us to think and talk about abstract concepts which might otherwise be beyond our understanding, it is perhaps unsurprising that there is no historical delay between literal and metaphorical senses of deeply embedded metaphors of this kind. None of this entirely resolves the difficulty of the historical picture, though, and it remains to be seen whether any more satisfactory and conclusive account will be formulated in the future. Further work may be stimulated by the 'Mapping Metaphor' project at the University of Glasgow, which uses the structure of *HTOED* to link source and target concepts, and may uncover patterns and historical trends that have been difficult to identify in the past (see further Chapter 10).

9.5 Metonymy and motivation

Although metonymical mappings are motivated by a different kind of connection between source and target, there seem to be some parallels between the ways metaphorical and metonymical mappings are motivated. The source and target in a metonymy belong to the same domain, and are related by contiguity; in other words, they are concepts that belong to the same area of experience. This means that the motivation for metonymy tends to be fairly transparent, although this does not mean it is always immediately obvious why some sources are selected rather than others. In the discussion of animal metaphors above, we saw that particularly salient features of an animal's behaviour often form the basis of mappings between animals and humans. Salience also seems to be the most important factor in a large proportion of metonymical mappings. If we look again at some of the examples we have discussed in this chapter, we can see that many sources tend to relate to particularly distinctive, noticeable aspects of the target entity they refer to. This is certainly true for PRODUCER FOR PRODUCT mappings like *a Jackson Pollock* for 'a painting by Jackson Pollock' or *a Dickens* for 'a novel by Dickens', and it is interesting that objects are most likely to be metonymised by their brand names where these are particularly valued. We find examples such as *Nikes* for 'trainers made by the brand Nike', since this is a high-profile sports brand which makes expensive trainers, but it is much less likely that we would find *Primarks* for 'trainers made by the fashion retailer Primark' (the European chain): this is not a brand associated specifically with sportswear or footwear, and the shoes they manufacture are very much less expensive. (You can confirm this by comparing the results of Google searches for 'wearing Nikes' and 'wearing Primarks'.) For a different reason, MATERIAL FOR OBJECT metonymies tend to occur where what the object is made of is particularly significant or conspicuous. In some cases, objects are made almost entirely from one material, like *canvas* 'tent' and *glass* 'drinking vessel'. In others, the material used is what makes the object different from similar objects, like *iron* and *wood* 'golf club'; if there was only one type of golf club these names would not make sense, since they differentiate a specialised club by contrast with other clubs. Yet another type of example is *glasses* 'spectacles', where the key part of the object is made of a particular material, and it would be difficult for other materials to replace this (or at least this would have been true at the time when the object was named).

Another commonality between the motivation for metaphor and metonymy is the propensity for mappings with an abstract target to have a concrete source. The opposite is much less likely, and again this can be explained by the tendency to think of abstract concepts in terms of familiar, physical things. One very famous example of metonymy is the phrase *the pen is mightier than the sword*, defined by the *OED* as 'the written (or spoken) word is more effective than violence' (*pen*, noun[3] 1d). Here, two concrete objects, the pen and the sword, are mapped to the abstract concepts of the written word, or more accurately the power to persuade or influence, and physical violence, or more accurately physical violence as a means to control. In each case there is a kind of two-stage metonymy based on the functions of each object, and the metonymy makes for a very succinct, condensed way to express the idea. Other more commonplace metonymies show that some of the same concepts that are frequent sources for metaphor can also be involved in metonymy, such as the body. *Tongue* is often used to mean 'language', for example in phrases like *mother tongue* and *foreign tongue*, and other body parts also conventionally stand for the functions they enable: *to eye (up)* means 'to look at', *to shoulder* means 'to carry', and *to finger* means 'to touch' or 'to steal'. Some of these expressions also have metaphorical meanings by a further mapping. *To shoulder a burden* can either mean 'to (physically) carry a heavy load' or 'to take responsibility for something difficult, costly, etc.', and similarly *to finger* can mean 'to identify', in phrases such as a recent headline on various news websites, 'Soot fingered as climate threat'.

We can identify some patterns that account for a large number of metonymies, such as PRODUCER FOR PRODUCT and MATERIAL FOR OBJECT. The list below includes a few of the most common, with examples of each. Two of the most general of these are PART FOR WHOLE and WHOLE FOR PART, and traditionally the term used for these mappings is **synecdoche**. This is still a common term, and some scholars treat synecdoche as a separate category from metonymy, but it seems to us to be a class of metonymy, and this is the way it is treated by many cognitive linguists.

PART FOR WHOLE:	I like your new *wheels* (= 'car'), the football coach brought in fresh *legs* (= 'players')
WHOLE FOR PART:	I polished the *car* (= 'outside shell'), we have the *family* visiting (= 'some members of the family')
CONTAINER FOR CONTENTS:	She has an elegant *wardrobe* (= 'clothes'), the *kettle's* boiling (= 'water in the kettle')

PRODUCER FOR PRODUCT:	Where's the *hoover*? (= 'vacuum cleaner'), I like to write with a *biro* (= 'pen')
OBJECT FOR USER (OR CONTROLLER):	the *trains* are on strike (= 'train drivers'), a hired *gun* (= 'assassin')
MATERIAL FOR OBJECT:	I used *plastic* to pay (= 'credit card'), he polished the *silver* (= 'cutlery')
PLACE FOR PEOPLE:	*Scotland* voted in the independence referendum (= 'Scottish people'), *the hall* gave the soloist a standing ovation (= 'the audience')

A more complete list is given in Kövecses (2010: 179–84), and Handl (2011: 86–96) discusses typologies of metonymy in more depth. In many cases there may be more than one way to classify a particular instance, and more than one type of metonymy might be involved simultaneously. One of the examples in the fire safety text was *call the police*, and we suggested that this was a metonymy of the pattern INSTITUTION FOR PERSON, but we might also argue that this could be treated as a WHOLE FOR PART mapping, since the target is one or more members from the whole collection of people that makes up the police force. Not all metonymies fit into categories like the ones listed here, but it seems significant that we can identify clear patterns, and finding cases in which the relationship between source and target is similar is often a helpful starting point for comparisons between the semantic histories of different words.

9.6 Conclusion

We began this chapter by saying that metaphor and metonymy are important triggers for semantic change, and the examples we have discussed give some sense of how many semantic histories include shifts in meaning that involve these processes. The examples also show the ubiquity of metaphorical and metonymical polysemy in the lexicon of English, and the kind of patterns that can be found across mappings of each kind. Some source domains, like the body, are particularly important for conventional metaphors and metonymies, and this is consistent with current ideas about the role of metaphor and metonymy in thought, which stress the role of familiar entities and experiences in our understanding of more obscure phenomena. In fact, some concepts are sources for a large number of mappings: for example, we considered the conventional use of *head* to mean 'top of a mountain' in section 9.4, but *head* also has a range of other meanings triggered by metaphor and metonymy. Via metonymy, it can mean 'a person', in phrases like *cost per head* or the expression *two heads are better than one*, where it specifically refers to a person's capacity for thought. Via metaphor, it can mean 'part of a plant', like *a head of broccoli*, or 'part of a tool', like *the head of a hammer*, or 'the end of a table', or 'the top of a page', or 'a person in a senior position', like *the head of the company*. The *OED* entry for *head* gives a large number of other senses that also show metaphor and metonymy, including some that are now obsolete.

We can make a number of observations therefore about the kinds of sources and targets that are typical in metaphor and metonymy, and go some way towards understanding the motivation for particular cases. However, the range of cognitive, cultural and lexical factors that can be involved means that we cannot predict future metaphorical and metonymical mappings that might trigger semantic change, nor explain why some mappings that appear to be possible do not occur. For example, we have seen that MATERIAL FOR OBJECT is a common type of metonymy, but it is difficult to see why there is no conventional use of *wood* for 'table'. In fact, *board* developed this meaning by metonymy, though it is obsolete except in restricted contexts now, as the *OED* entry for *board* records (noun 5a). (*Table* is discussed further in Allan 2010: 174–5.) Similarly, *cotton* for 't-shirt' seems plausible, but is not recorded. In many respects, change triggered by metaphor and metonymy is like any other kind of semantic change, and the kind of language-internal and language-external factors that we discussed in Chapter 5 can interact with mapping processes with unpredictable results.

Finally, it is important to remember that the semantic history of any one word can involve multiple stages of change, so that both metaphor and metonymy can be involved at different times, and can interact with one another.[2] A neat example can be seen in the development of the noun *carpet*, which is borrowed into English from French or Latin in the mid-fourteenth century. The earliest meaning attested in the *OED* is 'a thick fabric'; by metonymy, it is also used to mean 'a table cloth', and, slightly later, 'a floor covering' (as well as the material this is made of). From the end of the sixteenth century onwards, a number of metaphorically motivated senses are also recorded, which develop from the metonymical sense. The first of these is 'an expanse of grass or flowers', and several others are specialised uses in particular registers: 'the surface of the field' is the meaning of the term used in cricket (from the very late nineteenth century), 'the ground' is found in aeronautical slang (first attested in 1918), and 'a layer of a road surface' in civil engineering (attested from 1920). Most recently, a further metaphorical meaning is found which perhaps results from a perceived similarity with a different aspect of a literal carpet, its density: from 1944 there are instances of the meaning 'a large number of bombs dropped to damage an area intensively'. Interestingly, the verb *to carpet* develops the metaphorical sense 'reprimand', and this seems to show influence from the expression *to walk the carpet* 'said of a servant summoned for reprimand' (*OED carpet*, noun 2d, verb 4). With the exception of the earliest use 'thick fabric, table cloth', all of these metaphorical and metonymical senses co-exist in PDE. The semantic histories of many other words show similar but much more complicated polysemy; try looking at the *OED* entries for *paper* or *bed* for some challenging but fascinating examples.

Exercises

1. In this chapter we looked at the metaphorical link between temperature and emotion, evidenced by expressions like *ardent desire, burning passion, a warm smile*, and *cold-hearted*. Can you think of other examples that fit this pattern? You might be able to find some relevant historical metaphors; try using *HTOED* to look for possibilities.
2. The history of the noun *toilet* includes some interesting semantic shifts. Give an account of how the earliest meaning evolved into the frequent current sense 'sanitary ware' (i.e. the thing you flush!), and identify any stages which involve metonymy. (You might also be interested to look at the discussions of other expressions for 'toilet' in Fischer [2004] and Crystal [2014, chapter 5], which are mentioned in section 5.7.3 and the further reading section for Chapter 5 respectively.)
3. Identify whether metaphorical or metonymical polysemy is involved in each of the following examples. Can you explain the motivation for the mapping in each case?
   * According to the media, women still find it difficult to break through the glass ceiling.
   * I usually read the paper online when I get to work.
   * Political commentators have suggested that this could be the current president's Watergate.

Further reading

As discussed above, Lakoff and Johnson's *Metaphors We Live By* is still a key work on metaphor in Cognitive Semantics, with some discussion of metonymy; the 2003 edition includes an afterword on more recent work in the field. Another accessible introduction which is more up to date (and which has several chapters on metonymy) is Kövecses' textbook *Metaphor: A Practical Introduction* (2nd edition, 2010). There are also a number of more historically informed studies. Allan (2008) considers the metaphorical and metonymical motivation for nouns and adjectives in the semantic field *Intelligence*; Tissari (2003 and subsequent work) takes a similar look at the lexis of emotions, and there are papers in Winters et al. (2010) by Trim, Fabiszak and Hebda, and Tissari which look at the expression of emotion over time with particular attention to metaphor and metonymy. Winters et al. (2010) also includes a paper on metonymic polysemy by Allan. Papers by Koch, Blank, Goossens and Jäckel in Panther and Radden (1999) examine metonymy from a historical perspective. Finally, several studies by Geeraerts and collaborators (some collected together in Geeraerts 2006) have a historical focus, often with particular attention to the role of culture in mappings.

Notes

1. Michael Reddy's paper 'The Conduit Metaphor – A Case of Frame Conflict in our Language about Language' discusses the metaphor LANGUAGE IS A CONTAINER FOR THOUGHTS, and this is also a key text for cognitive metaphor theory (Reddy 1979).
2. In some cases, metaphor and metonymy may be involved at the same time; Goossens (1990) coined the term *metaphtonymy* for cases where a mapping seems to result from interaction of both processes.

10 The big picture and a look ahead

10.1 Introduction

We have tried throughout this book to give you a sense of the pleasures and challenges of working with historical data. We have also tried to show how ideas from theoretical linguistics, especially Cognitive Linguistics, can be used to shed new light on topics such as polysemy, metaphor and categorisation. In fact, the gap between traditional philological approaches to language history and modern linguistic methods may not be as great as the relative neglect of Historical Semantics in recent times might suggest. Geeraerts makes this point when he writes:

> First, cognitive semantics and traditional historical semantics share, by and large, a psychological conception of meaning. Second, both approaches start from an encyclopedist conception of meaning, in the sense that lexical meaning is not considered to be an autonomous phenomenon, but is instead inextricably bound up with the individual, cultural, social, and historical experience of the language user. Third, both are specifically interested in the flexibility and polysemy of meaning and the mechanisms underlying those phenomena . . . (2010: 277)

This sense of continuity of endeavour corresponds very much with our own perceptions when writing this book.

10.2 The big picture

The chapters and exercises throughout this book have offered suggestions for exploring the lexis of English in different ways and from different perspectives. We have discussed individual word histories, and the ways these reflect and illuminate the historical development of the language as a whole. We have considered the nature of word meaning, and the relationship between the multiple senses of a word both synchronically and diachronically. We have thought about the tendencies in semantic change that are only apparent if we compare large numbers of word histories. We have also examined the semantic relationships that structure the lexicon as a whole, and the ways in which the senses of one word connect to and interact with senses of other words. Along the way, we have emphasised the role of context in every aspect of semantic change, and the crucial influence of both cognition and culture. One way of bringing all these ideas together is to consider one word in detail, and suggest ways of exploring its semantic history in relation to the topics and issues we have discussed. The word that we will consider is the adjective *green*; the sketch we present here might give you a starting point for a more detailed treatment of this word, and encourage you to consider other words in a similar way. The more practice you have at using the various resources we have mentioned, the more you will be able to exploit their potential, and the more interesting your investigations will become.

10.3 *Green* as an example

Green is a native English word which has always had a complex and overlapping range of meanings. As we saw in Chapter 7, it has been a BCT since the OE period, when it also had senses relating to plants: it could mean 'verdant, flourishing' (and had more specialised meanings in this semantic area), but also 'fresh', 'unripe' and 'raw'. This is exactly the kind of polysemy we might expect from a BCT, and suggests that the prototype for the colour category is found in the grass or foliage of the natural world. Look at its entry in *DOE*, under the headword *grene*, to see the full range of senses in OE; the etymology section of the *OED* shows that cognate forms in related languages have a similar range of senses. Interestingly, the *HTOED* section in which the colour term appears, 01.04.09.07.04 in the print edition, shows that there are no synonyms in the OE period, although there are a number of compounds for hyponyms of *green* such as *eallgrene* 'bright green'. In fact, synonyms and hyponyms of *green* which are not compounds nor derived forms are not attested until the EModE period, when we find synonyms including *verdant, sinople* and *viricund*. Think about what synonyms and hyponyms are available in PDE (you might like to look at some paint charts for inspiration!), and look at the sections for other BCTs in *HTOED* to see how these compare in different periods.

If we look at the later history of *green* in the *OED* and *MED*, we can see that most of the meanings recorded in OE survive into ME, and there are some interesting semantic developments. *MED* sense (1c) under *grene* defines the colour green specifically 'as symbolic of inconstancy or envy', and this is a sense that we are still familiar with, often in the phrases *green with envy* or *jealousy* (*OED green*, adj., phrase 7), and *the green-eyed monster*, meaning 'jealousy' (*OED green-eyed*). This shows an interesting cultural change, since (as noted in the *OED* at sense 3) traditionally yellow is the colour associated with jealousy. You might like to do some research to find out more about the associations of these colours and others, and the ways in which they have changed historically. You can also trace the way in which envy is expressed onomasiologically by looking at *HTOED*, section 02.02.26 *Jealousy/envy* in the print edition; look out for any colour terms.

The polysemy shown by *green* in different periods exemplifies many of the tendencies in semantic change that we examined in Chapter 5. For example, we noted the sense 'raw' that exists from OE onwards, and the *OED* lists several other specialised senses that develop from this sense by narrowing in (6) 'That has not been prepared or treated for consumption or use', including (6g) 'Of coffee beans: unroasted' (first attested 1761). This use shows the impact of cultural change on the lexicon, since coffee is not a substance that has always been familiar to English speakers (see the *OED* entry for *coffee*). Another branch of meaning shows pejoration: the OE sense 'unripe' seems to give rise to the meanings recorded in (8) 'Immature, undeveloped', which includes neutral senses like (8a) 'Of a thing, esp. something immaterial, such as a thought, plan, etc.: not fully developed or elaborated', attested from around 1300, but also the later, more negative sense (8d) 'Of a person: naive, gullible', attested from 1605. The noun converted from the adjective shows a number of metonymically motivated senses that we might describe as COLOUR FOR MATERIAL/OBJECT, such as 'Money' (1e), 'Green vegetables' (6d, in the plural), and 'In snooker and similar games: a green ball' (12). You might like to compare the polysemous senses of other colour terms in different periods using any of the dictionaries we have mentioned, and see whether they show similar extensions of meaning.

In Chapter 7 we noted that BCTs are particularly likely to show metaphorical extensions of meaning, and *green* is typical in this respect. Going back to the adjective *green*, the *OED* records the sense (4a) 'Designating or relating to a green-coloured signal, such as a light, flag, etc., used to give permission to proceed or to indicate safety', often in the expression *green light*; as a note indicates, this use gives rise to the metaphorical sense of *green light*, 'permission to proceed on a particular course of action', thus showing a combination of metonymy and metaphor. *Green light* is one of many expressions treated as a headword in its own right in the *OED*, and many others are listed and defined 'in special applications' in the entry for *green*. Look through some of these and find out which sense of *green* applies in each case, and see how many other examples of metaphorical uses you can find.

Finally, a very interesting recent development shown by *green* is almost the last sense recorded in the *OED*: 'Of, relating to, or supporting environmentalism, esp. as a political issue' (13a), and the closely related meaning 'Of a product, service, etc.: designed, produced, or operating in a way that minimizes harm to the natural environment' (13b). Can you account for the emergence of this meaning? It appears to have become very frequent in PDE, and one way to gauge its rise in frequency is to examine some of the uses of *green* in corpora that include recent material, such as the Google Books Corpus. Many of these corpora, including all of the Brigham Young University resources, show when particular collocations undergo significant increases in frequency. This can be indicative of the rise of new senses; for example, searching for the most frequent collocate immediately following *green* in both the British and American portions of the Google Books Corpus shows that *green revolution* has a huge rise in frequency from the 1970s onwards. Links to the quotations in different decades show that most uses in the 1970s relate to farming techniques, but more recent quotations from the 2000s commonly use the expression to refer to the environmental movement. Take some time to explore the use of *green* in some of the corpora mentioned at the end of Chapter 4 (see pp. 66–7). You might also find it interesting to compare this meaning of *green* to uses of semantically related terms such as *environmentally-friendly* and *eco-*, and consider the extent to which these are synonymous.

10.4 Looking ahead

Looking to the future, we expect input from Cognitive Linguistics to become an increasingly strong force in Historical Semantics, and for further account to be taken of developments in sister disciplines such as Historical Pragmatics and Historical Sociolinguistics, with their emphasis on social and cultural factors. With the advent of more powerful and sophisticated electronic resources, we also expect the input of Corpus Linguistics to grow in importance, as described below. Work in Psycholinguistics on how meanings are created and stored in our mental lexicons will also generate new ideas. Overall, research in Linguistics, and therefore Historical Linguistics, will continue to benefit from its fuzzy boundaries with other subjects.

New resources may be developed out of those that are already available; for example, the framework devised for *HTOED* could be adapted to create a thesaurus from another historical dictionary. The greater sophistication of electronic resources has already enabled new research questions to be asked, and has suggested new ways of displaying the results.[1] A recently completed project at the University of Glasgow is 'Mapping Metaphor with the Historical Thesaurus', which starts from the premise, discussed in Chapter 9, that metaphor involves the mapping of one domain of experience onto another. Since *HTOED* is already organised in domains, it was possible to use automatic computing routines to identify all the categories where there is lexical overlap, and which might therefore contain metaphorical links, such as the link between intense thinking and physical violence, recorded from the sixteenth century onwards in expressions like *beat, break, cudgel, hammer* or *rack one's brains*. A strong link such as this would suggest the presence of a conceptual metaphor. Of course, computers can't actually recognise metaphors, and a good deal of uninteresting 'noise' was generated at the start of the project by factors such as polysemy and homonymy. These were eliminated by statistical methods and by human coders, who had the last word in deciding whether an expression identified by the computer was metaphorical or not. (This exercise in itself challenged many preconceptions about metaphor – such as historical directionality, the metaphoricity of highly abstract concepts like shape and space, and the metaphor/metonymy boundary – when the coders were faced by historical data in bulk.) The results are presented online in a variety of ways, including a series of 'Metaphor Maps' visualising the category links. As far as metaphor research goes, the 'Mapping Metaphor' data are only a beginning, but the project demonstrates, as others have done, what computers and human beings can achieve together (see further Alexander and Bramwell 2014).

Before computing can really come into its own in historical linguistic research, however, two further substantial problems have to be solved. The first of these is the problem of spelling variation, discussed in Chapter 2. Irregular spelling across the history of English is a challenge for any automatic system which attempts to deal with unedited original texts. Only recently (and to some extent in OE) has English spelling been standardised; if we were to use the *HTOED* database to search for all the words from a particular semantic category in, say, a seventeenth-century text or a text written in Yorkshire dialect, we would miss any variants that we had not trained the computer to recognise. Considerable advances in solving this problem have been made at Lancaster University, which produced the VARD software, a system for analysing and regularising non-standard English texts, particularly in the EModE period. This system has been integrated into the annotation software of the SAMUELS project (Semantic Annotation and Mark-Up for Enhancing Lexical Searches), a research programme carried out jointly by the Universities of Glasgow and Lancaster (Alexander et al. forthcoming 2015). Thanks to the co-operation of Oxford University Press, the system includes the comprehensive database of variant spellings derived from *OED* data files, which contain a large number of both common and rare spellings organised by date.

Overall, our capacity for searching non-standard texts has been greatly enhanced, and along with it our capacity for undertaking Historical Corpus Linguistics on the massive new datasets which are becoming available. A case in point is a project at the Universities of Sheffield, Glasgow and Sussex, 'The Linguistic DNA of Early Modern Thought: Paradigmatic Terms in English, 1500–1800'. Information is extracted from a database of approximately 37 million pages of text and semantic and conceptual patterns are identified in order to aid understanding of the evolution of early modern thought. As with SAMUELS, *HTE* is an integral part of this resource.

The second major problem is that of polysemy and homonymy. As we've seen throughout this book, it is a natural condition of English words to have more than one meaning, sometimes many more. If one is using *HTOED* to search a text for words for weapons, including the word *piece*, it would be useful if the search returned occurrences of *piece* only in that meaning and not the twenty-four other main meanings and many sub-meanings recorded in the *OED* (or the many meanings of its homophone *peace*, with which it shares some spellings). If one were interested only in EModE, it would also be useful to be able to exclude any words in the *HTOED* category which don't occur in that period. In other words, such corpus searches could be executed much more successfully if the words in the text had first been tagged semantically and by date, in the same way as texts can be automatically tagged for parts of speech. The SAMUELS project has produced a semantic tagger, HTST (Historical Thesaurus Semantic Tagger), which performs this function, again building on work done at Lancaster University, which developed the UCREL Semantic Annotation System (USAS) for such a purpose (see Rayson 2008). Other semantic taggers have been developed for different purposes elsewhere, but SAMUELS is the first to adapt the fine-grained semantic hierarchy of *HTOED* for both synchronic and diachronic text searches. Its tagger proceeds on the principle that texts generally have topics, and that senses of words can be determined by tagging them with *HTOED* categories relevant to that topic. For example, in the extract from *Bleak House* at the end of Chapter 6, the word *yard* is polysemous, and would need to be tagged in the meaning of 'an enclosure attached to a prison' (*OED yard*[1], noun 1d) rather than any of its other meanings. The homonym *yard* 'a unit of measurement' would also have to be excluded.

One further outcome of the march of digital humanities may be worth mentioning: the blurring of the lines of demarcation between different kinds of resources. The *OED* is undoubtedly a dictionary, as anyone who has viewed its paper volumes can attest, and yet increasingly it also fulfils the functions of corpus and thesaurus, the first through quotations from texts and the second through its links with *HTOED*. Online access renders the alphabetical format of the traditional dictionary largely redundant, except where the user is interested in morphologically related groups of words. It may well be that the online 'dictionary' of the future will consist of a range of kinds of information, including semantic categorisation, with a facility for searching it in different ways, so that ultimately the user will be able to customise the resource according to his or her current requirements. Tools developed from the ideas discussed above may well form part of such a resource, as will others that have not yet been thought of.

Note

1. Details of how to access the projects discussed below can be found in the References section (pp. 191–9).

Glossary of key terms

achromatic refers to the tone range which in English includes black, white and grey.

acronyms are words composed of initial letters, for example *NATO* for *Northern Atlantic Treaty Organisation*. Sometimes a distinction is made between acronyms, which are pronounced as single words (following the usual rules of English phonology), and initialisms like *BBC* (*British Broadcasting Corporation*) for which each initial letter name is pronounced.

active vocabulary is a term for the vocabulary a speaker normally uses. **Passive vocabulary** is understood by an individual but not frequently used.

affixes are elements which can be attached to the beginning or end of a word (or part of a word) to change the meaning or word class. **Prefixes** attach to the beginning of a word, for example *un-* in *unhappy*, *pseudo-* in *pseudoscience*, and **suffixes** attach to the ends of words, for example *-ment* in *embankment*, *-y* in *tricky*.

amelioration (occasionally called **melioration** or **elevation**) occurs when words acquire more positive connotations, moving either from a negative or neutral meaning to a positive one, or from a negative meaning to a neutral one, for example *sinful* 'full of sin' ameliorating to 'bad, unacceptable', as in *a sinful waste of money*. Contrasted with **pejoration**.

antonymy occurs when two or more words or senses of words (**antonyms**) contrast in one element of their meaning. **Antonymous** words are sometimes divided into sub-types. *Happy* and *sad* are **graded antonyms** or **polar terms** which refer to positions on a scale, in this case a scale of emotions. *True* and *false* are **true antonyms**, also called **binary antonyms** or **complementary terms**, which describe an either/ or situation; something is either one or the other.

archaisms are words or phrases which sound old-fashioned and tend to be used in historical contexts, for example *forsooth* 'in truth', *wireless* 'radio'.

back-formations are verbs formed from nouns rather than vice versa because these nouns appear to be suffixed (although historically are not), for example *burgle* from *burglar*, *edit* from *editor*.

basic colour categories (**BCCs**) are the principal divisions of the colour space which underlie the **basic colour terms** (**BCTs**) of a particular speech community. A BCC is an abstract concept which operates independently of things described by terms such as *green* or *yellow*. BCCs are presented in small capital letters, for example GREEN. See also **macro-categories**.

basic colour terms (**BCTs**) are the words which languages use to name basic colour categories. A BCT, such as *green* or *yellow*, is known to all members of a speech community and is used in a wide range of contexts. Other colour words in a language are called **non-basic terms**, for example *sapphire*, *scarlet* or *auburn*.

binary antonyms see **antonymy**

bleaching see **grammaticalisation**

blends are words formed from the initial part of one word and the final part of another (which sometimes have some shared sounds or syllables), such as *smog* from *smoke + fog*, *metrosexual* from *metropolitan + heterosexual*.

borrowing is the process by which words (**loanwords**) or senses of words from one language are adopted by another, for example *chic* from French, *brother* 'member of a religious order' on the model of Latin *frater*. The form or pronunciation of a borrowed word is often naturalised in the borrowing language over time so that it looks or sounds more like a native word, for example *beef* from Old French *boef*, *potato* from Spanish *patata*.

brightness refers to the amount of light contributed to a colour impression by an object producing or reflecting light.

broadening see **widening**

categorisation is the process by which people group similar things together under a shared name. **Basic level categories** are those, such as *Chair* or *Anger*, which people most readily use to conceptualise and name things in their interaction with the world around them. They are contrasted with more general **superordinate categories**, such as *Furniture* or *Emotion*, and more specific **hyponymic categories**, such as *Armchair* or *Rage*.

chaining describes the development of a **polysemous** word form which has semantically linked senses, for example *attractive* from literal meanings of 'absorbing' or 'pulling towards' to more abstract meanings of 'inspiring admiration, affection, sympathy', etc. Also called radiation.

citations are quotations in a dictionary that exemplify a defined sense of a word.

classical categorisation theory is associated with Aristotle's theory of categorisation, where category membership is clear-cut and binary. Membership is based on a set of criteria, **necessary conditions**, which all members must fulfil and which together constitute **sufficient conditions** for category membership. Thus, in order to be a member of the category of *Aunts*, someone must be female and the sister of a parent. All members of a category are equal, with no better or worse examples. Contrasted with **prototype theory**.

clipped (cut) describes a word form that has been shortened, for example *uni* for *university*, *phone* for *telephone*.

clippings (abbreviations) are **clipped** word forms.

cognate describes either forms or languages that share a common source, for example English *flower*, French *fleur* and Italian *fiore*, or the English, German and Dutch languages.

Cognitive Linguistics is a discipline which combines insights from linguistics and psychology, focusing on the connection between mental processes and the production and understanding of language.

Cognitive Semantics is a branch of Cognitive Linguistics and is particularly concerned with categorisation and the relationship between meaning and thought.

co-hyponym see **hyponymy**

collocations are strings in which particular words occur together or **collocate**, for example *salt and pepper*, *environmentally friendly*; these words are known as **collocates** or sometimes **collocators**.

colour in the technical language of Colour Studies denotes all the elements which combine to create a particular colour experience, including **hue**, **saturation**, **brightness** and **tone**.

common refers to the ancestor language of words that occur in various forms in a group of related languages; for example English *go* and *staff* can be traced back to **Common Germanic**.

complementary terms see **antonymy**

components are units of meaning smaller than a word, for example [+human] is a component of the meaning of *man* and *woman*. **Componential Analysis** (**CA**) uses components to formulate semantic distinctions.

composite categories see **macro-categories**

compounding is the process by which two (or occasionally more) independent words are joined to make a new form or **compound**, for example *phonebox* from *phone + box*.

conceptual domains (sometimes called **conceptual fields**) are areas of experience in the external world, such as farming or pleasure, which provide reference points for the language used to discuss them.

conceptual metaphors are metaphors which are systematic in that they are found in many different linguistic expressions; for example, the conceptual metaphor TIME IS A PHYSICAL SUBSTANCE is reflected in the expressions *have time, save time* and *waste time*.

connotative meaning is opposed to **denotative meaning** and refers to meaning that varies according to factors such as speaker and social context, where the **connotations** of a word are said to differ.

constant reference is a property of words or phrases that refer to a unique entity, for example *Dubai, Eric Cantona*.

conventional metaphors or **metonymies** are metaphors or metonymies which have been established in the linguistic system for some time and might not be noticeable to speakers because they are so frequently used, for example *see* 'understand'.

converse terms or **conversives** are **antonyms** which denote a reciprocal relationship, for example *over/under, sister/brother*.

conversion occurs when one part of speech is 'converted' to use as another; for example, the noun *access* can be used as a verb (*to access information*).

core vocabulary is the basic vocabulary of everyday life which is known by most speakers, used in most contexts, and likely to remain stable over long periods of time.

degeneration see **pejoration**

denotative meaning is opposed to **connotative meaning** and refers to a word's **denotation** or basic core meaning, which is generally agreed by speakers of a language and appears in dictionaries. Contrasted with **connotation**.

derivation is the process by which a word is created or **derived** from a historically earlier word or **root**. The derivation of ModE *right*, for example, is OE *riht*.

descriptivism is the view that linguists should be concerned with describing how language is used rather than prescribing 'correct' usage. Contrasted with **prescriptivism**.

deterioration see **pejoration**

diachrony refers to the study of the **diachronic** development of language, i.e. its development over time. Contrasted with **synchrony**.

Discourse Analysis, also called **Text Linguistics**, is the academic discipline concerned with the study of linguistic relationships within texts.

domain see **conceptual domains**

domain matrix see **profiling**

dysphemism occurs when a serious or frightening topic is treated in an inappropriately light-hearted way, for example *bite the dust* for *die*.

elevation see **amelioration**

entailments are the correspondences between aspects of a source and target in a metaphorical mapping; for example, the metaphor ARGUMENT IS WAR, found linguistically in expressions like *we fought on every point* and *she wouldn't back down*, has entailments including THE PEOPLE ARGUING ARE OPPONENTS IN CONFLICT and BEING PERSUADED IS DEFEAT IN BATTLE.

eponymous forms come from trade-names or the names of inventors or famous people, for example *escalator, hoover, scrooge*.

etymology can refer either to the study of the origins of words or to an account of the history of a particular word.

etymon refers to a word from which another word has developed, for example ModE *heavenly* from its OE etymon *heofon* 'heaven' + the suffix -*lic*.

euphemism occurs when an unpleasant or taboo topic is named by a word (a **euphemism**) which disguises its unpleasant aspects, for example *little girls' room* for 'lavatory'.

evolutionary sequence is a formula which claims to display the order in which **basic colour categories** are likely to develop in different languages, as revealed by the identification of their **basic colour terms**.

expert taxonomies are systems of classification devised by people with specialised knowledge such as scientists. As in **classical categorisation theory**, membership is on an either/or basis. Contrasted with **folk taxonomies**.

fade-out describes the fact that our knowledge of a system, such as kinship, tends to disappear as that system loses salience in our lives.

folk taxonomies are systems of classification based on the way things are perceived and grouped together in everyday life. A **folk taxonomy** of a conceptual domain such as *Animals* or *Plants* is likely to differ from an **expert taxonomy** of the same topic.

frame is the term used for the body of knowledge speakers need in order to understand and produce the language used in particular situations such as 'shopping in a supermarket'. Frames are described in **scripts**, which set out the necessary contextual and linguistic information.

fuzzy set theory introduced the idea that categories have a clear core but less clear boundaries. Members of categories thus range from best examples to least good examples.

generalisation see **widening**

graded antonyms see **antonymy**

grammaticalisation occurs when a word loses some of its semantic content and becomes part of the grammatical system, for example the modal auxiliary verbs *can* and *must*. A more general term for loss of semantic content, like that which has affected the adjectives *awesome* and *ghastly*, is **bleaching**.

headword refers to the word at the beginning of a dictionary entry, which the entry defines and describes.

holonym see **meronymy**

homographs are words which are spelled the same but pronounced differently, for example *minute* of time and *minute* 'small'.

homonymy occurs when words share the same form but derive from different roots, for example the **homonyms** *fair* 'pretty' and *fair* 'a market'. **Homonymic clash** occurs when the meanings of homonyms are likely to be confused in context; in such cases one or more senses of a homonym may undergo semantic change or die out. **Homographs** and **homophones** are sub-types of homonyms. Contrasted with **polysemy**.

homophones are words which are pronounced the same but spelled differently, for example *flour* and *flower*, *great* and *grate*.

hue in the technical language of colour studies is one of the elements which make up **colour**. **Hue** refers to the range of different impressions perceived on the spectrum of visible light, designated by both **BCT**s and **non-basic terms**, for example *green, blue, indigo, violet*.

hyperonym see **hyponymy**

hyponymy or **inclusion** refers to the relationship between the general and the specific which occurs in hierarchies of meaning represented by words such as *animal, mammal, cow*, where *animal* is the **superordinate** or **hyperonym** and *mammal* and *cow* are **hyponyms** in a **hyponymous** or **hyponymic** relationship to it. **Co-hyponyms** are words which occur at the same level in a hierarchy of meanings, for example *apple, pear* and *banana* in a category of *Fruit*. They are variously referred to as **contiguous**, **partially synonymous** or **incompatible** terms.

image metaphors are metaphors motivated by visible similarities between **source** and **target**, such as similarities of shape or size; for example, a *finger* of toast, a *carpet* of flowers.

Indo-European is a large language family stretching from India to Europe. One of its branches is **Germanic**, which includes English, Dutch, Frisian, German and the Scandinavian languages.

invited inferencing occurs when an utterance has a possible meaning in context that is more than the surface meaning of the individual words; for example, *He fainted when you arrived* invites the interpretation 'He fainted because you arrived'.

kennings are metaphorical compounds found in OE poetry, for example *hwælweg* 'whale + way = the sea'.

lexeme see **word**

lexical field see **semantic domains**

lexical gaps occur when a language lacks a word or established phrase to express a concept. The lack may become apparent when new objects or ideas are introduced, or when a foreign word or phrase with no native equivalent is conventionally used, for example *rendezvous*.

lexical item see **word**

Lexical Semantics is the academic discipline concerned with the study of word meaning in its various aspects.

lexical sets are groups of words relating to aspects of particular areas of experience. They combine to form **semantic fields**, as, for example, the set of cooking terms contributes to the field of *Food*.

lexicalisation refers to the situation where a language already has or acquires a word or established phrase to express a concept. Cultural change may lead to new concepts being lexicalised.

lexicon is sometimes used as a synonym for *dictionary* or for any systematic presentation of vocabulary, such as a **thesaurus**; it is also used to mean the complete vocabulary of a language. **Mental lexicon** is used to describe an individual's vocabulary.

linguistic determinism see **Sapir-Whorf Hypothesis**

linguistic relativity see **Sapir-Whorf Hypothesis**

linguistic universals are features that are so fundamental to human thought and experience that we might reasonably expect to find them in all languages. It would, for example, be strange to find a language that had no way of expressing negation.

loanword see **borrowing**

macro-categories or **composite categories** are broader than **basic colour categories**. They occur when speakers perceive groups of similar hues, such as red, brown, orange, pink and purple, as belonging to a single category and refer to it by a single **basic colour term**.

mapping refers to a link between two concepts which involves 'projecting' aspects of one onto the other, so that it is described or thought of in terms of that concept; for example, the metaphor *fight* 'argue' **maps** physical conflict onto verbal disagreement, so that verbal disagreement is described and thought of as physical conflict.

melioration see **amelioration**

meronymy refers to the relationship between wholes and parts, as in *finger* and *thumb* being **meronyms** of the **holonym** *hand*, which refers to the whole.

metalanguage is the technical terminology used to discuss a subject.

metaphor refers to a type of **mapping** between two concepts, often based on a perceived similarity between the **source** and **target**, or some association in basic human experience, for example *monkey* 'cheeky child', *I see* 'I understand'.

metaphorical polysemy is polysemy triggered by **metaphor** where both the literal and the metaphorical meanings survive, for example *carrot* 'vegetable, reward'.

metonymical polysemy is polysemy triggered by **metonymy** where both the literal and the metonymical meanings survive, for example *glass* 'material, drinking vessel'.

metonymy refers to a type of **mapping** between two concepts where one is used to refer to the other because they are associated in experience, for example *the crown* 'the monarch', *an elegant wardrobe* 'elegant clothes'.

monosemy occurs when a word is a **monoseme** with a single sense. Contrasted with **polysemy**.

monosyllabic words consist of a single syllable.

morphemes are linguistic units which cannot be analysed into smaller meaningful units. The word *outlandish* consists of three morphemes, *out-land-ish*. **Morphology** refers either to the study of morphemes or to the morphological structure of individual words.

motivation refers to the basis or explanation for a metaphorical or metonymical **mapping**, or for any kind of semantic change; for example, the metaphor *mouse* 'shy person' is **motivated** by a perceived similarity between the behaviour of mice and that of shy people.

narrowing or **specialisation** occurs when the meaning of a word (or of one of its senses) becomes more restricted and specific over time, for example *meat* 'food' narrowing to mean 'flesh'.

necessary conditions see **classical categorisation theory**

non-basic colour terms see **basic colour terms**

Old Norse (ON) was the language spoken by the Scandinavian invaders of Britain.

onomasiology is concerned with the form or forms used to express a particular meaning. A conceptually organised **thesaurus** can be described as **onomasiological**. Contrasted with **semasiology**.

ontological metaphors are metaphors in which the targets – abstract states, processes or relations – are 'seen as' physical entities with substance that can be manipulated, for example TIME IS A PHYSICAL SUBSTANCE, UNDERSTANDING IS GRASPING.

opaque see **transparent**

ostensive definition occurs when a speaker points to something and says the word used to refer to it, i.e. defines it by giving an example.

overstatement (**hyperbole**) is used to draw attention to something by using exaggerated language, for example by saying *I loathe tomatoes* when you merely dislike eating them.

paradigmatic relationships are formed by items which can occur in the same position in a grammatical structure, as many adjectives can in the frame *The _____ woman looked up*. Contrasted with **syntagmatic** relationships.

passive vocabulary see **active vocabulary**

pejoration (sometimes called **deterioration** or **degeneration**) occurs when words acquire more negative connotations, moving either from a neutral or positive meaning to a negative one, or from a positive meaning to a neutral one, for example *peasant* 'agricultural worker' pejorating to 'unsophisticated person'. Contrasted with **amelioration**.

polar terms see **antonymy**

polysemy occurs when a single form has two or more senses, all deriving from the same root, for example the many meanings (**polysemes**) of the **polysemous** form *book* which have developed during the course of its history. If there is a risk of polysemes being confused in context, one or more of them may undergo semantic change or die out. Contrasted with **monosemy** and **homonymy**.

polysyllabic words have more than one syllable.

Pragmatics is the academic discipline concerned with the study of language in everyday interaction.

prefix see **affixes**

prescriptivism is the view that language use should be regulated in order to exclude 'incorrect' usage. Contrasted with **descriptivism**.

productive is a term applied to linguistic processes which are still in use at a given time. In ModE, for example, the processes of affixation and compounding are still productive in creating new words.

profiling refers to imposing structure on a conceptual domain in order to present information in a particular way. The various ways in which a domain can be profiled are referred to as its **domain matrix**. Any particular profile of a domain is referred to as a **schema**.

proto- is attached to the names of languages and language families to indicate their earliest form, whether attested or reconstructed.

prototype refers to the best or most typical example of a category. When confronted with potential members of a category, we judge them consciously or unconsciously by their **prototypicality** or degree of likeness to central members. Thus for many speakers an apple would be a more **prototypical** example of the category *Fruit* than a pomegranate. This approach to categorisation is known as **prototype theory** and is contrasted with **classical categorisation theory**. **Prototype effects** recognised by speakers include degrees of category membership and the **fuzzy** nature of category boundaries. Where a form develops more than one meaning in the course of its history, **prototype split** is said to have taken place.

radiation see **chaining**

reference is the relationship between the words we use (**referring expressions**) and the things we are talking about (the **referents** of the words).

reflex refers to the surviving form of an earlier form, for example ModE *heaven* is the reflex of OE *heofon*. Reflexes often have different meanings from their earlier forms.

register is the language appropriate for use in a particular context. *I was proceeding towards the entrance* would be acceptable in a formal or legal register, but less so in the register of colloquial speech.

root refers to the ultimate source of a word, which may itself be a word (an **etymon**) or a unit smaller than a word (a **morpheme**). The root of OE *fisc* 'fish' lies in Common Germanic and is the base from which ModE words such as *fish*, *fishy* and *fisherman* are formed.

salience is roughly synonymous with *prominence* or *importance*. Languages often have detailed vocabularies for things that are **salient** in the lives of their speakers.

Sapir-Whorf Hypothesis refers to views on the relationship between language and culture arising from the work of Edward Sapir and Benjamin Lee Whorf. Most discussions make a distinction between **linguistic determinism**, the view that language imposes categories on the world, and **linguistic relativity**, the weaker claim that languages reflect the world-views of their speakers.

saturation refers to purity of **hue**, for example a fully-saturated, vivid blue compared with a dull, greyish blue.

schema see **profiling**

script see **frame**

semantic change refers to change in the meaning or meanings of a word in the course of its history.

semantic domains are large groupings of words related to a particular area of experience, for example the vocabulary of *Sport or Education*. These are also called **lexical fields** or **semantic fields**, although sometimes these terms refer particularly to groupings of words structured by **sense relationships**.

semantic field see **semantic domains**

semantic space is a way of conceptualising the vocabulary of a language as objects occupying a metaphorical space.

semasiology is concerned with the meaning or meanings attached to individual word forms. An alphabetically-organised dictionary, listing forms and definitions, can be described as **semasiological**. Contrasted with **onomasiology**.

sense refers to the meaning or one of the meanings of a word, as in 'the six main senses of the noun *carpet* in the *OED*'. It also refers to the connections (**sense relationships**) which words have with other words in the language system such as their **synonyms** or **antonyms**.

Sociolinguistics is the academic discipline concerned with the study of language use among different groups in society.

source (or **vehicle**) in a metaphor or metonymy refers to the concept **mapped** onto, or used to talk or think about, something else (the **target**); for example, in the metaphorical expression *you are an angel*, *angel* is the source.

specialisation see **narrowing**

stem refers to the part of a word which remains unchanged when affixes are added. Thus *place* is the stem in words such as *placing*, *placed* and *replace*.

stereotype refers to a list of typical features, or an imagined entity with those features, which can be abstracted from a **prototype** and used in assessing category membership.

Structuralism refers to an approach to Linguistics associated with the work of Ferdinand de Saussure. **Structuralist** Semantics views word meanings as forming semantic networks.

sufficient conditions see **classical categorisation theory**

suffix see **affixes**

superordinate see **hyponymy**

synchrony refers to the study of language at a single stage in its development. **Synchronic** research takes no account of what led up to or followed this stage. Contrasted with **diachrony**.

synecdoche is the traditional term for **metonymies** where a part stands for the whole or the whole for a part, for example *his career on the stage* ('in the theatrical profession') or *the theatre was good to him* ('the institution of the theatre').

synonymy occurs when two or more words or senses of words (**synonyms**) share all or most of their meaning. Truly **synonymous** words (true or perfect synonyms) are extremely rare. Even pairs like *radio* and *wireless*, which refer to the same object, are differentiated by the contexts in which they are used.

syntagmatic relationships are formed by items, often referred to as **collocates**, which occur together in a grammatical structure, for example *boy* and *kicked* and *kicked* and *ball* in the sentence *The boy kicked the ball*. Contrasted with **paradigmatic** relationships.

systemic regulation occurs when a language changes in order to accommodate new developments, as when the introduction of a new word leads to change in the meaning of one or more existing words.

target (or **tenor**) in a metaphor or metonymy refers to the concept which is described in terms of something else (the **source**); for example, in the metonymical expression *I like your wheels* 'I like your car', 'car' is the target.

Text Linguistics see **Discourse Analysis**

thesaurus is the term applied to a book of words organised according to the concepts they express, for example *Roget's Thesaurus of English Words and Phrases*.

tone refers to the amount of black or white which is perceived as being involved with a **hue** in a visual impression, for example *pale* or *light green* compared with *dark green*.

transparent describes words such as **compounds** when the meaning of the whole is obvious from the meaning of the parts, for example *toast-rack* 'a rack in which to put toast'. Where the meaning is not obvious, as in *paperback* 'a book with a soft cover', it is described as **opaque**.

true antonyms see **antonymy**

understatement (**litotes**) is used to downplay the seriousness of a situation, for example by saying *Mary is a bit upset* when in fact she is extremely angry.

variable reference is a property of words or phrases that refer to sets of referents, for example *mouse, village*.

vogue expressions are those which pass quickly in and out of fashion.

widening (sometimes called **broadening** or **generalisation**) occurs when the meaning of a word (or of one of its senses) becomes more general over time, so that it can be used to refer to a broader, less specific concept, for example *bird* 'young bird' widening to mean 'bird (of any age)'.

word is notoriously difficult to define as a technical term of Linguistics despite being unproblematic in everyday language. In this book we define it as a linguistic unit which expresses a single concept (or group of concepts). In most cases, such units are single forms, separated from each other by spaces in modern typography. Sometimes, however, they may be multiword expressions such as phrases (*in fact*) or idioms (*pleased as punch*). Some writers use the term **lexeme** to cover both single and multiword forms. Others use **lexeme** in a more abstract way to refer to the base form of a word (*walk*) and any inflected or derived forms (*walked, walking, walker, walkway*). The accompanying term for each realisation of the base form is **lexical item**.

References

1. Dictionaries and thesauruses

An American Dictionary of the English Language (1828), ed. Noah Webster, New York: S. Converse.

Anglo-Norman Dictionary (*AND*) (2nd edn 2005–), general editor William Rothwell; ed. Stewart Gregory, William Rothwell and David Trotter, London: Maney, http://www.anglo-norman.net/

A Concise Anglo-Saxon Dictionary ([1894] 1960), ed. J. R. Clark Hall, Toronto: University of Toronto Press.

A Dictionary of Canadianisms on Historical Principles Online (2013), based on Avis et al. (1967), ed. Stefan Dollinger, Laurel J. Brinton and Margery Fee, http://dchp.ca/DCHP-1/

A Dictionary of the English Language (1755), ed. Samuel Johnson, London.

Dictionary of Old English A-G (*DOE*) (2008), ed. Angus Cameron, Ashley Crandell Amos, Antonette diPaolo Healey et al., Toronto: Pontifical Institute of Mediaeval Studies, http://www.doe.utoronto.ca; also available to subscribers to the *OED* website.

A Dictionary of the Older Scottish Tongue (*DOST*) (1931–2002), ed. William A. Craigie, A. J. Aitken, J. A. C. Stevenson, H. D. Watson and M. G. Dareau, Oxford: Oxford University Press.

Dictionary of the Scots Language (*DSL*), http://www.dsl.ac.uk

Dictionary of Selected Synonyms in the Principal Indo-European Languages ([1949] 1988), ed. Carl Darling Buck, Chicago and London: University of Chicago Press.

An Essay Towards a Real Character, and a Philosophical Language ([1668] 1968), by John Wilkins, Menston: Scolar Press.

Historical Thesaurus of English (*HTE*), www.glasgow.ac.uk/thesaurus

Historical Thesaurus of the Oxford English Dictionary (*HTOED*) (2009), ed. Christian Kay, Jane Roberts, Michael Samuels and Irené Wotherspoon, 2 vols, Oxford: Oxford University Press, www.glasgow.ac.uk/thesaurus; also available to subscribers to the *OED* website.

Middle English Dictionary (*MED*) (1956–2001), ed. H. Kurath, S. M. Kuhn and R. Lewis, Ann Arbor: University of Michigan Press, http://quod.lib.umich.edu/m/med/; also available to subscribers to the *OED* website.

Oxford Advanced Learner's Dictionary (2000), ed. A. S. Hornby and Sally Wehmeier, Oxford: Oxford University Press.

Oxford Dictionary of English (*ODE*) (2010), ed. Angus Stevenson, Oxford: Oxford University Press and Oxford Dictionaries Online.

Oxford Dictionaries Online, http://www.oxforddictionaries.com

The Oxford English Dictionary (*OED*), ed. Sir James A. H. Murray, Henry Bradley, Sir William A. Craigie and Charles T. Onions 1884–1928. *Supplement and Bibliography* 1933. *Supplement* 1972–1986, ed. Robert W. Burchfield. 2nd edn 1989, ed. John A. Simpson and Edmund S. C. Weiner. *Additions Series* 1993–1997, ed. John A. Simpson, Edmund S. C. Weiner and Michael Proffitt, Oxford: Oxford University Press. 3rd edn (in progress) *OED Online*, March 2000–, ed. John A. Simpson (2000–2013), Michael Proffitt (2013–), www.oed.com

Roget's Thesaurus of English Words and Phrases. 150th Anniversary Edition (*Roget*) ([1852] 2002), ed. George W. Davidson, London: Penguin.

The Scottish National Dictionary (*SND*) (1931–1976), ed. William Grant and David Murison, Edinburgh: Scottish National Dictionary Association.

A Table Alphabeticall, Conteyning and Teaching the True Writing, and Understanding of Hard Usuall English Words ([1604] 1997), by Robert Cawdrey, ed. Raymond E. Siemens, Toronto: University of Toronto Library, http://www.library.utoronto.ca/utel/ret/cawdrey/cawdrey0.html

A Thesaurus of Old English (*TOE*) ([1995] 2000), ed. Jane Roberts and Christian Kay with Lynne Grundy, Amsterdam: Rodopi, http://oldenglishthesaurus.arts.gla.ac.uk/

2. Online corpora and websites

British National Corpus http://corpus.byu.edu/bnc/

Corpus of Contemporary American English (COCA) http://corpus.byu.edu/coca/

Corpus of Historical American English (COHA) http://corpus.byu.edu/coha/

Corpus of Modern Scottish Writing (CMSW) http://www.scottishcorpus.ac.uk/cmsw/

Corpus Resource Database (CoRD) http://www.helsinki.fi/varieng/CoRD/corpora/HelsinkiCorpus/

Early English Books Online (EEBO) http://eebo.chadwyck.com/

Google Books Corpus http://googlebooks.byu.edu/

Hansard http://www.parliament.uk/business/publications/hansard/ and http://hansard.millbanksystems.com (Historic Hansard)

Internet Shakespeare Editions http://internetshakespeare.uvic.ca/

Learning with the Online Thesaurus of Old English http://www.gla.ac.uk/schools/critical/research/fundedresearchprojects/learningwiththeonlinethesaurusofoldenglish/

A Linguistic Atlas of Late Mediaeval English (LALME) http://www.lel.ed.ac.uk/ihd/elalme/elalme.html

The Linguistic DNA of Early Modern Thought: Paradigmatic Terms in English, 1500–1800 http://hridigital.shef.ac.uk/linguistic-dna-of-modern-thought

Mapping Metaphor with Historical Thesaurus of English http://www.gla.ac.uk/metaphor

SAMUELS (Semantic Annotation and Mark-Up for Enhancing Lexical Searches) http://www.glasgow.ac.uk/samuels

Scottish Corpus of Text and Speech (SCOTS) http://www.scottishcorpus.ac.uk

TIME Magazine Corpus of American English http://corpus.byu.edu/time/

World Color Survey http://www1.icsi.berkeley.edu/wcs/

Word Webs: Exploring English vocabulary http://www.glasgow.ac.uk/word webs

WordNet http://wordnet.princeton.edu/

3. Books and articles

Adams, Michael (ed.) (2010), *Cunning Passages, Contrived Corridors: Unexpected Essays in the History of Lexicography*, Monza: Polimetrica.

Alexander, Marc (2010), 'The Various Forms of Civilization Arranged in Chronological Strata: Manipulating the *HTOED*', in Adams (ed.), 309–24.

Alexander, Marc (2015), 'Words and Dictionaries', in *The Oxford Handbook of the Word*, John R. Taylor (ed.), Oxford: Oxford University Press, 38–52.

Alexander, Marc and Ellen Bramwell (2014), 'Mapping Metaphors of Wealth and Want', in *Studies in the Digital Humanities* 1, Clare Mills, Michael Pidd and Esther Ward (eds), http://www.hrionline.ac.uk/openbook/chapter/dhc2012-alexander

Alexander, Marc and Christian Kay (2014), 'The Spread of RED in the Historical Thesaurus of English', in Anderson et al. (eds), 126–39.

Alexander, Marc, Fraser Dallachy, Scott Piao, Alistair Baron and Paul Rayson (forthcoming 2015), 'Metaphor, Popular Science and Semantic Tagging: Distant Reading with the Historical Thesaurus of English', *Digital Scholarship in the Humanities*.

Allan, Kathryn (2008), *Metaphor and Metonymy: A Diachronic Approach* (Publications of the Philological Society 42), Chichester: Wiley-Blackwell.

Allan, Kathryn (2010), 'Tracing Metonymic Polysemy through Time: MATERIAL FOR OBJECT Mappings in the *OED*', in Winters et al. (eds), 163–96.

Allan, Kathryn (2012), 'Using *OED* Data as Evidence', in Allan and Robinson (eds), 17–39.

Allan, Kathryn (2013), 'An Inquest into Metaphor Death: Exploring the Loss of Literal Senses of Conceptual Metaphors', *Cognitive Semiotics* 5.1–2: 291–311.

Allan, Kathryn and Justyna A. Robinson (eds) (2012), *Current Methods in Historical Semantics*, Berlin and Boston: De Gruyter Mouton.

Anderson, Earl R. (1997), 'The Seasons of the Year in Old English', *Anglo-Saxon England* 26, 231–63.

Anderson, Earl R. (2003), *Folk-taxonomies in Early English*, Madison, NJ: Fairleigh Dickinson University Press.

Anderson, Wendy and Ellen Bramwell (2014), 'A Metaphorical Spectrum: Surveying Colour Terms in English', in Anderson et al. (eds), 140–52.

Anderson, Wendy and John Corbett (2009), *Exploring English with Online Corpora: An Introduction*, London: Palgrave Macmillan.

Anderson, Wendy, Carole P. Biggam, Carole Hough and Christian Kay (eds) (2014), *Colour Studies: A Broad Spectrum*, Amsterdam and Philadelphia: Benjamins.

Barber, Charles, Joan C. Beal and Philip A. Shaw (2009, 2nd edn), *The English Language: A Historical Introduction*, Cambridge and New York: Cambridge University Press.

Battig, William F. and William E. Montague (1969), 'Category Norms for Verbal Items in 56 Categories', *Journal of Experimental Psychology* Monograph 80: 3, 2.

Baugh, Albert C. and Thomas Cable (2013, 6th edn), *A History of the English Language*, London: Routledge.

Bergs, Alexander and Laurel J. Brinton (eds) (2012), *The Historical Linguistics of English: An International Handbook*, vol. 1, Berlin: Mouton de Gruyter.

Berlin, Brent and Paul Kay (1969), *Basic Color Terms: Their Universality and Evolution*, Berkeley: University of California Press.

Biggam, C. P. (1993), 'Aspects of Chaucer's Adjectives of Hue', *Chaucer Review* 28.1: 41–53.

Biggam, C. P. (1997), *Blue in Old English: An Interdisciplinary Semantic Study*, Costerus New Series 110, Amsterdam and Atlanta: Rodopi.

Biggam, C. P. (1998), *Grey in Old English: An Interdisciplinary Semantic Study*, London: Runetree Press.

Biggam, C. P. (2010), 'The Development of the Basic Colour Terms of English', in *Interfaces between Language and Culture in Medieval England: A Festschrift for Matti Kilpiö*, Alaric Hall, Olga Timofeeva, Ágnes Kiricsi and Bethany Fox (eds), The Northern World 48, Leiden and Boston: Brill, 231–66.

Biggam, C. P. (2012), *The Semantics of Colour: A Historical Approach*, Cambridge: Cambridge University Press.

Biggam, C. P. (2014), 'Prehistoric Colour Semantics: A Contradiction in Terms', in Anderson et al. (eds), 3–28.

Brewer, Charlotte (2007), *Treasure-House of the Language: The Living OED*, New Haven, CT: Yale University Press.

Burnley, David (2000, 2nd edn), *The History of the English Language: A Source Book*, Harlow: Longman.

Burnley, J. D. (= Burnley, David) (1976), 'Middle English Colour Terminology and Lexical Structure', *Linguistische Berichte* 41: 39–49.

Cruse, Alan (2006), *A Glossary of Semantics and Pragmatics*, Edinburgh: Edinburgh University Press.

Cruse, D. A. (= Cruse, Alan) (1986), *Lexical Semantics*, Cambridge: Cambridge University Press.

Crystal, David (2014), *Words in Time and Place*, Oxford: Oxford University Press.

Davies, R. T. (1966), *Medieval English Lyrics: A Critical Anthology*, London: Faber & Faber.

Deutscher, Guy ([2010] 2011), *Through the Language Glass: Why the World Looks Different in Other Languages*, London: Arrow Books.

Durkin, Philip (2009), *The Oxford Guide to Etymology*, Oxford: Oxford University Press.

Durkin, Philip (2014), *Borrowed Words: A History of Loanwords in English*, Oxford: Oxford University Press.

Fischer, Andreas (1994), '"Sumer is icumen in": The Seasons of the Year in Middle English and Early Modern English', in *Studies in Early Modern English*, D. Kastovsky (ed.), Berlin and New York: Mouton de Gruyter, 79–95.

Fischer, Andreas (2002), 'Notes on Kinship Terminology in the History of English', in *Of Dyuersitie & Chaunge of Langage: Essays Presented to Manfred Görlach on the Occasion of his 65th Birthday*, Katja Lenz and Ruth Möhlig (eds), Heidelberg: Winter, 115–28.

Fischer, Andreas (2004), '"Non olet": Euphemisms We Live by', in *New Perspectives on English Historical Linguistics, vol. 2: Lexis and Transmission*, Christian Kay, Carole Hough and Irené Wotherspoon (eds), Amsterdam: Benjamins, 91–107.

Fischer, Andreas (2006), 'Of *fæderan* and *eamas*: Avuncularity in Old English', in *The Power of Words: Essays in Lexicography, Lexicology and Semantics in Honour of Christian J. Kay*, Graham D. Caie, Carole Hough and Irené Wotherspoon (eds), Amsterdam and New York: Rodopi, 67–77.

Geeraerts, Dirk (1997), *Diachronic Prototype Semantics*, Oxford: Clarendon Press.

Geeraerts, Dirk (2006), *Words and Other Wonders: Papers on Lexical and Semantic Topics*, Berlin: Mouton de Gruyter.

Geeraerts, Dirk (2010), *Theories of Lexical Semantics*, Oxford: Oxford University Press.

Geeraerts, Dirk and Stefan Grondelaers (1995), 'Looking back at Anger: Cultural Traditions and Metaphorical Patterns', in *Language and the Construal of the World*, John Taylor and Robert E. MacLaury (eds), Berlin: Mouton de Gruyter, 153–80.

Gevaert, Caroline (2002), 'The Evolution of the Lexical and Conceptual field of ANGER in Old and Middle English', in *A Changing World of Words: Studies in English Historical Semantics and Lexis*, Javier E. Diaz-Vera (ed.), Amsterdam: Rodopi, 275–99.

Goody, Jack (1983), *The Development of the Family and Marriage in Europe*, Cambridge: Cambridge University Press.

Goossens, Louis (1990), 'Metaphtonomy: The Interaction of Metaphor and Metonymy in Expressions for Linguistic Action', *Cognitive Linguistics* 1.3: 323–40.

Grady, Joseph E. (1997), 'Foundations of Meaning: Primary Metaphors and Primary Scenes', PhD thesis, University of California.

Hamilton, Rachael (2014), 'Exploring the Metaphorical Use of Colour with the

Historical Thesaurus of English: A Case Study of Purple and Lavender', in Anderson et al. (eds), 153–66.

Handl, Sandra (2011), *The Conventionality of Figurative Language: A Usage-Based Study*, Tübingen: Narr Verlag.

Hough, Carole (2012), 'Linguistic Levels: Onomastics', in Bergs and Brinton (eds), 212–23.

Hughes, Geoffrey (1988), *Words in Time: A Social History of the English Vocabulary*, Oxford: Blackwell.

Hughes, Geoffrey (2000), *A History of English Words*, Oxford: Blackwell.

Jackson, Howard and Etienne Zé Amvela (2000), *Words, Meaning, and Vocabulary: An Introduction to Modern English Lexicology*, London and New York: Continuum.

Jucker, Andreas and Irma Taavitsainen (2013), *English Historical Pragmatics*, Edinburgh: Edinburgh University Press.

Kay, Christian (2000), 'Historical Semantics and Historical Lexicography: Will the Twain Ever Meet?', in *Lexicology, Semantics and Lexicography in English Historical Linguistics: Selected Papers from the Fourth G. L. Brook Symposium*, Julie Coleman and Christian Kay (eds), Amsterdam: Benjamins, 53–68.

Kay, Christian (2010), 'Classification: Principles and Practice', in Adams (ed.), 255–70.

Kay, Christian (2012), 'Old English: Semantics and Lexicon', in Bergs and Brinton (eds), 313–25.

Kay, Christian (2013), 'Footprints from the Past: The Survival of Scots Kinship Terms', in *Language in Scotland: Corpus-based Studies*, Wendy Anderson (ed.), Amsterdam: Rodopi, 145–65.

Kay, Christian (2015), 'Words and Thesauri', in *The Oxford Handbook of the Word*, John R. Taylor (ed.), Oxford: Oxford University Press, 53–67.

Kay, Christian and Marc Alexander (forthcoming 2015), 'Historical and Synchronic Thesauruses', in *The Oxford Handbook of Lexicography*, Philip Durkin (ed.), Oxford: Oxford University Press.

Kay, Christian and Kathryn Allan (forthcoming 2015), 'Lexical Change', in *The Cambridge Handbook of English Historical Linguistics*, Merja Kytö and Paivi Pahta (eds), Cambridge: Cambridge University Press.

Kay, Christian and Margaret Mackay (eds) (2005), *The Edinburgh Companion to the Dictionary of the Older Scottish Tongue*, Edinburgh: Edinburgh University Press.

Kay, Paul and Luisa Maffi (1999), 'Color Appearance and the Emergence and Evolution of Basic Color Lexicons', *American Anthropologist* 101.4: 743–60.

Kay, Christian and Jeremy Smith (eds) (2004), *Categorization in the History of English*, Amsterdam: Benjamins.

Kay, Christian and Irené Wotherspoon (2005), 'Semantic Relationships in the Historical Thesaurus of English', *Lexicographica* 21: 47–57.

Kay, Paul, Brent Berlin, Luisa Maffi, William Merrifield and Richard Cook (2009), *The World Color Survey*, CSLI Lecture Notes 159, Stanford: CSLI Publications.

Kornerup, A. and J. H. Wanscher (1978, 3rd edn revised and introduced by Don Pavey), *Methuen Handbook of Colour*, London: Eyre Methuen.

Kövecses, Zoltán (2000), *Metaphor and Emotion: Language, Culture and the Body in Human Feeling*, Cambridge: Cambridge University Press.

Kövecses, Zoltán (2010, 2nd edn), *Metaphor: A Practical Introduction*, New York: Oxford University Press.

Lakoff, George and Mark Johnson ([1980] 2003), *Metaphors We Live By*, Chicago and London: University of Chicago Press.

Lehrer, Adrienne (1969), 'Semantic Cuisine', *Journal of Linguistics* 5: 39–55.

Lehrer, Adrienne (1974), *Semantic Fields and Lexical Structure*, Amsterdam and London: North Holland.

Los, Bettelou (2015), *A Historical Syntax of English*, Edinburgh: Edinburgh University Press.

Lucy, John A. (1992), *Language Diversity and Thought; A Reformulation of the Linguistic Relativity Hypothesis*, Cambridge: Cambridge University Press.

MacLaury, Robert E. (1997), *Color and Cognition in Mesoamerica: Constructing Categories as Vantages*, Austin: University of Texas Press.

McWhorter, John (2014), *The Language Hoax*, Oxford: Oxford University Press.

Minkova, Donka and Robert Stockwell (2009, 2nd edn), *English Words: History and Structure*, Cambridge: Cambridge University Press.

Mugglestone, Lynda (2005), *Lost For Words: The Hidden History of the* Oxford English Dictionary, New Haven, CT: Yale University Press.

Mugglestone, Lynda (ed.) (2006), *The Oxford History of English*, Oxford: Oxford University Press.

Müller, Cornelia (2008), *Metaphors Dead and Alive, Sleeping and Waking: A Dynamic View*, Chicago: University of Chicago Press.

Murphy, M. Lynne (2003), *Semantic Relations and the Lexicon*, Cambridge: Cambridge University Press.

Murphy, M. Lynne (2010), *Lexical Meaning*, Cambridge: Cambridge University Press.

Murphy, M. Lynne and Anu Koskela (2010), *Key Terms in Semantics*, London and New York: Continuum.

Murray, K. M. Elisabeth ([1977] 1995), *Caught in the Web of Words: James A. H. Murray and the* Oxford English Dictionary, New Haven, CT: Yale University Press.

Nida, Eugene A. (1975), *Componential Analysis of Meaning*, The Hague: Mouton.

Niemeier, Susanne (2000), 'Straight from the Heart: Metonymic and Metaphorical Explorations', in *Metaphor and Metonymy at the Crossroads: A Cognitive Perspective*, Antonio Barcelona (ed.), Berlin: Mouton de Gruyter, 195–214.

Nunberg, Geoffrey D. (1978), *The Pragmatics of Reference*, Bloomington: The Indiana University Linguistics Club.

O'Hare, Cerwyss (2004), 'Folk Classification in the HTE Plants Category', in Kay and Smith (eds), 179–91.

Panther, Klaus-Uwe and Günther Radden (eds) (1999), *Metonymy in Language and Thought*, Amsterdam: Benjamins.

Perelman, Chaïm and Lucie Olbrechts-Tyteca (1969), *The New Rhetoric: A*

Treatise on Argumentation, trans. John Wilkinson and Purcell Weaver, Notre Dame and London: University of Notre Dame Press.

Pinker, Steven (1994), *The Language Instinct*, London: Allen Lane.

Plag, Ingo (2003), *Word-Formation in English*, Cambridge: Cambridge University Press.

Rayson, Paul (2008), 'From Key Words to Key Semantic Domains', *International Journal of Corpus Linguistics* 13.4: 519–49.

Reddy, Michael J. (1979), 'The Conduit Metaphor: A Case of Frame Conflict in our Language about Language', in *Metaphor and Thought*, Andrew Ortony (ed.), Cambridge: Cambridge University Press, 284–310.

Rees, Abraham (1819), *The Cyclopædia; or, Universal Dictionary of Arts, Sciences, and Literature*, vol. 34, London: Longman, Hurst, Rees, Hurst and Brown.

Richards, I. A. (1936), *The Philosophy of Rhetoric*, New York: Oxford University Press.

Robinson, F. N. (ed.) ([1957] 1978), *The Complete Works of Geoffrey Chaucer*, Oxford: Oxford University Press.

Robinson, Justyna A. (2012a), 'A *Gay* Paper: Why Should Sociolinguistics Bother with Semantics?', *English Today* 28.4: 38–54.

Robinson, Justyna A. (2012b), 'A Sociolinguistic Perspective on Semantic Change', in Allan and Robinson (eds), 199–231.

Rosch, Eleanor (1973), 'Natural Categories', *Cognitive Psychology* 4: 328–50.

Ross, Alan S. C. (1956), 'U and non-U', in *Noblesse Oblige: An Enquiry into the Identifiable Characteristics of the English Aristocracy*, Nancy Mitford (ed.), London: Hamish Hamilton, 11–36.

Salzmann, Zdenek (1993), *Language, Culture, & Society*, Boulder: Westview Press.

Samuels, M. L. (1972), *Linguistic Evolution, with Special Reference to English*, Cambridge: Cambridge University Press.

Sapir, Edward (1929), 'The Status of Linguistics as a Science', *Language* 5: 207–14. Reprinted in David Mandelbaum (ed.) (1949), *Selected Writings of Edward Sapir*, Berkeley: University of California Press.

de Saussure, Ferdinand ([1916] 2013), *Course in General Linguistics*, trans. Roy Harris, London: Bloomsbury.

Smith, Jeremy (1996), *An Historical Study of English: Function, Form and Change*, London and New York: Routledge.

Sweetser, Eve E. (1990), *From Etymology to Pragmatics: Metaphorical and Cultural Aspects of Semantic Structure*, Cambridge: Cambridge University Press.

Taylor, John (2003a, 3rd edn), *Linguistic Categorization*, Oxford: Oxford University Press.

Taylor, John (2003b), 'Category Extension by Metaphor and Metonymy', in *Metaphor and Metonymy in Comparison and Contrast*, René Dirven and Ralf Pörings (eds), Berlin: Mouton de Gruyter, 323–49.

Tissari, Heli (2003), *LOVEscapes: Changes in Prototypical Senses and Cognitive Metaphors since 1500*, Helsinki: Société Néophilologique.

Traugott, Elizabeth Closs (2012), 'Linguistic Levels: Semantics and Lexicon', in Bergs and Brinton (eds), 164–77.

Traugott, Elizabeth Closs and Richard B. Dasher ([2002] 2005), *Regularity in Semantic Change*, Cambridge: Cambridge University Press.

Tremaine, Hadley P. (1969), 'Beowulf's *Ecg Brun* and Other Rusty Relics', *Philological Quarterly* 48: 2, 145–50.

Ullman, Stephen (1962), *Semantics: An Introduction to the Science of Meaning*, Oxford: Blackwell.

Ungerer, Friedrich and Hans-Jörg Schmid (2006, 2nd edn), *An Introduction to Cognitive Linguistics*, Harlow: Pearson Education.

Walker, Warren S. (1952), 'The *Brūnecg* Sword', *Modern Language Notes* 67: 516–20.

Whorf, Benjamin Lee (1956), *Language, Thought and Reality: Selected Writings of Benjamin Lee Whorf*, ed. J. B. Carroll, Cambridge, MA: MIT Press.

Wild, Kate (2010), 'Angelets, Trudgeons and Bratlings: The Lexicalization of Childhood in the *Historical Thesaurus of the Oxford English Dictionary*', in Adams (ed.), 289–308.

Winchester, Simon (1999), *The Surgeon of Crowthorne: A Tale of Murder, Madness and the* Oxford English Dictionary, London: Penguin (US edition 1999, *The Professor and the Madman: A Tale of Murder, Insanity and the Making of the* Oxford English Dictionary, New York: Harper Perennial).

Winchester, Simon (2003), *The Meaning of Everything: The Story of the* Oxford English Dictionary, Oxford: Oxford University Press.

Winters, Margaret, Heli Tissari and Kathryn Allan (eds) (2010), *Historical Cognitive Linguistics*, Berlin: Mouton de Gruyter.

Wotherspoon, Irené (2010), 'The Making of the *Historical Thesaurus of the Oxford English Dictionary*', in Adams (ed.), 271–87.

Wrenn, C. L., ed., rev. W. F. Bolton (1973, 3rd edn), *Beowulf with the Finnesburg Fragment*, London: Harrap.

Zadeh, Lotfi A. (1965), 'Fuzzy sets', *Information and Control* 8: 338–53.

Index

Page numbers followed by 'n' indicate notes. Page numbers in *italics* indicate figures.

EU Authorised Representative: Easy Access System Europe Mustamäe tee 5
0, 10621 Tallinn, Estonia gpsr.requests@easproject.com

Printed and bound by CPI Group (UK) Ltd, Croydon, CR0 4YY

16/04/2025

01846999-0001